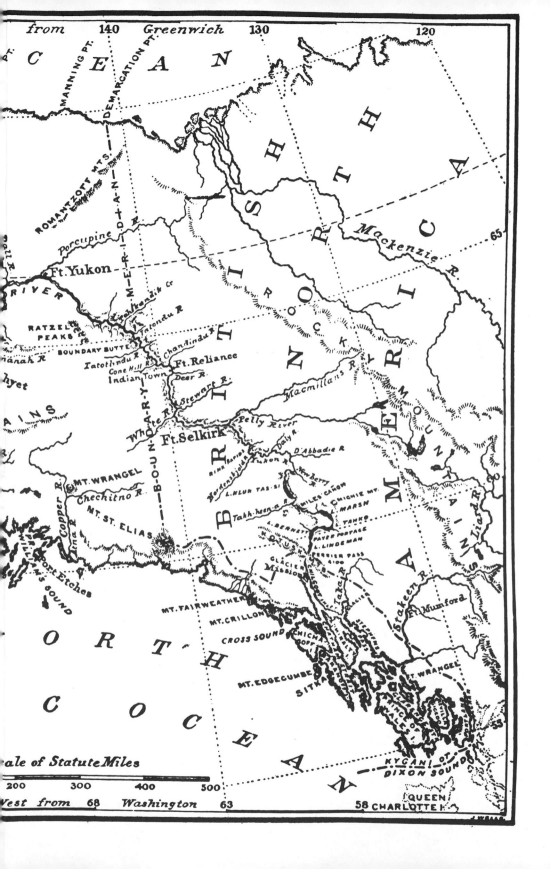

from 140 Greenwich 130 120

O C E A N

MANNING PT.

DEMARCATION PT.

ROMANTZOFF MTS.

Porcupine R.

Ft. Yukon

RIVER

RATZEL PEAKS

BOUNDARY BUTTE

Tatothndu R.

Cone Hill R.

Indian Town

Ft. Reliance

Deer R.

Stewart R.

White R.

Ft. Selkirk

MT. WRANGEL

Chechitno R.

MT. ST. ELIAS

Copper R.

Tina R.

Port Etches

PRINCE WILLIAM'S SOUND

MT. FAIRWEATHER

MT. CRILLON

CROSS SOUND

MT. EDGECUMBE

SITKA

B R I T I S H   N O R T H   A M E R I C A

Mackenzie R.

R O C K Y   M O U N T A I N S

Macmillans R.

Pelly River

Daly R.

D'Abbadie R.

Newberry R.

B O U N D A R Y

Takh-heen-a R.

MILES CANON

MARSH

TANKO

PAYER PORTAGE

L. BENNETT

L. LINDEMAN

PERRIER PASS 4100

Takou R.

GLACIER Mission

Stikeen R.

Ft. Mumford

CHICH OFF

Liard R.

QUEEN CHARLOTTE

MT. WRANGEL

KYGANI OR DIXON SOUND

65

55

Scale of Statute Miles

200   300   400   500

West from 68   Washington   63   58

EXPLORATION OF ALASKA

1865-1900

by Morgan B. Sherwood

Preface by Terrence Cole

University of Alaska Press
Fairbanks, 1992

University of Alaska Press
P.O. Box 756240
Fairbanks, AK 99775-6240
888.252.6657
fypress@uaf.edu
www.uaf.edu/uapress

Library of Congress Cataloging-in-Publication Data

Sherwood, Morgan B.
    Exploration of Alaska, 1865–1900 / by Morgan Sherwood : preface
        by Terrence Cole
    p. cm.
    Originally published: New Haven : Yale University Press, 1965.
    Includes bibliographical references and index.
    ISBN 0-912006-62-5
    1. Alaska--Description and travel--1967-1896. 2. United States--Ex-
        ploring expeditions. I. Title.
    F908.S6   1992
    917.9804'4--dc20   92.26287
                                              CIP

This book was printed on acid-free, recycled paper that meets the
requirements of ANSI/NISO Z39.48-1992.

Book design by John O. C. McCrillis.
Cover design by Keith Swarmer, IMPACT Graphics, University of Alaska
    Fairbanks. Line illustrations by A. Fraser.
    Front cover: An artistic conception of Chilkoot Pass.
    Back cover: Lieutenant Frederick Schwatka's raft shooting the Miles
    Canyon rapids in 1883.

Frontispiece map: An 1885 map of Alaska made following Frederick
    Schwatka's 1883 exploration of the Yukon.

For Mom and Dad

Contents

Preface to the 1992 Edition

MORGAN SHERWOOD's *Exploration of Alaska 1865-1900* was first published in 1965, the one hundredth anniversary of the first systematic American exploration of interior Alaska. His book was a pioneering, in-depth historical analysis of Alaskan exploration and has become one of the milestones of Alaska's historical literature. Like the 19th century soldiers, sailors and scientists whose exploits he described, Sherwood discovered a vast unexplored historical terrain and filled in one of the largest blank spaces on the map of Alaskan history. It was a story that he felt had to be told "before the country is wounded and scarred by the ax and the bulldozer."

Sherwood refuted the common wisdom, spouted for years by Alaskan political historians and still today by Alaskan politicians pitching for votes, that the root cause of virtually all Alaskan problems is federal neglect of Alaska. He challenged the notion that "Alaska was a victim of conspiratorial neglect by the federal government." In his view this "paranoid delusion" was fostered by the narrow focus of historians on the minutiae of politics in southeastern Alaska which had blinded them to the larger realities of northern conditions. "That same concentration on political evolution," he wrote, "tends to obscure the significance of exploration, which should be the focal point of Alaskan history in the nineteenth century."

By both inclination and education, Sherwood was a natural candidate to explore the role of the U.S. government in Alaskan exploration. Born in 1929 in Anchorage, where his father worked for the U.S. government-built Alaska Railroad, he grew up in a town that survived on its federal payroll. After graduating from Anchorage High School in 1947 and four years of college, he received a baccalaureate degree from San Diego State College. Subsequently he served as a counterintelligence agent in the U.S. Army in Korea He then spent two years working in Hamburg, Germany, before he began graduate study in history at the University of California, Berkeley, where he earned a Ph.D. in 1962. His main scholarly interest was the history of science. Sherwood's mentor at

Berkeley, A. Hunter Dupree, the author of *Science in the Federal Government*, encouraged his Alaskan protégé to combine his love of the north and his fascination with science in a dissertation on the scientific exploration of Alaska, eventually published in 1965 by Yale University Press as *Exploration of Alaska 1865-1900*.

Using many sources never utilized before, including scores of scientific papers, private correspondence and archival records, Sherwood analyzed the general patterns of Alaskan exploration from the Western Union Telegraph Expedition of 1865 to the investigations of the U.S. Geological Survey in 1900 and placed the Alaska experience into the broader context of American history. "Alaska's separation from the rest of the country made it a freak in American development," Sherwood wrote, "the first important colonialist effort of the European variety." Viewed in that more general perspective, he found Alaska had not been the neglected victim often portrayed in the literature. "In an era devoted to laissez-faire, it is a wonder that the government promoted any exploration at all in unoccupied Alaska." Sherwood concluded that the federal government was almost exclusively responsible for the vast increase in the world's knowledge of Alaska in the last third of the 19th century. Just because large-scale economic development and population increases did not occur did not mean that the country had been neglected by the federal government.

A modern analogy to Sherwood's thesis is that if Alaska was neglected, it was only in the sense that Americans have neglected the moon since Neil Armstrong stepped off his spacecraft in 1969. Like Alaska of the 19th century, the moon is a cold, dangerous and distant place where travel is costly and usable resources have yet to be discovered; other more hospitable locales are closer at hand. Yet the fact that lunar settlements have not followed in the wake of the Apollo Mission should not obscure the extent of NASA's achievement in landing a man on the moon. So too, according to Sherwood's logic, the fact that waves of settlers did not follow Alaska expeditions by the U.S. Army, U.S. Navy, Revenue Marine, Coast and Geodetic Survey, Geological Survey or Smithsonian Institution should not detract from the achievements of the U.S. Government in opening up Alaska to the rest of the world.

Sherwood's book describes a lively cast of characters who explored Alaska between the Civil War and the turn of the century, such as William H. Dall, the scholar-adventurer who became America's leading authority on Alaska; Ivan Petroff, the con man, plagiarist and forger who "authored" two of the three most influential books on Alaska in the 19th century; Frederick Schwatka, the swaggering, boastful polar explorer who floated down the Yukon in 1883, giving new names to every geographical feature he saw; and Henry T. Allen, an ambitious young army officer whose 1,500-mile journey in 1885 on the Copper, Tanana and Koyukuk Rivers was called the greatest overland expedition on the continent since that of Meriwether Lewis and William Clark eighty years earlier.

Following the publication of *Exploration of Alaska*, Morgan Sherwood went on to produce numerous other articles and books about Alaska and the history of science, including a history of Alaskan sport hunting which, he said, was inspired by "the small and big game animals of Alaska, whose company I have enjoyed off and on for more than forty years." After teaching for 26 years in the History Department at the University of California, Davis, Professor Sherwood recently retired. But he still comes back to Alaska almost every year to a summer home on Kachemak Bay where he and his wife enjoy the natural beauty that so captivated the 19th century explorers whose adventures fill the pages of this book.

—Terrence Cole

Acknowledgments

I HAVE TRIED here to describe man's earliest exposure to nature's temptations in the interior of the Far Northwest. The story should be told before the country is wounded and scarred by the ax and the bulldozer.

Though I am responsible for all errors of detail and interpretation, I am indebted to many for inspiration and constructive criticism. To A. Hunter Dupree of the University of California, Berkeley, I extend special thanks for encouragement to undertake the study in the first place, for critical direction of my research and writing, and for providing in appropriate sections of his classic work, *Science in the Federal Government*, the logical institutional framework in which the story was set. Professors Walton Bean and Clyde Wahrhaftig, also of the University of California, read and criticized the manuscript in dissertation form. My friends and colleagues James Lal Penick, Carroll W. Purcell, and Donald C. Swain all made intelligent substantive and stylistic suggestions. Franklin W. Burch gave me some valuable advice. Vera Chadwick kindly helped me to proofread the revised manuscript, and my wife Jeanie helped me to read the printed proofs.

I want also to thank the staffs of the following institutions for expert assistance and warm hospitality: Bancroft Library of the University of California; the National Archives; the library of the Division of Mollusks at the Smithsonian Institution; the U.S. Geological Survey, Alaska Branch, Menlo Park, California; the Smithsonian Institution Archives; the Manuscript Division of the Library of Congress; the U.S. National Museum Library; the library of the U.S. Geological Survey, Washington; the Alaska State Historical Library at Juneau; the Sheldon Jackson Junior College Library, Sitka; the Jackson Library at Stanford University; and the California Historical Society Library, San Francisco. Members of the staff of Bancroft Library not only gave me access and aid but also provided me with a large and convenient desk which served as my headquarters during the first year of research.

Mrs. Madeleine Adams of Berkeley granted me permission to quote from a manuscript by George Russell Adams which is on microfilm in the

Bancroft Library. The following publishers gave me permission to quote copyrighted material: *Pacific Northwest Quarterly* (1941), C. L. Andrews, "Some Notes on the Yukon by Stewart Menzies," and (1949), R. G. Athearn, "An Army Officer's Trip to Alaska in 1869"; *Bulletin of the Geological Society of America* (1926), P. S. Smith, "Memorial of Alfred Hulse Brooks"; *California Historical Society Quarterly* (1956), H. F. Taggart, "Journal of George Russell Adams"; *British Columbia Historical Quarterly* (1946), C. Mackay, "The Collins Overland Telegraph"; American Council of Learned Societies for C. Ginsburg's translation of A. I. Andreyev, *Russian Discoveries in the Pacific and in North America in the Eighteenth and Nineteenth Centuries;* Fleming H. Revell Company for S. Hall Young, *Hall Young of Alaska;* Alfred A. Knopf Incorporated for Pierre Berton, *The Klondike Fever;* University of Oklahoma Press for S. R. Tompkins, *Alaska: Promyshlenik and Sourdough;* Harvard University Press for A. H. Dupree, *Science in the Federal Government;* Houghton Mifflin Company for John Muir, *Travels in Alaska* and *John of the Mountains;* and the Arctic Institute of North America for D. G. Knapp and E. B. Roberts, "Geomagnetism—Cosmic and Prosaic," in *Science in Alaska, 1950.* The chapter on Ivan Petroff appeared in the July 1963 issue of the *Journal of the West.* Additional bibliographical information appears in the appropriate footnotes.

M.B.S.

Cincinnati, Ohio
October 1964

List of Illustrations

Maps

Chronology

1865	Russian American Telegraph Expedition
1866	Death of Kennicott at Nulato
1866, summer	Yukon reconnaissance by Ketchum, Lebarge, and Lukeen
1867, March–May	Winter sledge trip to Ft. Yukon by Ketchum and Lebarge
1867, summer	Yukon reconnaissance by Dall and Whymper
	Telegraph Expedition suspended
1867	Purchase of Alaska
	Davidson's coastal investigation aboard the *Lincoln*
1867–68	Dall remains in Alaska
1867–77	Period of Army rule in Alaska
1868	Thomas Minor aboard the *Wayanda*
1869	General Thomas' summer tour of Alaska
1869, summer	Raymond's Yukon reconnaissance
1871–74	Dall's coastal surveys for the USCS
1874	Lucien Turner of Signal Service assigned to Alaska
1875	General Howard's summer inspection tour
1877	C. E. S. Wood fails to reach Mt. St. Elias
1877–79	Period of Treasury Department rule in Alaska
1877–81	Nelson of the Signal Service explores the lower Yukon and Kuskokwim
1879, summer	Muir and Young investigate Glacier Bay
1879–84	Period of Navy rule in Alaska
1880	Dall and Baker return to coastal Alaska for a season
	Petroff's census of Alaska
1881, summer	Nelson and Muir aboard the *Corwin*
1882	General Miles visits southeastern Alaska
1882, summer	Krause explores Chilkoot and Chilkat passes
1883, summer	Schwatka's Yukon reconnaissance
	From the *Corwin*, Stoney investigates the lower Kobuk
1884	Alaska's First Organic Act
1884, summer	Cantwell's Kobuk expedition
	Stoney's Kobuk expedition
	Abercrombie attempts to explore the Copper River basin
1885, summer	Allen explores the Copper, Tanana, and Koyukuk rivers

	Cantwell's second Kobuk expedition
	S. B. McLenegan explores the Noatak River
1885–86	Stoney's expedition on the Kobuk and in adjacent country
1886	Schwatka's New York *Times* expedition to Mt. St. Elias
1887–88	Dawson, Ogilvie, and McConnell explore and survey parts of the Yukon District
1888	Topham's English expedition to Mt. St. Elias
1889	I. C. Russell's Yukon reconnaissance
1889–90	McGrath and J. H. Turner of USC&GS on the 141st meridian
1890–91	Leslie expedition (Glave, Schanz, and Wells)
1890, 1891	Russell's expeditions to Mt. St. Elias
1890, 1892	Reid at Glacier Bay
1891	Schwatka and Hayes investigate upper White River, Skolai region, and the Chitina
1893	Funston's Yukon reconnaissance
1895	USGS mineral survey of coast by Dall and Becker
1896	USGS mineral survey of Yukon diggings by Spurr, Schrader, and Goodrich
	Dickey ascends Susitna River and names Mt. McKinley
1898	Abercrombie's USA expedition on the Copper (Mahlo, Lowe, Schrader)
	Glenn's USA expedition in Susitna basin (Kelly, Learnard, Yanert, Castner, Mathys, Mendenhall)
	Barnard, USGS, maps Fortymile region
	Brooks and Peters, USGS, explore White and upper Tanana
	Eldridge and Muldrow, USGS, explore through Broad Pass
	Spurr and Post explore Yentna, Kuskokwim, for USGS
1899	Abercrombie's expedition on the Copper, with Rohn
	Glenn's expedition in Susitna basin (Van Schoonoven, Griffith, Yanert, Mathys, Herron)
	Peters and Brooks explore north base of St. Elias Mountains, Nabesna, and upper Fortymile
	Schrader, Gerdine survey Chandalar and Koyukuk basins
	Harriman Alaska Expedition
1900	Schrader and Spencer map Chitina copper district
	Barnard, Brooks, Peters, and Mendenhall map portions of Seward Peninsula mining district

Abbreviations

AAAS   American Association for the Advancement of Science
AGO   Adjutant General's Office
BCHQ   *British Columbia Historical Quarterly*
BE   Bureau of Ethnology
CHSQ   *California Historical Society Quarterly*
DAB   *Dictionary of American Biography*
JAGS   *Journal of the American Geographic Society*
JG   *Journal of Geography*
NA, RG   National Archives, Record Group
NAR   *North American Review*
NGM   *National Geographic Magazine*
PHR   *Pacific Historical Review*
PNQ   *Pacific Northwest Quarterly*
RGS   Royal Geographic Society
SI   Smithsonian Institution
USCS   United States Coast Survey
USC&GS   United States Coast and Geodetic Survey
USGS   United States Geological Survey
USN   United States Navy
USNM   United States National Museum
USRM   United States Revenue Marine

1. Introduction

> The learning of one man does not subtract from the learning
> of another, as if there were a limited quantity of unknown truth.
> Intellectual activity does not compete with other intellectual ac-
> tivity for exclusive possession of truth; scholarship breeds schol-
> arship, wisdom breeds wisdom, discovery breeds discovery. . . .
> The laws of political economy do not belong to the economics
> of science and intellectual progress.
>
> JOHN WESLEY POWELL[1]

HENRY T. ALLEN, in a modest afterthought on his own memorable
achievement, wrote in 1886: "It is a very remarkable fact that a region
under a civilized government for more than a century should remain so
completely unknown as the vast territory drained by the Copper, Tanana,
and Koyukuk Rivers."[2] Allen had reason to wonder. The Copper River of
Alaska was discovered in 1783, and various attempts were made thereafter to explore the stream. Topographic, climatic, and natural barriers
were formidable, but if, as Powell believed, discovery breeds discovery,
then a century seemed a long time indeed. Physiographic barriers are of
minor importance in explaining the lag between discovery and exploration. The true reasons for the lag are more fundamental.

The pace and extent of Russian and American exploration in Alaska
were intimately related to the social and political atmosphere in the parent
nations. During the Russian period, political attitudes in St. Petersburg
were not congenial to the promotion of inland exploration or science. In
1796 Gregory Shelikof, whose firm formed the nucleus of the Russian
American Company, instructed his chief manager to "note down where
anything may be found in the entrails of the earth, and where beasts and

1. W. B. Allison *et al*. [Allison Commission], "Testimony before the Joint Commission to Consider the Present Organization of Certain Bureaus," *Senate Miscellaneous Document 82, 49th Congress: 1st session* (2345), 1082.
2. H. T. Allen, *Report of an Expedition to the Copper, Tanana, and Koyukuk Rivers in the Territory of Alaska, 1885* (U.S. Army, Washington, 1887), p. 15.

birds and curious sea-shells, and other things may be found."[3] Though
Shelikof himself made reliable observations on natural history and ethnology, his men displayed slight concern for "birds and curious sea-shells";
but they did pay attention to "beasts" that wore fur coats. When the sea
otter retreated, the easy income disappeared, and with it Imperial interest
in Alaska save as a pawn in the game of international politics.[4]

The succession of naval officers to company management after 1818
saw some notable work, for example by Ferdinand von Wrangell in geography, Ilia Voznesenskii in natural history, Peter Doroshin in mineral investigation, and Father Veniaminov and H. J. Holmberg in ethnology;[5]
but in general Russian science in Alaska was spotty and uncoordinated.
Russian inland exploration fared no better. A few probes were made along
the lower Yukon, Kuskokwim, Susitna, and Copper rivers. The investigations hardly ever extended beyond the area immediately adjacent to the
stream. Toward the end of the Russian period, P. N. Golovin reported officially: "The explorations that were undertaken at different times in the
colonies were exceedingly superficial and wholly confined to the coast;
the interior, not only of the continent but also of Sitka Island, is today still
unexplored."[6]

When the United States bought the territory in 1867, it was a vast *terra
incognita*. Basic information was needed before anything like an intelligent understanding of the country could be entertained. In the years that

3. A. I. Andreyev, editor, *Russian Discoveries in the Pacific and in North America
in the Eighteenth and Nineteenth Centuries*, translated by Carl Ginsburg (Ann Arbor,
Mich., 1952), p. 52.

4. S. B. Okun, *The Russian-American Company*, translated by Carl Ginsburg (Cambridge, Mass., 1951).

5. Wrangell, *Statistische und ethnographische Nachrichten über die Russischen
Besitzungen an der Nordwestküste von Amerika* (St. Petersburg, 1839). C. Grewingk,
*Beitrag zur Kenntniss der Orographischen und Geognostichen Beschaffenheit der Nord-
West-Küste Amerikas, mit den Anliegenden Inseln* (St. Petersburg, 1850), p. 346.
A. L. Isotoff, "Russian Contributions to the Geographical Knowledge of Alaska and the
Adjacent Islands and Seas," typescript MS thesis in geography (Eugene, University of
Oregon, 1942), p. 112. P. Doroschin, "Einige Beobachtungen und Bemerkungen
über das Goldvorkommen in den Besitzungen der Russisch-Amerikanischen Compagnie,"
Archiv für wissenschaftliche Kunde von Russland, 25 (1866), 229–37. H. J. Holmberg,
"Ethnographische Skizzen über die Völker des Russischen Amerika," *Acta Societatis
Scientiarum Fennicae*, 4 (Helsingfors, 1856), 281–421.

6. P. N. Golovin, "Ueber die russischen Colonien an der Nordwestküste von
Amerika," *Archiv für wissenschaftliche Kunde von Russland*, 22 (1862), 47–70.

followed, the Americans did a competent job of amassing knowledge of Alaska, especially in light of contemporary attitudes at home about the country and attitudes about the role of government in the primary development of virgin land.

In the first place, Alaska has been a victim of the icebox myth. "Though less than one-third of Alaska lies within the Arctic Circle," reported a popular magazine in 1896, "the impression has long prevailed that the whole country north of Mt. St. Elias bares [sic] the Arctic aspect the mental picture of which suggests thoughts of viscid alcohol thermometers and a diet of sealskin boots and the like."[7] By 1886, southeastern Alaska was regularly visited by tourists, who wrote about the glaciers and marveled in print at the impenetrable forests that clothed the perpendicular slopes of the fiords. "The very encomiums which enraptured tourists have bestowed upon her Alpine scenery . . . served to discourage settlement or adventure."[8]

This myth, originating with a few newspapers objecting to the Cession, was perpetuated unintentionally by popular writers who were only slightly acquainted with the country, and deliberately by better informed authors who unwisely distorted the public concept of Alaska. Alaska is neither an icebox nor a garden. Large parts of it are as hospitable as other more heavily populated regions of the world.

Clearly the public misconception was based on the location. Alaska is in the high latitudes; it is nearer the Pole than North Dakota and therefore, many people reasoned, all of it must be colder. Professorial talk in 1867 about warm currents and warped isothermal lines—talk often based on insufficient data—was ineffective in dispelling the myth. The political satirist Petroleum V. Nasby said of President Andrew Johnson:

> The president wuzn't favorably inclined. He wuz full uv the old fogy idea that it wuz rather chilly there than otherwise. He hedn't faith in the isothermal line, and wuz skepticle about the Gulfstream. It wuz his experience that the further north yoo got the colder it wuz. For instance, he remarkt, that while people wuz warm toward him in Virginy and Maryland, last fall, they become very cold ez he got north. Wher wuz the isothermal line and the gulf stream then?

7. R. Stein, "The Gold Fields of Alaska," *Review of Reviews 13* (1896), 697.
8. C. Hallock, *Our New Alaska* (New York, 1886), page ii.

William Seward tried to remove the objection, Nasby reported.

> The isothermal line wuz more accomodatin ther than in any other
> part of the world. It cork-screwed through the territory so ez to grow
> fine peaches for exportation to the states and ice to the Sandwich
> islands side by side. He drawd a picter uv the white bear a rushin
> over the line and disportin hisself in fields uv green peas. Imagin, he
> remarked, the delicacy uv polar meat fattened on strawberries—
> think uv the condishn the sea lions must be in wich leav their watry
> lairs to feed on turnips wich grow above the 60th parallel.[9]

Other geographical realities contributed to the myth. Alaska's separation from the rest of the country made it a freak in American development
—the first important colonialist effort of the European variety. A glance
at the world map may suggest that Alaska is a logical geographic entity,
but its Canadian border is artificial, since no continuous range or river
divides it from Canada. This fact served to complicate an understanding
of the territory. Also, Alaska was remote and therefore exotic. It was not
only a long distance away, but the distances within the country were not
easily grasped at home. The immense size of the land frustrated a thorough
and immediate appreciation of its worth. Writers visited one part and returned to write about the whole. If they touched at the Aleutians only, all
Alaska was represented as treeless, foggy, and wind-blown; if they visited
the Alexander Archipelago, Alaska was another Norway; if they went
ashore at Point Barrow, Alaska was an Arctic wasteland; and so on.

The myth of the icebox fed on ignorance. Only the accumulation, dis-
semination, and acceptance of knowledge can overcome deeply embedded
misconceptions. The explorers of Alaska both gathered and disseminated
their facts. To publish on Alaska was easy enough because of the novelty
of the subject, but increased knowledge did almost nothing to dispel the
novelty, for the reports were not widely read. An irate Alaskan exploded:
"If those Senators and Congressmen don't know any more about the tariff
and the other things they help to discuss than they do about Alaska, the
Lord help the rest of the United States! Their ignorance of the commonest
facts of geography would disgrace any little siwash at Fort Wrangell

9. Newspaper clip, dated April 14, 1867, in "Alaska Miscellany," Bancroft Scraps,
81, 49, 50, Bancroft Library, University of California, Berkeley.

school. What have they paid for all these special government reports for, if they don't ever read them?"[10]

Though explorers are usually followed by settlers, in Alaska the correlation was not always precise. Settlement did not keep pace because the territory's remoteness keyed its economic growth to the exploitation of natural resources that were unique or superabundant. Before the 1890s, the economy of Alaska depended upon the fur business and fishing—enterprises not requiring a large permanent population. More important, the myth of the icebox persisted. The intellectual and social climate of America during the last half of the nineteenth century was not receptive to the knowledge so carefully gathered by explorers.

People in the United States between 1867 and 1898 were hostile to the development of distant, newly acquired, vacant land. There were other pressing matters nearer home. Technological progress and rapid industrialization promised a good life to the American who stayed at home to tend the machine. Before the century ended, the ideal Jeffersonian freeholder became a "farmer," and "farmer" came to connote "hick." The new frontiers of opportunity were far removed from nature's wilderness; they were, rather, the aisles of the factory or of the stock exchange. The hero of the period carried a brief case instead of a long rifle. While industry grew and diversified, thanks in part to technological innovation, technology sharpened the contrast between wilderness, or rural life, and metropolitanism. "Civilization" became a tangible commodity that made life easier, and the commodity was not available in the bush or on the farm. American interest in the wilderness frontier as a source of opportunity diminished with a heightened interest in technological frontiers, and the old dream that Alaska's "free land" would serve the function of the Old West, in a Turnerian sense, all but vanished.

The period had its own philosophy conducive to further mechanization and money-making—a philosophy born, ironically, in the myth and the reality of the frontier. Success was survival not in the struggle against nature but in the struggle at the market place. To this philosophy pure science unwittingly contributed, as it did to the rush of technological progress. Social Darwinism was a rationalization of the rough-and-tumble economic competition of the day. The Carnegies, the Rockefellers, the

10. Quoted in K. Field, "Our Ignorance of Alaska," *NAR*, *149* (1889), 79.

Morgans were allegedly the fittest because they were the richest. Selection of the fittest required a free market unhampered by government intervention. In an era devoted to laissez-faire, it is a wonder that the government promoted any exploration at all in unoccupied Alaska. For while a railroad subsidy in the States might be advocated as the social overhead cost of primary development between two economically important points, an inland expedition in Alaska before 1898 started nowhere and arrived at the same place.

Specific political concerns also influenced the intensity of interest in Alaska, though to a lesser degree. Between 1867 and 1877 the nation was struggling with one of its greatest missions—reconstruction after the Civil War. In a sense, the South and Alaska were both colonial possessions begging for assimilation. How could the north country claim priority on the political agenda or in the public imagination when the day-to-day problems of reconstruction absorbed the time and attention of Washington? In 1877, the Army was withdrawn from Alaska as it was from the South and, like the South, Alaska was not yet assimilated.

The period after 1877 was devoted to a headier pursuit of wealth—a chase that often led to ugly political involvement. This age of monopoly and the justification of monopoly was also reflected in Alaskan exploration and development. The territory had its Alaska Commercial Company just as Pennsylvania had Standard Oil. The parallel should not be overdrawn, however. The A. C. Company influenced legislation on Alaska and now and then inhibited political development, but its role vis-à-vis exploration is debatable. The proclivity of Alaskan historians to make a bête noire of the A. C. Company is connected to their emphasis on political considerations. That same concentration on political evolution tends to obscure the significance of exploration, which should be the focal point of Alaskan history in the nineteenth century. For even as discovery breeds discovery, so does discovery precede development.

The organization, fortunes, and rationale of the American scientific establishment had a heavy impact on activity in the Far Northwest. The 1880s saw a clear exposition of laissez-faire in science. The influential John Wesley Powell objected to the intrusion of the "laws of political economy" in the economics of science, but the eminent Alexander Agassiz believed that "moderate centralization, allowing of great competition, is the ideal of scientific activity."[11] Such dogma, if adhered to, would obviously have had major consequences for science in Alaska as in the country as a whole.

The views of Agassiz and Powell were expressed during a crisis in governmental science. Political and economic considerations forced a close examination of the role of scientific bureaus and agencies. The questions of duplication, of jurisdiction, of civil versus military science arose to harry the scientist in government. When the first Democrat since before the Civil War assumed the presidential office in 1885, the old Coast Survey was thoroughly shaken.[12] Scrutiny of the bureaus brought a shuffling of duties and functions that was reflected in Alaskan exploration.

Almost as important in determining the governmental impact on science was the massive influence of John Wesley Powell. Powell ran the Colorado River in 1869 and was satisfied thereafter that pioneer exploration in the United States was complete; turning his attention to the desert, he produced an important study of irrigation that brought science to bear on reclamation. Alaskan exploration was further relegated to the background by a national policy that emerged in the last years of the eighth decade, formulated by a special committee of the National Academy of Sciences and strongly reflecting the views of Powell. Further, the U.S. Geological Survey, headed by Powell, displayed only indifferent regard for Alaska until 1895, despite Powell's broad interpretation of his statutory authority to direct "the classification of the public lands, and examination of the geological structure, mineral resources, and products of the national domain."

In sum, intellectual, political, and institutional attitudes at home influenced the intensity and character of scientific exploration in the Far Northwest. The exploration provided a central thread for the region's history during the nineteenth century, and it occupied an important corner in the mural of American history. How it was similar to and how it differed from the American pattern of science and discovery are major questions that will be examined in the following pages.

Another purpose of the study is to correct certain errors prevalent today.

11. Quoted in A. H. Dupree, *Science in the Federal Government* (Cambridge, Mass., 1957), p. 221.
12. Ibid., pp. 215–31.

One is the misconception that all problems of gross geography in America were solved at least by 1890—perhaps when Powell shot the Colorado rapids in 1869. Another is the fallacious idea—encouraged by A. W. Greely, who as author of a special report on the territory should have known better—that science in Alaska received only trivial support from Washington and that the principal researches were made independently of the government.[13] Still another is the view that Alaska was a victim of conspiratorial neglect by the federal government. Students have been led toward this latter viewpoint by overemphasis on the political aspects of Alaskan history; the theme of neglect reached paranoid dimensions in twentieth-century literature.

It is a fundamental thesis of the present study that exploratory activities by the federal government in Alaska were extensive in light of contemporary social attitudes in the United States, and in view of the territory's infinitesimal population, which rendered Alaskan history essentially apolitical during the nineteenth century. This does not mean exploration was as rapid as it should have been, but only that it proceeded as rapidly as it could in the context of the time. If Dr. Jeannette Nichols is correct in stating that, up to 1884, Alaska was administered far better by the Russians than by the United States,[14] equally valid is an observation by Ivan Petroff in 1892: "At a comparatively insignificant expense to the Government we have learned more of Alaska's geography and topography, its people and its resources, in twenty-five years than Russia learned or tried to learn in one hundred and twenty-six years of possession."[15] Finally, a few writers imply that the pace of exploration in Alaska was slower than the pace for North America generally. The conclusion is doubtful.

The subject could be described either institutionally or biographically. Or, it might be preferable to combine these approaches and write a slim institutional synthesis with a hasty reference here and there to the principal actors in the drama. But this would be far from adequate. The stories of the Alaskan explorers have not been told, and they deserve to be; for these men constitute a genus as vigorous and as fit as any hearty type that ever sought to penetrate the wilderness of North America. It may come as a surprise that so many courageous men have so long been hidden behind

13. *Handbook of Alaska* (New York, 1909), p. 224.
14. *Alaska* (Cleveland, 1924), p. 86.
15. "Twenty-five Years of Alaska," *NAR, 154* (1892), 628.

the curtain of unwritten history. Furthermore, to do justice to the subject, the story must be more than a mere string of high adventure tales. Alaskan scientific exploration was part of a total social phenomenon characterized by shifting relationships between science and government, between science and society, between one scientific activity and another. The goal therefore is a balance between the impersonal institutional approach and excessive attention to individual heroism.

Because the story is new, an equally important goal in telling it is to achieve a balance between information about the physical facts of the Far Northwest as they were established and an intellectual history of the men and institutions responsible for the acquisition and interpretation of the knowledge gathered.

The study is limited by area and time. It is confined for the most part to the inland sub-Arctic regions, that is, the territory south of the Brooks Range. (Discovery in the Arctic itself has already caught the attention of many capable writers.) By date, the study begins with 1865, when the first systematic exploration was made by Americans, and concludes with 1900. The terminal date is arbitrary though based on a number of considerations. Problems in gross geography had largely been solved by 1900. That does not mean that Alaska was officially "explored"; the United States Geological Survey was occupied with original, detailed exploration well into the twentieth century. It does mean that important mountain ranges had been outlined and the major rivers traced.[16] The year 1900 marks roughly the ascendancy of the USGS as the major agency devoted to scientific exploration in Alaska. Thereafter the Army was less concerned with exploration, though it continued to push trails, telegraph lines, and roads into the interior. The Coast and Geodetic Survey, except for geodesy, was confined to the coast. The Revenue Marine (Coast Guard) no longer ventured inland after its Yukon revenue steamer was decommissioned, and the Navy had lost its bid for jurisdiction a few years earlier. In 1900, after two years of systematic exploration, the Geological Survey paused to undertake detailed surveys of important mining districts. Within Alaska, 1900 was the year of the Nome Rush, though Alaska had for three years been overrun by hopeful Klondike prospectors. In 1901 the new president, Theodore Roosevelt, brought to office much of the reform sentiment

16. A. H. Brooks, *The Geography and Geology of Alaska*, USGS Professional Paper No. 45, (Washington, 1906), p. 12.

accumulated during a half-century of uninhibited business expansion. Before long he sought to protect Alaskan wildlife as enthusiastically as he destroyed wildlife (albeit for the Smithsonian) in Africa. An act to protect Alaskan game was approved in 1902. The new century, furthermore, conveniently delimits certain trends in American science. Smithsonian leadership in fundamental research was being clearly challenged by the universities.[17] After 1900, division of labor among the various institutions of science solidified;[18] specialization was accepted as a matter of course. Scientific articles on Alaska were esoteric more often than they were comprehensible to laymen. William Healey Dall was by then a "malacologist" rather than a "natural historian," and Brooks, his successor to the title of Dean of Alaskan Experts, was a geologist first and a geographer incidentally.

The term "science" is used here chiefly to mean what the Vannevar Bush Report calls "background research," as distinguished from "pure research" and "applied research." Background research covers the preparation of topographic and geologic maps, the collection of meteorological data, the description of animal and plant species, and the location and identification of minerals. Such knowledge is essential to progress in "pure" and "applied" research.[19] Original geographic exploration is akin to "pure research" in that goals are obscure and the best instructions do nothing more than point an investigator in a general direction. Further, just as a scientific experiment is successful only if when duplicated it yields the same results, so an exploration may for our purposes be termed successful if another investigator can, with the aid of information supplied by the explorer, travel the same route, see the same country, and arrive at the same destination without getting lost.

The term "Far Northwest" will often be used synonymously with "Alaska" and "Yukon Territory," though each term has its drawbacks. Alaska or Alaska-Yukon denotes a specific political area, and the denotation may tend to diminish the area. Alaska has always suffered from lack

17. Dupree, *Science in the Federal Government*, pp. 296, 297.

18. A. H. Dupree, "Influence of the Past: An Interpretation of Recent Development in the Context of 200 Years of History," *Annals of the American Academy of Political and Social Science*, 327 (1960), 24.

19. V. Bush, *Science: The Endless Frontier* (Washington, 1960; originally published 1945), pp. 81, 82.

of geographical perspective by outsiders,[20] and perspective is essential to an appreciation of the problems and achievements of institutions and individual explorers. The technique of superimposing an outline of the territory on a map of the United States is a cartographic cliché in books on Alaska, but some such device is necessary. "The dimensions of the Territory are of continental magnitude. This basal fact must be clearly comprehended by him who would understand the country," wrote Brooks in 1925,[21] and no amount of verbal or pictorial emphasis of the point is excessive. It would be instructive to superimpose the territory's profile on a map of the Trans-Mississippi West, on the Eastern United States, on Scandinavia, and on Western Europe. Alaska is one-half larger than the thirteen original American colonies, nearly twice the size of California, Oregon, and Washington together, and as large as Great Britain, Denmark, Sweden, Norway, and the old German Empire combined. It sprawls over 16 degrees of latitude and, excluding most of the Aleutian Islands, about 36 degrees of longitude. The Yukon River drains an area in Alaska and Canada roughly equal to the combined area of California, Washington, Utah, Nevada, and Idaho—that is, most of the Far West. All this is not a flight of neo-Texan pride in bigness. If perspective of size is not clearly grasped at the outset, the exploits outlined below will be relegated to the realm of regional puttering. Hence the use of the label "Far Northwest," which conveys the continental proportions better than the political name.

Within Alaska and Yukon Territory the natural barriers to exploration are similar to the geographical obstacles faced by explorers of the United States proper, though with a few special complications.[22] The northern winter climates are often more rigorous, and the summer is shorter. Topographically, all four main physiographic divisions of western North America—the Great Plains, the Rocky Mountain system, the central

20. E. Gruening, in *The State of Alaska* (New York, 1954), cites an example on p. 60.

21. "The Value of Alaska," *Geographical Review, 15* (1925), 29.

22. A. H. Brooks' "The Influence of Geography on the Exploration and Settlement of Alaska," *Bulletin of the American Geographical Society, 38* (1906), 102–05, was useful in preparing this brief general section on geographical considerations, though the Brooks article is directed more toward an explanation of exploratory activities during the Russian period.

plateau, and the Pacific mountain system—are found compressed in Alaska.

The mountains of Alaska guard the interior like great concentric walls of a medieval fort, forming arcs parallel to the southern coast. North of the Yukon River, the Brooks Range arches slightly in the opposite direction, parallel to the Arctic Circle. In between, the Yukon runs first north by northwest to the Circle, then west by southwest, following the axis of the central plateau.

The Yukon, unique in that it is navigable for virtually its entire length, early became the main highway of the Far Northwest. North and south of the Yukon in Alaska, and west of the Yukon in Canada, the river's four major tributaries flow in several directions. The White in Canada runs almost due north, the Tanana of Alaska flows west northwest, and the Koyukuk and Porcupine run southwest. Some northern tributaries flow southward or, like the Chandalar, southeast. The second big navigable stream of Alaska, the Kuskokwim, flows southwest, and in one lowland area runs near the Yukon. The Copper and Alsek—neither of them navigable—drain the coastal mountains. The Susitna is navigable for a short distance, but it passes through the broadest part of the Pacific mountain system in Alaska. In short, the drainage system of Alaska is complex beyond the experience of North American explorers. About one-fifth of the territory is drained south toward the Pacific, one-half toward the Bering Sea, and the remainder toward the Arctic Ocean.

Still another peculiar feature is the way in which the affluents of large rivers interlock, or are connected by lakes, though the rivers into which they empty may flow in different directions. Some of the passes and portages went unnoticed by explorers because they were so easily traversed; broad, low passes in the central plateau, for example, serve as the heads for important tributaries of the Susitna and Tanana rivers in the region between the complex coastal mountains and the Alaska Range. Other divides were more striking and yet produced confusion. A military explorer in 1898 reported that a party of miners started out for a tributary of the Koyukuk by ascending a northern affluent of the Yukon. For two and a half months they dragged their supplies up the branch. Over the divide they came upon a stream flowing north, and they selected it as a logical highway to the Koyukuk. The miners built rafts, loaded them with equipment and provisions, and, without paying much attention to direction, descended the stream until they reached a broad river, which, they learned from a passing steamboat captain, was the Yukon! They had traveled up one tributary of the Yukon and descended another, coming out some ten miles above where they left the Yukon three months before.[23]

Alaskan explorers were confronted by almost every environment found elsewhere in North America except the desert. There were thickly timbered valleys, swamps, mountains and plains, muskeg and hard surfaces. There were great stretches of seemingly flat land, sometimes on a plateau or high pass, which were actually a type of swamp occupied by tufts of grass or hummocks of bog moss; these stretches, variously designated, were termed *têtes de femmes* by voyageurs. One variety of this cover was called "waltzing grass" in 1898 by a military explorer:

> It grew in bunches or tufts that projected a foot or more above the water surrounding it. Each tuft is separated from its neighbor by a space of from 4 to 6 inches, in which there is water 2 or 3 feet in depth, so that one is compelled to step on the top of one of these bunches to avoid getting into the water. The surrounding space admits of considerable movement or vibration, so that one requires a steady nerve to balance himself on top of the bunch he selects for planting his foot. It made one literally dance about to retain his equilibrium, in which he too frequently failed. . . . A mile of this sort of travel not only fatigues and shakes up a man very badly, but spoils the best disposition on earth.[24]

Another impediment to exploration was the infamous Alaskan mosquito. One explorer wrote: "I have never seen their equal for steady and constant irritation in any part of the United States, the swamps of New Jersey and the sand hills of Nebraska not excepted. It was only when the wind was blowing and well out on a lake or wide portion of the river that their abominable torment ceased."[25] Clouds of mosquitoes swarming on target could hinder the explorer from shooting game for food, could pre-

23. J. C. Castner, in E. F. Glenn and W. R. Abercrombie, *Report of Explorations in the Territory of Alaska (Cooks Inlet, Sushitna, Copper, and Tanana Rivers) 1898* (War Department, Washington, 1899), pp. 250, 251.

24. Glenn, in ibid., p. 66.

25. F. Schwatka, "Report of a Military Reconnaissance Made in Alaska in 1883," *Compilation of Narratives of Explorations in Alaska* (Washington, 1900), p. 299.

vent sextant observations, and might drive pack animals and dogs quite mad. Alfred Brooks said of the mosquito: "While every other hardship of Alaska travel is often grossly exaggerated, it is hardly possible to do this one justice. Men capable of enduring heat and cold, hunger and fatigue without murmuring, will become almost savage under the torture."[26] As a European ethnological collector in Alaska remarked: "No philosophy protects against the mosquito."[27]

Such were some of the natural obstacles to Alaskan exploration that combined with general social conditions to hinder geographical discovery in the Far Northwest. In spite of them, the government compiled an admirable record of achievement in exploration. The following study aspires to record the achievement as chapters in the history of American science, the history of North American exploration, the history of westward expansion, and—incidentally but not least—the history of Alaska.

26. "An Exploration to Mount McKinley, America's Highest Mountain," *JG*, 2 (1903), 452, 453.

27. *Gegen Mosquitos schützt keine Philosophie:* Captain J. A. Jacobsen, in A. Woldt, editor, *Capitain Jacobsen's Reise an der Nordwestküste Amerikas, 1881–1883* (Leipzig, 1884), p. 168.

2. Young Wine in New Bottles

Doubtless Colonel Bulkley's preference for youth, activity, and "go" is that of Americans generally. Here, in England, I have sometimes thought that youth was considered more of a crime than a recommendation, and that you were nowhere until you had—like old port—acquired "body" and "age!"

FREDERICK WHYMPER[1]

IT IS APPROPRIATE and symbolic that the Yukon of Alaska was officially explored by an international party—an American adventurer, a Russian Creole, a French-Canadian, an English artist, and a Yankee scientist. Their combined background represented the past, the present, and the future of North America. Equally appropriate were the setting, the time, the sponsor, and the purpose of the exploration: The region was a part of Russian America, the last corner of the continent to be explored, and it was examined shortly before its transfer to the United States by a blossoming American monopoly that aimed to link Europe to the United States by telegraph.

The intercontinental telegraph was a project in the tradition of American expansionism, for which the slogan—Manifest Destiny—was coined in the 1840s and which had its last spectacular overt expression in the Spanish-American War near the end of the century. A sense of mission impelled the American westward to spread his civilization, particularly his commerce, from shore to shore. Territorial acquisition from Atlantic to Pacific was only the first phase of a larger geopolitical design to control the trade of Asia. The harbors of California and Oregon were gateways to the Orient, and the islands of Alaska and Hawaii were ports of call and coaling stations on the seaway to the wealth of Asia. Much of what was done or not done in the exploration of Alaska between 1865 and 1900 can be tied to the waxing and waning of expansionist sentiment. The first systematic American investigation of interior Alaska was undertaken in search of

1. *Travel and Adventure in the Territory of Alaska* (New York, 1869), p. 92.

a path for the telegraph, and one of the last scientific surveys in the century was sponsored by Edward Harriman, the railroad magnate.

In 1861 the Western Union Telegraph Company joined the Atlantic and Pacific coasts with a transcontinental telegraph. The first coast-to-coast railroad, authorized in 1862—half a dozen years after the Army's Topographical Engineers had explored the routes west—was completed after the Civil War. Once the continental United States had been welded together by wire and rail, the way was open for the western movement to become international, and Americans with a world view sought more actively to extend their commercial influence to Asia. There were two ways of tapping the wealth of the Orient by sea: from Pacific ports via the tropical Pacific islands to the littoral of eastern Asia, and the more direct Great Circle route via the North Pacific. The road was cleared by Commodore Matthew Perry, who opened feudal Japan to trade in 1854, and by Captain John Rodgers, who explored the North Pacific during the mid 1850s. By land in 1856, Perry McDonough Collins traveled from St. Petersburg, Russia, into Siberia and down the Amur River to the Pacific. Collins was an East Coast businessman whose entrepreneurial drive was cosmopolitan. He envisioned a telegraph line arching from the United States along the Great Circle land route in North America to Siberia and the Amur basin, there to connect with a Russian wire from Europe. It was in fact a vision of the first commercially feasible "northwest passage."

Collins' scheme was supported by the ardent expansionist William H. Seward of New York, later Lincoln's Secretary of State. In 1857, after the first of Cyrus Field's five unsuccessful attempts to lay an Atlantic cable for the American Telegraph Company, Collins sought and obtained a charter from the Russians and approval from the British for the international line. When on the recommendation of Seward the Congress of the United States authorized the project, Collins merged with Western Union.[2]

The enterprise was nothing if not ambitious. The line was to pass through British Columbia and Yukon Territory, through Russian Amer-

2. American expansionism has been examined by several authors. For example, Vilhjalmur Stefansson discusses the Northwest Passage as telegraph and railroad in *Northwest to Fortune* (New York, 1958), pp. 243–322. The Collins line as an enterprise in continentalism is treated in Charles Vevier, "The Collins Overland Line and American Continentalism," *PHR*, *28* (1959), 237–53. See also H. F. Taggart, editor, "Journal of William H. Ennis, Member, Russian-American Telegraph Exploring Expedition," *CHSQ*, *33* (1954), 2. Ennis' Journal is concluded in ibid., *33* (1954), 147–68.

ica, and through Siberia for thousands of miles; a large portion of the route was unexplored wilderness. Two wires handling 1,000 messages a day at $25 per message could gross $9 million annually.[3] Small wonder that Western Union invested so heavily in the project.

Plans called for three divisions, one in Canada, one in Russian America, and one in Asia. Colonel Charles Bulkley was given over-all command, and Captain Charles M. Scammon, on leave of absence without pay from the U.S. Revenue Marine, was second in command and in charge of the marine service for the expedition.[4] The directors chose Robert Kennicott, the only available American "expert" on Alaska, to head the Russian American division.

Kennicott was born in New Orleans and raised in Illinois. From his physician father he acquired an early interest in natural history. After studying under J. E. Kirtland of Cleveland, a natural scientist, and P. R. Hoy, the ornithologist, Kennicott undertook a natural history survey of Illinois in 1855. In 1857 he became curator of the Northwestern University museum of natural history. His collection activities for the University took him to the Red River of the North and to the Smithsonian Institution in Washington. In 1859 he resolved to explore and collect in Canada and Russian America.

Under the auspices of the Smithsonian Institution and the Chicago Academy of Sciences, Kennicott came to Alaska by way of the Mackenzie and Porcupine Rivers, and remained at Fort Yukon during the winter of 1860–61. His trip could not have succeeded without the generous hospitality of the Hudson's Bay Company.[5] Satisfaction was mutual. The Company provided room and transportation, such as it was in that country at that time, and Kennicott provided its traders with enthusiasm for a new avocation in a lonely land, plus a clear chance for immortality. Part of his Yukon collection was lost, but the over-all result of his work and the work of his recruits was staggering.[6] In 1863 alone, Spencer Baird of the Smith-

3. W. H. Depermann, "Two Cents an Acre," NAR, 245 (1938), 128.

4. Scammon to Secretary of the Treasury McCulloch, June 25, 1865; Scammon to Bulkley, June 6, 1865; both in C. M. Scammon Papers, MSS, Bancroft Library. See also Taggart, "Journal of William H. Ennis."

5. SI, Annual Report, 1859, p. 66. Ibid., 1861, pp. 59, 61. J. A. James, The First Scientific Exploration of Russian America and the Purchase of Alaska (Evanston and Chicago, 1942), pp. 1–12.

6. Kennicott to R. McFarlane, April 15, 1864, in W. H. Dall, Spencer Fullerton Baird (Philadelphia, 1915), p. 377.

sonian reported the arrival of forty boxes and packages weighing in the aggregate around a ton and a half. Of the ethnological materials, said Baird, "It is believed that no such series is elsewhere to be found of the dresses, weapons, implements, utensils, instruments of war and of the chase . . . of the aborigines of Northern America"; of the zoological collections, he wrote: "The materials . . . will serve to fix with precision the relationships of the arctic animals to those of more southern regions, their geographic distribution, their habits and manners."[7] Kennicott worked for a year on his collections at the Smithsonian, and in 1864 he became curator of the Chicago Academy of Sciences.

For the Western Union expedition, Kennicott requested permission to engage a few other naturalists, organized as a "Scientific Corps" designed to gather data and specimens as official duty permitted. Professional opportunity in lieu of fabulous pay induced half a dozen men to enlist. J. T. Rothrock was signed on as botanist; insects were to be Ferdinand Bischoff's specialty; Henry W. Elliott and Charles Pease were assigned to birds and small animals, Henry M. Bannister to paleontology, and William Healey Dall to invertebrates and fishes.[8] The Scientific Corps had its own flag, a scallop outlined on a blue cross. The banner was a fringe benefit, for the salary was infinitesimal. "It probably was a fair expression of the estimate placed upon scientific endeavor by the business end of the enterprise," wrote a Corpsman many years later.[9] Kennicott was both Chief ("Major") of the Russian American Division and head of the Scientific Corps. His old sponsors, the Smithsonian Institution and the Chicago Academy of Sciences, contributed toward the scientific outfit.

Although Robert Kennicott's sojourn with the Hudson's Bay Company had been pleasant and fruitful, his association with Western Union was futile, tense, and ultimately tragic. Kennicott was first a naturalist and accidentally a company representative. He worked best alone with no responsibility other than the demands of science. Burdened with the schedules of a business venture and the necessity of cooperating with ambitious men concerned only with their own company record, Kennicott's young

7. SI, *Annual Report, 1863*, p. 53.

8. Dall's Notebooks, William Healey Dall Papers, Division of Mollusks, U.S. National Museum, Washington, D.C.

9. J. T. Rothrock in a letter dated January 11, 1913, quoted in C. Mackay, "The Collins Overland Telegraph," *BCHQ*, 5 (1946), p. 197n.

ideals shattered, and he finally broke under the strain. He was the right man by regional experience and the wrong man by temperament. This remarkable, intelligent, sensitive, and devoted young scientist (he was thirty in 1865) was in a way sacrificed to the pecuniary busyness of the nineteenth century.

The signs of a troubled personality appeared early. Dall (who never bore an iota of malice toward Kennicott) wrote of him on the journey out to San Francisco: "He is certainly in a great state of excitement or else he was intoxicated. I should say of another man judging from the same data that he was either insane or incapable of doing the work set before him. . . . He is absurdly suspicious of everyone."[10] Kennicott was the only man in the party with any practical qualifications for the job of exploration, and he had a reputation in science. Both conditions made him an object of jealousy among the other officers. His reaction was neurotic. From San Francisco, he mailed a statement to Spencer F. Baird: "should anything happen to me on this Exped[ition] so that I never return it might be that some evil disposed person should by misrepresentations make it appear that I have not done my duty by the Company." Bulkley, he went on, might cloud the record because some of his "subalterns are jealous of me." It was all probably a "money question," and he thought there was a "screw loose somewhere." Members of his Scientific Corps, he wrote, were being flattered into defection and encouraged to distrust him and doubt his competency. In the same breath, with a near manic-depressive symptom, he said: "The 'Carcajous' (my men) are all true blue—gentlemen—tough, nervous, and ready for hard work, fun, or anything that comes up —I'd bet on them . . . to discover the open polar sea."[11]

The hectic organization of the expedition at San Francisco in 1865 would have frayed the nerves of an iron personality. There was the matter of a route to be followed, for example. Kennicott thought the line should go via the Mackenzie River, but Bulkley ordered it built from the head of the Fraser.[12] There was the problem of recruitment. There were needless delays and difficulties, the import of which only Kennicott could fully appreciate. There was the silly attention to uniform and to military disci-

10. Dall's Diaries, May 10, 1865, Dall Papers.

11. Kennicott to Baird, June 4, 1865, in Russian Telegraph Expedition Collection, MSS, U.S. National Museum Library, Washington, D.C.

12. Ibid., handwritten copy of a telegram from Kennicott to the Director.

pline. The officers were given military rank. The uniform was a single-breasted coat with staff buttons, a silver snowshoe as shoulder strap, and a silver canoe on the cap. The uniform failed to hide a lack of *esprit de corps*.

Moreover, the function of the Scientific Corps was not clearly established. There was among Company men a lack of interest in science except when it served practical ends. Dall wrote to Baird at the end of the year: "They [Bulkley, *et al.*] mean to get a vessel (steamer) out of the Revenue Service, through the Sec'ry of the Treasury. They rely much on the aid to be furnished by yourself and Dr. Torrey who is a personal friend of McCullough [sic]. Of course on the ground of the assistance done to science etc. etc. These men should furnish us if they expect such help, with an . . . [idea] of what they will do next year for the N. H. [natural history] work in the way of out-fit."[13] Kennicott's equipment for the telegraph work, he complained, was "abominable." "I'm going to *succeed fully by God if it is only to put myself in a position to punish* those who have been the cause of this absurd outfit."[14] From the time he boarded the boat for San Francisco, throughout his layover there, until he was put ashore in the fall at St. Michael, Kennicott was like Sam McGee in a "fiery furnace"[15] of confusion, pettiness, and inefficiency.

Once in Russian America, a number of circumstances further conspired to break Kennicott's spirit. A small river steamer, the *Lizzie Horner,* was taken to St. Michael to be employed on the Yukon. The engineer left the *Lizzie's* exhaust pipe at Sitka, and another had to be made.[16] When finally repaired, the *Lizzie* still would not run. Then the hapless little steamer parted her chain and was washed on the rocks.[17] Also, the expedition was left with Army rations. "One of us could eat, up there, as much as four soldiers."[18] More catastrophic was the scarcity of sled dogs. "Things

13. Ibid., Dall to Baird, December 16, 1865.

14. Ibid., Kennicott to Baird, September 16, 1865.

15. Ibid., Dall to Baird, September 26, 1866.

16. Ibid., Dall to Baird, October–November 1865.

17. Ennis to Bulkley, June 30, 1866, in C. S. Bulkley, "Journal of the U.S. Russo-American Telegraph Expedition, 1865–1867," microfilm, Bancroft Library, of a copy in possession of the Library Association of Portland, Oregon. Another copy of Bulkley's Journal is in the U.S. National Museum Library, Washington, D.C.

18. Ferdinand Westdahl, MS dated Olympia, W.T., 1878, Bancroft Library.

don't look at all pleasant and I wish I were quite alone with a small outfit of my own choosing," Kennicott revealed. "I could then go in with a lighter heart than I now do when I have the safety and comfort of the others to look after."[19] As a loner the "Major" was a grand success; as the leader of a large expedition with practical goals, he was melancholic and a worrier.

Procurement of local help was another difficulty that confronted Kennicott. Russian interpreters and guides got a dollar a day on the road and half a dollar in camp, an inflated wage for the time and place. At least one of them was worth it—Lukeen.

Much of the history of Russian inland exploration can be tied to the name Lukeen, either Simon Lukeen or his son Ivan. The Lukeens were "Creoles"—persons with mixed Russian and Alaskan native blood—who were fur traders and served incidentally as explorers. The Russian American Company relied almost exclusively on Creoles for exploration. They were the true *coureurs de bois*, the Mountain Men, the voyageurs of Alaska.

At what time the first Lukeen died and the second succeeded to his father's peripatetic existence is not known, for the available sources often give only the surname. There was a Lukeen (probably Simon) with Korsakov, who founded a redoubt on the Nushagak River, and with Vasilief, who, a decade later, in 1829, explored the Holitna and lower Kuskokwim rivers. In 1834 Lukeen, from his post on the Kuskokwim, aided the Russian explorer Andrei Glazunov. Glazunov came overland from St. Michael and attempted unsuccessfully to reach Cook Inlet by ascending the Stony River. The most extensive Russian inland exploration was led by Lieutenant Laurenti Alexiev Zagoskin, who examined parts of the Yukon in 1842 and 1843; in 1844 he was accompanied by Lukeen on a trip up the Kuskokwim to a point near present-day McGrath. In 1863 Ivan Lukeen was chosen by the chief Russian trader at St. Michael to learn more about the English operation on the upper Yukon. Lukeen traveled with the regular Russian trading party to Nukluklayet, then continued alone to the Hudson's Bay post at Fort Yukon. There, posing as a defector from the Russian company, he gathered information on the extent of British trade

19. Kennicott in a note attached to a letter from H. M. Bannister to Baird, December 5, 1865, Russian Telegraph Collection.

in Alaska. Lukeen is thus the first one on record to trace the Yukon from
the sea to the Porcupine River. His findings were not disseminated.[20]

Two years later the same Lukeen and George Russell Adams of the
Telegraph Expedition, accompanied by an Eskimo, were ordered to ascend
the Unalakleet River in a three-hole kayak and investigate the portage to
the Yukon. Lukeen, Adams reported, could read and write Russian, and
spoke Eskimo, Ingalik, and one other Indian language fluently; he swore
in Russian. "Going up the river . . . I saw an animal running along the
shore and called Lukine's attention to it. . . . As the wolf came opposite
. . . , about one hundred feet away, I took a shot at it with my revolver. I
missed it and the animal bounded off. Then I heard some violent language
from Lukine. . . . I got a number of words from the incident for my Rus-
sian-English vocabulary and also some Russian cuss words that it was just
as well for the harmony of our expedition that at the time I was not able to
interpret." Lukeen was an excellent shot, as illustrated by another incident
on the same trip. Beaching the kayat, the men heard a fluttering in a
nearby spruce grove. Lukeen, "pouring a handful of shot into a barrel of
his musket, rammed a piece of cloth down on the shot and started for the
trees. He crept around until he got the position he wanted, with several of
the birds well in line, and with one shot brought down four partridges."
Very shortly two of the birds were picked, cleaned, and set to boiling over
a new fire.[21]

The Russian-American phase of the telegraph work was divided in two
sections, one to explore the Yukon east from Nulato and connect with the
party working north through Canada, and the other to investigate the

20. For a study of inland exploration during the Russian period see Brooks, *The
Geography and Geology of Alaska*, or Brooks, *Blazing Alaska's Trails* (University of
Alaska and Arctic Institute of North America, 1953), which contain similar accounts.
In Chapter 2 of my doctoral dissertation, "American Scientific Exploration of Alaska,
1865–1900" (University of California, Berkeley, 1962), the subject is coupled with a
survey of scientific activities during the period.

21. G. R. Adams, "A Story of the First American Exploring Expedition to Russian
America," microfilm, Bancroft Library, of a typescript MS in the possession of Mrs.
Oliver Adams, Berkeley, California, pp. 67–70. The MS was written by Adams later in
life with his diaries at hand. See H. F. Taggart, "Journal of George Russell Adams,
Member, Exploring Expedition in Russian America, 1865–67," *CHSQ*, 35 (1956),
305, n. 1. The original diaries are in the University of Washington Library, Seattle.
The "four bird" story is credible to anyone who has observed the behavior of the
Alaskan ptarmigan.

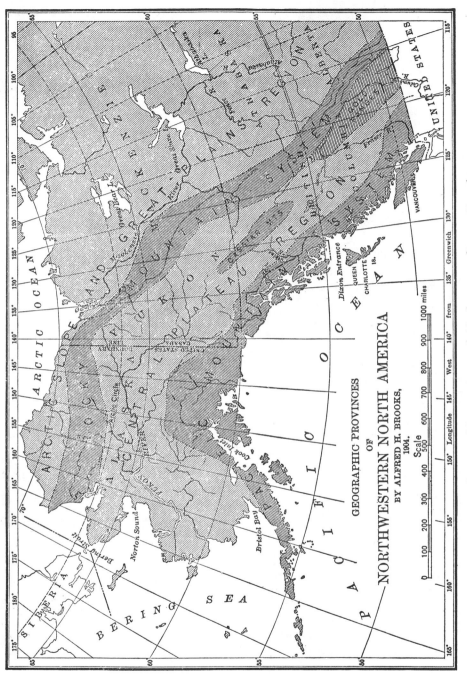

1. Geographic Provinces of Alaska, according to Brooks

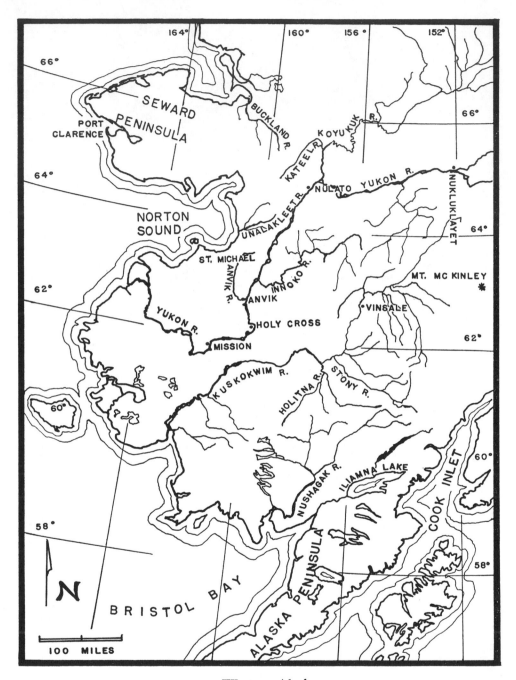

2. Western Alaska

area between the Yukon and Bering Strait. During the first year, the region between the Koyukuk and Norton Bay and parts of the Seward Peninsula were explored by the western party. Kennicott, Lukeen, and Adams, in the eastern party, moved their advance post to Nulato.

The Carcajous scattered. Rothrock and Elliott went to the Canadian Division, where they accomplished little scientific work; Elliott eventually became a telegraph operator.[22] Pease was in Alaska with Kennicott. Henry Bannister, who had been transferred from Canada to Kennicott's command, remained at St. Michael to make meteorological observations and collections for the Smithsonian, and to tend the stores. Dall stayed aboard a Company ship as Acting Surgeon, collecting specimens wherever the ship touched in Russian America or Siberia; his first trip yielded 5,160 specimens belonging to 451 species.[23] Also, he was Acting Chief of the Scientific Corps while Kennicott worked in Alaska.[24] Ferdinand Bischoff, the one older man in the group, fell ill and on the trip northward was left at Sitka, where he gathered a large and valuable collection of natural history materials that were later forwarded to the Smithsonian.[25]

Bischoff was a thoroughly likable individual with a lonesome drive not unlike that of his youthful chief, Kennicott. "Bischoff has stood out like a man," wrote Dall to Spencer Baird, "against seasickness, arsenical poison and poor fare. I am proud to call the old Dutchman my friend and I have no doubt the old man would die if he thought he could advance Natural History by so doing. When some officious asses were trying to soothe him when sick, by crying down K.[ennicott] for bringing him out at all; the old man spoke up stoutly and said he came of his own choice and would not go back if he could, but that if he made good collections, he was satisfied; they might drop him overboard, he had no friends! ... He will make his record I have no fear about it."[26] The old man did make his record. He was one of two men with Alaskan experience to testify before a Senate committee on the purchase of the territory. (The other witness, young Bannister, once back in the States, would have no more of the North;

22. Elliott to Joseph Henry, April 30, 1869, SI Archives, Washington, D.C.
23. P. Bartsch, H. A. Rehder, and B. E. Shields, *A Bibliography and Short Biographical Sketch of William Healey Dall*, Smithsonian Miscellaneous Collections, *104*, No. 15 (Washington, 1946), 5.
24. Kennicott to Baird, September 16, 1865, Russian Telegraph Collection.
25. SI, *Annual Report*, 1867, p. 42.
26. Dall to Baird, October–November 1865, Russian Telegraph Collection.

Bischoff, however, returned to Alaska and to his scientific work. Under the auspices of the Smithsonian and the Chicago Academy, he collected in Siberia and at Kodiak and Kenai. In 1869 he was visited at Kenai by General George H. Thomas, whose aide reported: "He barely makes a living and works for the love of his Science. He is known here as the 'bug catcher.' "[27] Bischoff passed into history in a manner consistent with his lonely, eccentric life. Eventually he made his way back to the States, where—characteristically alone—he wandered off into the New Mexico desert and was never heard from again.)[28]

From Kennicott's earlier journeys in the Far Northwest had emerged the dream of his life: to explore Russian America, identifying the fauna and establishing its relation to the fauna of Siberia and Japan.[29] As a first part of the project, he planned a winter trip to Fort Yukon, but was forced at length to abandon it as impracticable. There followed a period of inactivity, and he became depressed. Then one day in May of 1866, near Nulato, he strolled off and failed to return. Pease and Lebarge later came upon his body lying on the river beach. "He must have died suddenly and without pain. A pocket compass lay near him, and a diagram of the points of the compass was traced out in the sand. . . . He had, it seems, been taking the bearings of the landmarks in view."[30] Apparently he died from a heart attack, though Adams thought he might have committed suicide. Dall, learning of his friend's death in the fall when he arrived at St. Michael, formed his own view and wrote home in an explosion of grief that Kennicott had "Died last May of disease of the heart on a desolate northern beach, alone! He was murdered; not by the merciful knife but by slow torture of the mind. By ungrateful subordinates, by an egotistic and selfish commander, by anxiety to fulfil his commands, while those that gave them were lining their pockets in San Francisco. I am so nervous from rage and grief that I can hardly write."[31] Whatever the cause, Kennicott had a

27. R. G. Athearn, editor, "An Army Officer's Trip to Alaska in 1869," *PNQ*, 40 (1949), 51, 52.

28. Dall, *Spencer Fullerton Baird*, p. 377 n.

29. W. H. Dall, "Alaska as It Was and Is," *Bulletin of the Philosophical Society of Washington*, 13 (1895), 124, 125.

30. Bannister to Baird, October 12, 1866, Russian Telegraph Collection.

31. Dall to Miss E. M. (Lizzie) Merriam, September 28, 1866, Dall Papers. Dall claimed that Kennicott "was badgered to death": Dall to Baird, September 26, 1866, Russian Telegraph Collection.

premonition of his own death. That very morning he had drafted a plan for continuing the work should anything happen to him: Frank Ketchum was placed in charge of the Yukon section,[32] and William H. Ennis was to command the region west of Nulato to the Strait.[33]

Pease and Lukeen constructed a coffin of boards ripped from the sides of the old Nulato fort.[34] Pease, Kennicott's boyhood friend, escorted the body south. A year later, at Nulato, Dall carved an inscription on an oak tablet: "In memory of Robert Kennicott, Naturalist, who died near this place May 13, 1866, aged thirty."[35]

William Dall succeeded Kennicott as Chief of the Scientific Corps— "a funereal sort of honor." The science department of the Western Union Telegraph Expedition had all but disintegrated. Bannister had frozen his face on the only excursion he made during the previous winter and been sent home.[36] Pease was gone. Bischoff, after a year in Sitka, traveled to Washington. Rothrock and Elliott were out of touch in Canada; although Bulkley had promised Dall that Elliott would help in Alaska with the scientific work, Elliott preferred the greater emoluments of the telegraph. Dall was Chief, but there were no Indians.[37]

Final conquest of the Yukon was left to Frank Ketchum. On May 26, 1866, he set out on his initial voyage with Lukeen and Mike Lebarge in a three-holed kayak. Michael Lebarge had been on the same ship that carried Kennicott to San Francisco, and except for that coincidence might never have visited Alaska. He was, a comrade wrote, "An indefatigable

32. Adams, "First American Exploring Expedition," pp. 187–89. Committee of the Academy, "Biography of Robert Kennicott," *Transactions of the Chicago Academy of Sciences*, *1* (1867–69), 221.

33. Ennis to Bulkley, June 30, 1866, in Bulkley's Journal, p. 49. Also, Dall to his mother, September 26, 1866, Dall Papers.

34. J. H. A. Bone, "Russian America," *Atlantic*, *14* (1867), 741.

35. Dall's Diaries, May 13, 1867, Dall Papers. Kennicott was thirty-one.

36. Dall to his mother, September 26, 1866, Dall Papers.

37. Dall to Kennicott, July 28, 1866, Dall Papers. (Kennicott was dead when the letter was written.) Also, Elliott to Joseph Henry, April 30, 1869, SI Archives. There has been a little confusion on the matter of leadership after Kennicott's death. Dall has been accused of leaving the erroneous impression that he was in charge of the whole Russian American Division. A few writers have in fact assigned him that distinction after a light reading of his *Alaska and Its Resources* (Boston, 1870). Actually, Dall made no claim to any title other than Chief of the Scientific Corps, a natural "promotion" from the duties given him by Kennicott; and he specifically indicated that Ennis was in command west of Nulato and Ketchum was in command east. See pp. 6, 8.

traveler, a delightful companion *en route* or by the campfire, full of expedients whatever befell, tactful and adroit in his dealing with the natives,
generous and helpful to the inexperienced—in short, a capital voyageur
of the best type."[38] The Russian factor at Nulato went along with the
party as far as Nukluklayet on his annual summer trading mission. En
route they were supplied in part by Indian hunters; one Indian brought
thirty pounds of dried meat into camp, reported Ketchum, "for which he
modestly asked my coat, vest and pants." Arriving at Nukluklayet, the
party came upon the annual assembly of Tanana Indians gathered for
trade. There were two chiefs among them, one of whom was officially
recognized by the Russians and the other by the English. The explorers,
continuing their journey, overtook an English missionary thirty miles
above Nukluklayet, and traveled with him to Fort Yukon, the upper limit
of the voyage. Finding the head trader at the Fort absent, the American
party limited their visit to three days and began the return trip downstream. They arrived back at Nulato eight days later.[39]

On this initial voyage, which was a mere reconnaissance, it is difficult to
determine just how many fixes—if any—were taken. The two journeys
that yielded a rough survey of the river were not undertaken until the following year.

The winter of 1866–67 found Dall and the English artist Frederick
Whymper at Nulato, the former busily collecting and preparing specimens
and adding data to his ethnological notebooks. Collection was aided by a
good-natured, six-foot native named Kurilla who delighted in shooting at
anything he spied. Thanks to Kurilla, Dall obtained more specimens than
he had hoped for—"redpolls, downy and three-toed woodpeckers, pine
grosbeaks, titmice, hawkowls, and (strange to say) a bulfinch . . . , the first
ever shot on the American continent." Dall also trapped foxes, or tried to,
and he continued to add to his Indian vocabularies.[40] The collection of
ethnological data was a continuous and important operation, and one in
which Whymper also engaged. Whymper's vivid description of a Koyukuk
shaman's "medicine" was read to the Ethnological Society of London:

> A group of Indians encircled the invalid; in their midst burnt a
> dim fire. A monotonous chorus in an undertone was kept up, whilst

38. Dall, "A Yukon Pioneer, Mike Lebarge," *NGM*, 9 (April 1898), 138, 139.
39. Ketchum to Ennis, July 12, 1866, Bulkley's Journal, pp. 151, 153, 154.
40. Dall, *Alaska and Its Resources*, p. 57.

this man went through an elaborate performance: some details of which are absolutely revolting, and cannot be mentioned. Now he appeared to draw the evil spirit from the sick man, and wrestling with it, threw it on the fire, and then repelled, ran wildly from it with mock terror and affright. Now it has possession of him, and he gesticulated, groaned, and frothed at the mouth; the whole accompanied by recitative artistically managed in connection with the chorus. The whole affair was not unlike a weird scene in a sensation drama, taking into consideration the accessories, the over-hanging trees, the twilight, the low fire.

At last the performance assumed a gayer tinge, the chorus grew louder and livelier; the man was supposed to be dispossessed, and he hobbled from the scene.[41]

Indian opinion on their shaman's merit was divided: some considered it fine medicine and others regarded it as humbug. It was a matter of cultural perspective. If those same Indians had watched Dall's every move, they might have united to think him a trifle weird, if not downright evil. Waiting for a snowy day to cover his tracks, Dall sneaked upon a nearby native grave and removed the skull, carefully packing it away to avoid discovery by the Indians.[42] The pursuit of science often led down strange paths.

Whymper's main employment as an artist was hampered by the season. Sketching is an immobile occupation, and at thirty degrees below zero it can be a severe trial.

In November and December I succeeded in making sketches of the fort and neighborhood at times when the temperature was as low as thirty degrees below zero. It was done, it need not be said, with difficulty, and often by *installments*. Between every five strokes of the pencil I ran about to exercise myself, or went to our quarters for warmth. Several times I skinned my fingers, once froze my left ear, which swelled up nearly to the top of my head, and I was always afraid that my prominent nasal organ would get bitten. The use of water-colors was of course impracticable—except when I could keep

41. Whymper, "Russian America, or 'Alaska:' the Natives of the Youkon River and Adjacent Country," *Transactions of the Ethnological Society of London*, I (1869), 175, 176.

42. Dall, *Alaska and Its Resources*, p. 67.

a pot of warm water on a small fire by my side—a thing done by me
on two or three occasions when engaged at a distance from the post.
Even inside the house the spaces near the windows—as well as the
floor—were often below freezing-point. Once, forgetful of the fact
(and it is a fact of which you do become forgetful), I mixed some
colors up with water that had just stood near the oven, and wetting a
small brush, commenced to apply it to my drawing-block. Before it
reached the paper it was covered with a skin of ice, and simply
scratched the surface, and I had to give up for the time being.[43]

The two men occupied themselves profitably and not altogether uncom-
fortably. The Christmas meal, as reported by Whymper, was a feast:
Soupe a la Yukon—Roast Arctic Grouse—Alaska Reindeer Meat—Nu-
lato Cranberry Sauce—California (preserved) Peas and Tomatoes—Pies
—Dried Apple Pudding—Gingerbread a la Dall—Iced Cheese—Coffee,
Tea, Iced Water.

The big event of the winter was the departure of Ketchum and Lebarge
on an overland journey to Fort Yukon. The party, with four sleds, fourteen dogs, and four Indians, left Nulato on March 11, 1867, to the usual
shouting, firing of guns, and excitement that marked the beginning or end
of long trips in Russian America. J. T. Dyer had found a rusty, ancient
artillery piece in one of the old watch towers of the fort. With it he fired a
mighty salute to the travelers, a salute that nearly shook down the tower.[44]

The sledge trip to Fort Yukon was not completed until May 9th. A
snowfall during the first eighteen days slowed the explorers, but they
were lucky enough to keep supplied with caribou, moose, and small game
during the entire trip and to have eight of their fourteen dogs survive.
When the party finally arrived at Fort Yukon, no provisions were available there. Ketchum and Lebarge were forced to camp away for ten days,
living on a few wild geese. Then Trader McDougal, commander of the
Fort, was able to furnish them with a small supply of pemmican, and they
started upriver in birch canoes. On June 25, 1867, they reached Robert
Campbell's old Fort Selkirk, at the mouth of the Pelly, which marked the
upper limit of the exploration.

When they returned to Fort Yukon, Ketchum and Lebarge found that

43. Whymper, *Travel and Adventure*, p. 196.
44. Ibid., pp. 200, 203.

Dall and Whymper had arrived there by boat from Nulato a week before.[45] The Whymper-Dall expedition apparently originated with the
Englishman, who planned a summer sketching trip up the Yukon and
took Dall along, with Ketchum's approval.[46] One reason for the sanction
was Ketchum's hope that Dall could examine a coal seam above Nukluklayet. Dall had already reported that a deposit below Nulato was too small
to be useful.[47]

Whymper and Dall journeyed east in a skin boat when the river ice began to move. There were enough bergs still afloat to make the voyage
hazardous and exciting. Dall was also introduced to the pestiferous
northern mosquito: "The mosquitoes are like smoke in the air. Through
constant and enforced observation, I came to distinguish four kinds—a
large gray one, and another with white leg-joints, a very small dust-colored
one which held its proboscis horizontally in advance, and another small
one which carried its probe in the orthodox manner. All are distinguished
from the civilized species by the reckless daring of their attack." A blanket
was no defense; only "buckskin defied their art." Dall noted how the Indians placed in the bows of their canoes a dish of wet moss with a few hot
coals; when the canoes were in motion the smoke helped to disperse the
insects.[48] The mosquito, an object of levity to the inexperienced, was one
of the major hazards of exploration in the Far Northwest. "Cold is nothing compared to the mosquitos," one young explorer moaned; "of the two
give me fifty below zero."[49]

Dall also described the Indians along the way, especially the Tananas
with their blackened faces trimmed in vermilion, the dentalium orna-
ments in their pierced noses, the necklaces of bears' claws and teeth, sable
tails, wolf ears, or hawk and eagle feathers. At Nukluklayet the Tananas
performed the official greeting ceremony. "We formed in a line," Dall re-
counted, "with blank charges in our guns. The Indians did the same.
They advanced on us shouting, and discharged their guns in the air. We
returned the compliment, and they retreated to repeat the performance.
After ten minutes of this mock fight the tyone [chief] appeared between

45. Ketchum to Bulkley, July 25, 1867, Bulkley's Journal, pp. 224–26.
46. Draft letter from Dall to Bulkley, no date, in Dall's Diaries, Dall Papers.
47. Ketchum to Bulkley, March 6, 1867, in Bulkley's Journal, pp. 221, 222.
48. Dall, *Alaska and Its Resources*, pp. 92, 100.
49. Taggart, "Adams Journal," p. 302.

us. He harangued the Indians, who answered by a shout. Turning to us, he informed us that we were now at liberty to transact our business."[50]

On July 8th, Dall, Whymper, Ketchum, and Lebarge departed Fort Yukon together. Eating and sleeping as they drifted with the current, the party reached Nulato on the 13th. They were ordered to proceed immediately to St. Michael, where they learned that all operations were suspended: the Atlantic cable was at last in operation. Thus the Russian American Telegraph Expedition came to as abrupt and immature an end as its young commander had met.

Termination of the project was a disappointment to William Healey Dall. There was so much left to be done, however, that he resolved to stay. To supply himself with trading goods and provisions for the winter he asked Western Union for an order on the Russian American Company for part of the $775 in salary that the telegraph company owed him.[51] He hoped the Smithsonian might help; a meager $400 a year would cover expenses.[52]

Dall was well aware what he was letting himself in for. He knew the country was "the devil for nervous minds." One of his colleagues had gone quite mad the previous winter—the man had called himself "Beaver, Chief of the Kaviaks," and left Grantley Harbor with a small sled and an old squaw but no dogs or provisions.[53] Moreover, there was the Russian temperament to deal with. Sober, the Muscovites were good companions, but when their mighty thirst was slaked they were intolerable. One of them had stolen Dall's specimen alcohol containing arsenic and passed it around.[54] In a moment of exasperation, Dall wrote: "The Russians are *dogs;* if you come up bring plenty of rum & you can buy their *souls.*"[55] Any civilized person alone in that environment should be permitted an oc-

50. Dall, *Alaska and Its Resources*, pp. 93–95.

51. Dall to Baird, July 28, 1867, Dall Papers. According to a Dall memoir, the telegraph company refused to pay him when he arrived in San Francisco the following year. Ennis had lodged a complaint that Dall, as Acting Surgeon, had failed to come to the aid of Ennis' men who were suffering from scurvy during the winter 1866–67. Dall had had no medical supplies to administer, thanks to mismanagement in the Company, so he sent instructions to Ennis on all that could be done without supplies. A year later in Baltimore, Dall sued the Company for his salary and collected. See Dall, "Memoranda for My Grandchildren," typescript MS (1926), pp. 77, 71, 73, Dall Papers.

52. Bartsch et al., *Bibliography and Short Biographical Sketch*, p. 6.

53. Dall's Diaries, March 20, 1867, Dall Papers.

54. Whymper, *Travel and Adventure*, p. 264. Westdahl MS, p. 16.

55. Dall to Baird, August 21, 1867, Dall Papers.

casional explosion, a fit of petulance now and then, a small imagined ill-ness. Dall was not immune from slight symptoms of "bush disease"; at the same time, he was resilient, and his writings often reveal a humorous, philosophical resignation.

For the scientist, Alaskan wilderness had its advantages. There were all manner of rare plants and animals to be found, identified, and preserved. Dall searched for the emperor goose, and found eggs of a curlew not pre-viously located on the continent. Egg shells were preserved for science after their contents had been blown out and into a frying pan as omelets, prepared in caribou fat. "Duck roasted on a stick before a fire," Dall wrote, "is quite another thing from the embalmed remains which hotels offer us." Recruiting native help for his scientific activities was no problem. The abo-rigines were highly amused by the spectacle of a grown man eagerly chas-ing beetles and small animals, but the natives were "keenly alive to the fact that good specimens . . . [would] buy needles, caps, or tobacco." The In-dian himself was an object of Dall's interest. Ethnological investigation, absorbing in its own right, also gave him an opportunity to indulge his poetic proclivities; he translated a native song chanted in rhythm to the dipping paddles of a light canoe.[56]

On February 3, 1868, at Nulato, Dall heard news of an event that would mold his future. The usual commotion heralded the arrival of a party from afar. Lukeen and two traders brought a few supplies for the post and a keg of salted geese, a gift for Dall from the Chief Trader at St. Michael. Dall knew the arduous winter journey had not been made for so paltry a rea-son, but his inquiries met with a mysterious silence. Finally he coaxed the real reason for the trip from Lukeen, "a jolly little Creole." Official re-ports had arrived from Sitka via Nushagak and the Kuskokwim that Alaska had been sold to the United States. Dall immediately hoisted the Stars and Stripes in front of the fort, and had the supreme pleasure of ad-dressing letters to Trader McDougal at Fort Yukon, *United States of America*. The British held to the fiction that the fort was on Canadian soil.[57]

By a lucky accident, an American expedition that was exploring and

56. Dall, "Springtime on the Yukon," *American Naturalist*, 4 (1870), 601, 598.

57. Dall, *Alaska and Its Resources*, pp. 181, 182, 206. Lukeen disappears from the records soon after. A late mention of him by Dall was dated July 8, 1868. He was re-ported at the Kuskokwim with two Americans, formerly with Western Union and then trading privately. Dall's Diaries, Dall Papers.

collecting in the distant territory just prior to the purchase of Alaska had forwarded its materials to the Smithsonian Institution. For it was to the Smithsonian that Secretary of State William H. Seward turned for information on Alaska, after affixing his signature to the treaty. His ally in the Senate, Charles Sumner, (a strange political bedfellow), mined the Smithsonian and the libraries of Washington in preparing his memorable speech supporting the purchase.[58] Bannister and Bischoff testified before the Committee on Foreign Relations, and Spencer Baird provided important zoological data based on previous collections.[59] These activities gave rise to an unwarranted conclusion that the Telegraph Expedition was "largely responsible" for the acquisition of Alaska—a notion encouraged by Bannister and Dall and echoed by later writers.[60] Without doubt the resources in the Smithsonian helped advocates of the treaty to allay fears about the territory's value; but the scope of these resources was too limited to justify the role they came to assume. There were few original materials that had been properly worked over, and the Telegraph explorers had after all barely examined the country. Bischoff could report with authority on Sitka, to be sure, and Bannister's meteorological data were vital, since climate was a major point of attack for opponents of the treaty. Whether, however, the Telegraph information was of more actual value than Russian and English materials is a moot point. Seward would have contracted to buy the territory anyway, regardless of the recently collected Smithsonian data. There was heated debate over a House appropriations bill necessary to consummate the deal, much of it questioning the value of the territory. Dall did not return home in time to report favorably on this question, but Seward himself dispatched an official government expedition to Alaska under George Davidson to make its own investigation. The Davidson report, relying heavily on written materials, was used by proponents of the bill and was also credited by some with swaying the balance in favor of purchase.[61]

58. Joseph Henry to Seward, December 23, 1867, in U.S. House of Representatives, "Russian America," *House Executive Document 177, 40th, Congress: 2d session,* p. 86.

59. SI, *Annual Report,* 1867, p. 43.

60. James, *First Scientific Exploration,* p. 45. Dall, "Alaska as It Was and Is" (1895), p. 139. Dall, "The Discovery and Exploration of Alaska," *Harriman Alaska Expedition,* 2 (New York, 1902), 202, 203. Also W. H. Deperman, "Two Cents an Acre," p. 132.

61. M. B. Sherwood, "George Davidson and the Acquisition of Alaska," *PHR,* 28 (1959), 141–54.

The fact remains that every scrap of information about Alaska was welcome because so few scraps existed; but to connect any particular body of information with Seward's purchase and the votes of the Congress is a questionable procedure. Professor S. R. Tompkins' estimate of the Telegraph Expedition's role is more realistic: "It may indirectly have facilitated" the purchase of Alaska.[62]

There was no need to exaggerate the long-range scientific significance of the expedition. From it came numerous publications on geography and exploration, meteorology and hydrology, magnetism, history and bibliography, economics, geology and paleontology, faunal distribution, anthropology, zoology, and botany. Titles were usually connected with individual authors, not with the expedition, and many of the papers were the work of specialists in Washington, D.C., and elsewhere. The expedition thus served as an exercise for naturalists in and out of the territory, in the field and in the laboratory.

Most of the area touched by the expedition had been previously covered by the Russians or the English. One contribution of the Telegraph explorers was to coordinate earlier work. In addition, the Upper Yukon was reconnoitered and routes were established between Nulato and Bering Strait. Parts of Seward Peninsula and, more important, the Lower Yukon were mapped, the latter by Elijah Smith and J. T. Dyer.[63] The arcuate character of the Rockies in Alaska was confirmed, though the mountains were not penetrated. The westward bend of the range left a northern gap that helped to explain the general faunal distribution at that end of the continent.[64]

Determination of Alaska's fauna and flora and their relationship to the fauna and flora of Asia and North America had been Kennicott's primary goal in biology.[65] In 1865, Dall made the point to Bulkley: "The true scientific labor of late years has been in great part directed toward finding the boundaries of faunae, and accurately determining the habitat and value

62. S. R. Tompkins, *Alaska: Promyshlennik and Sourdough* (Norman, Okla., 1952), p. 182.

63. Dall, *Alaska and Its Resources*, p. 277. J. T. Dyer to Ketchum, July 7, 1867, Bulkley's Journal, pp. 228–30.

64. Dall, "On the Trend of the Rocky Mountain Range North of Lat. 60° and Its Influence on Faunal Distribution," AAAS, *Proceedings*, *18* (1870), 247. Dall, "Remarks upon the Natural History of Alaska," *Proceedings of the Boston Society of Natural History*, *12* (1868), 143–51.

65. Dall, "Alaska as It Was and Is," p. 141.

of species described. The mere addition of species supposed to be new to the already confused and crowded lists, is a work of far less value and dignity."[66] Consistent with that attitude, Dall noted the Canadian characteristics of northern Alaska fauna. Still, identification was necessary. Dall listed 77 mammalian species, 211 bird species, and 52 insect species obtained by the Scientific Corps in Alaska.[67]

J. T. Rothrock contributed an interpretive paper to help fulfill the other half of Kennicott's major plan. Adding the work of the Telegraph Expedition to the writings of Hooker and others, he came up with 732 Alaskan botanical species, including the cryptogamous plants. He also noted indications of a southward migration of northern plants during an ancient, frigid period, and remarked: "Whether we clothe this joint explanation of Messrs. Forbes and Darwin with all the dignity of a *theory* logically deduced from other and well-established facts, or reduce it to the rank of a mere *hypothesis,* it still remains the *only philosophical explanation* of these examples of widely-extended distribution along a given meridian."[68]

The achievement in geology was hardly less impressive, though based on limited evidence. Among Dall's 4,550 specimens were rocks collected from Fort Yukon to the sea, "sufficient to determine the geological formations for 1,300 miles."[69] For the *American Journal of Science,* he prepared a geologic cross-section of the river's course, though "having no pretenses to accuracy in detail."[70] Properly qualified in this way, it was a good beginning for geology in the Far Northwest. Dall and some of the Corpsmen had been tutored on glaciation by Louis Agassiz, the renowned glaciologist, before they left for Russian America. The instruction paid off. Dall noted the absence of indications of glacial action and concluded that north of the Alaska Range (as in parts of Siberia) there had been no glaciation. At the same time, he elaborated on the presence of ground ice a few feet below the surface, ice that yielded mammoth relics.[71] He also concluded tentatively that volcanism in Alaska was diminishing in violence, and that

66. Dall to Bulkley, November 6, 1865, Dall's Diaries, Dall Papers.

67. Dall, *Alaska and Its Resources,* pp. 576–78, 580–86, 587–89.

68. Rothrock, "Sketch of the Flora of Alaska," SI, *Annual Report,* 1867, pp. 439–41.

69. Dall, "Extracts from a Letter to the California Academy of Natural Sciences," *Proceedings of the California Academy of Sciences, 3* (1868), 367.

70. "Exploration in Russian America," *American Journal of Science [and the Arts],* ser. 2, 45 (1868), 96–99.

71. Ibid., p. 99. Also Dall, "Alaska as It Was and Is," pp. 140, 141.

the peninsular portion of the territory was undergoing a gradual elevation.[72]

Dall described coal deposits along the Yukon and reports of coal on
Cook Inlet. One notice in the reports of both Whymper and Dall anticipated the great gold rush of '98. Whymper wrote: "It is worthy of mention that minute specks of gold have been found by some of the Hudson's
Bay Company's men in the Yukon, but not in quantities to warrant a
'rush' to the locality." Similar specks were found by Telegraph personnel on Seward Peninsula.[73]

In addition to the bountiful scientific harvest, members of the expedition also passed along practical advice to future explorers. The Russian
skin boats used by Whymper and Dall rotted, tore, and required frequent
repairs; Whymper recommended using birch canoes instead. Better still,
with a small, flat-bottomed, stern-wheeled steamer, said Whymper, "a
comparatively inexpensive survey of the whole Yukon . . . might be easily
accomplished."[74]

Perhaps as significant a result as any was the light thrown on the opportunity for further exploration. Dall remarked: "The field now open to
Americans for exploration and discovery is grand. The interior everywhere needs exploration."[75]

The Western Union Telegraph Expedition was the first systematic scientific investigation of interior Alaska. Yet the term "Western Union" is
misleading. Without Dall's extra year the results would have been spotty.
Kennicott drew the blueprint for science; Dall carried it into the field.
And though members of the expedition sometimes credited the "liberality"
of the Company with making the work possible, Colonel Bulkley considered natural history little more than an off-duty recreation.[76] Thereafter
the job of exploration and science devolved mainly on the federal government.

72. Dall, "Observations on the Geology of Alaska," in G. Davidson, *Coast Pilot of
Alaska* (USCS, Washington, 1869), pp. 193, 194.

73. Whymper, *Travel and Adventure*, p. 258. Dall, "Account of Explorations,"
Proceedings of the California Academy of Sciences, 4 (1868), 35. H. L. Blake, "History of the Discovery of Gold at Cape Nome," *Senate Document 441, 56th Congress:
1st session* (3878), 1.

74. Whymper, *Travel and Adventure*, pp. 223, 267. Whymper to Ketchum, August
12, 1867, Bulkley's Journal, p. 232.

75. *Alaska and Its Resources*, p. 293.

76. Bulkley's Journal, p. 7.

3. William Healey Dall, Dean of Alaskan Experts

ALASKAN science and exploration between 1867 and 1900 may be divided into two broad phases. The first phase was spasmodic, often individual, microgeographical on land, decentralized, and uncoordinated, except for the loose connection of the Smithsonian with most of the investigative enterprises; it was strikingly consistent with Alexander Agassiz's "ideal" situation for scientific activity—"moderate centralization allowing of great competition." The second phase, which overlaps chronologically with the first, was comparatively systematic, though not continuous in time, and was dominated by two agencies in turn, the Army and the Geological Survey.

The impulse for the early phase came from five main sources: the need for coastal charts; the popularity of ethnological research, in which John Wesley Powell took a special interest south of the forty-ninth parallel; the appeal of tourism and mountaineering; the growing attractiveness of geology as a science and, particularly for Alaska, glaciological research; and the revolutionary concept behind the Tenth Census of the United States. The character of any given investigation during the period often reflected a combination of these motivations and was predetermined by social, intellectual, and economic considerations. Among the considerations were the current idea of laissez-faire, controversy over the role of science in government, and recognition of the need for geographical unification, a necessary precursor of the larger task of spreading American dominion over the entire Pacific. Though in 1867—the year Alaska was purchased— Congress authorized the geological exploration of the fortieth parallel, to produce geologic maps of the regions opened by the transcontinental railroad then in construction, and ordered the "Geological and Geographical Survey of the Territories," no systematic inland exploration of Alaska was put in motion for the next fifteen years. In brief, the first phase of science and exploration in the Far Northwest, excluding the start of Army work, was disjointed and uncoordinated.

The one thread of continuity for the early period was provided by the career of one man, William Healey Dall. The exploration of the Far Northwest between 1865 and 1900 in fact ran parallel to the biography of Dall. He undertook the first systematic examination of the territory after the United States acquired it in 1867, devoting four initial years to this work and thereafter returning periodically to make specific investigations. (His last visit of the century, in striking contrast to his first one, was made as a seasoned hand with the luxurious, private Harriman tour.) A government scientist-explorer, Dall was recognized as an Alaskan expert by all departments interested in Alaska-Yukon exploration, whether military or civilian. He actively represented three of the most important agencies concerned with science and exploration—the Coast Survey, the Smithsonian Institution, and the Geological Survey—and wrote for others—the Department of Agriculture and the Bureau of Ethnology, to name only two. Throughout his career he wrote prolifically, publishing reviews, articles, and critical comments for scientific and lay periodicals on matters of science and geography in Alaska, and eventually he compiled a history of Alaska. He took a vocal role in Alaskan politics, both as enacted in Washington and at the local level within the territory.

Dall's expertise was of course challenged—chiefly by an old colleague of the Scientific Corps, Henry Elliott. Dall was not always right. His geologic and ethnologic hypotheses were occasionally more bold than well advised. He erred by incorrectly estimating the height of Mt. St. Elias and, more broadly, by concluding that the Alsek River headwaters were the headwaters of the Copper River. Nevertheless his total achievement, considering the times and the circumstances and in comparison with the work of others, was magnificent. Dall's very presence was an important goad to careful, scientific accomplishment by Alaskan novitiates. Whatever was done, Dall would be there to examine, weigh, and judge—with his Alaskan experience, his scientific reputation in America and Europe, and his general historical and geographical erudition. William Healey Dall was the Dean of Alaskan Experts.

But he was much more than a regional specialist. He was a scientist, and the subject matter of science was international. His interest in Alaska was, like Kennicott's, related to the cosmopolitanism of science. Geographically, the Far Northwest was a bridge between the Old World and the New. It was a fertile, strategic, and virgin ground for testing big questions in biology, geology, and ethnology, an unused laboratory that promised to yield evidence confirming or refuting some of the great theories. Perhaps the evidence it veiled in unexplored wilderness might even relinquish a few new hypotheses. The evidence was at least worth recording, and Dall recorded a great deal of it. Unlike the work of many others, what he published was valuable, not merely because he was the first to pick up something and the first to describe it, but also because he was diligent and methodical and did not hesitate to draw large, tentative conclusions from his evidence. Even if some of the larger theses could not stand, the evidence was still pertinent.

William Dall was born on August 21, 1845, in Boston, the son of a Harvard-educated Unitarian minister and a scholarly and puritanical feminist. His father was devoted and gentle, his mother outspoken and strict; her ardent reformism brought William Lloyd Garrison, Susan Anthony, and Wendell Phillips to the Dall home. In 1855, his father was appointed Unitarian missionary to India, where he founded a school in Calcutta.

After attending Boston's English High School, young Dall became a student of Louis Agassiz at the Museum of Comparative Zoology, where he was fascinated by the mollusks. The special interest did not prevent him from developing the intellectual catholicity so common to the nineteenth-century "natural historian." The year 1863 saw Dall in Chicago as a clerk for the Illinois Central Railroad, and, given his interests, it was inevitable that he should meet Robert Kennicott at the Chicago Academy of Sciences. At nineteen, Dall accepted the Western Union job.[1] He returned to Washington too late to participate in the first official American exploration of Alaska.

William Henry Seward knew when he signed the treaty of annexation that more than Senate ratification was needed to consummate the purchase of Alaska. Traditionally, fiscal measures originated in the House, and Seward was afraid that unfavorable comment about the value of our newly acquired *terra incognita* might not dispose the House to make the funds available. He needed reliable information, and he moved rapidly. A Revenue Marine ship, the cutter *Lincoln*, was ordered north; aboard was a small group of Coast Survey scientists, headed by George Davidson, who had been instructed by the Smithsonian and enjoined by Seward to exam-

1. Bartsch et al., *Bibliography and Short Biographical Sketch*, pp. 1–4, 15. W. P. Woodring, "William Healey Dall," in National Academy of Sciences, *Biographical Memoirs*, 31 (1958), 93.

ine and report on the new territory. They touched the main island stations of Sitka, Kodiak, and Unalaska in a four-month cruise. Davidson's report was a masterpiece more of historical than of field research, but in the House debates it served Seward's purposes.[2]

While the Congress debated, Dall was winding up his first-hand Alaskan investigations with Western Union. He left St. Michael in August 1868. But the findings of the old Telegraph Expedition still needed a tidy and experienced hand. With assurance from Joseph Henry, secretary of the Smithsonian, that room and board could be had at the Institution, and with a small grant from the Boston Society of Natural History, Dall came to Washington at the end of 1868 to work over his collections and to write a book on Alaska. He ate at the Smithsonian boarding house and shared a room with Henry Elliott. For a time he shared Elliott's social life as well.[3] Whether Elliott's intellectual company was congenial to Dall is not recorded.

Dall's book, *Alaska and Its Resources,* was a narrative of his adventures and researches in Alaska with the Telegraph Company and a compilation of geographical, historical, and scientific information on the country. It established his reputation as an expert, though Dall knew the volume raised more questions than it settled. There were yawning gaps in the geographical and scientific knowledge of the territory.

With the encouragement of Spencer Baird, in 1870 Dall turned to the Coast Survey for support to continue the work of exploration. In line with the primary mission of the USCS, Dall submitted a proposal to concentrate first on the Aleutians, in order to determine points, survey the island coasts and navigable straits, gather data on currents and tides, and estimate altitudes when possible. Reconnaissance charts would be prepared. He also recommended the establishment of sailing directions for the various ports along the coast of Bering Sea, "as they are greatly needed by our traders." As a collateral duty, he suggested that the Coast Survey vessel might also apprehend smugglers. "If any captures were made," he explained, "the results might go some way toward paying the expenses of the

2. M. B. Sherwood, "George Davidson," pp. 141–54. As head of the Pacific division of the Coast Survey, Davidson exercised thereafter a leading role in the development of the territory. For an outline of his later activities see M. B. Sherwood, "A Pioneer Scientist in the Far North," *PNQ*, 53 (1962), 77–80.

3. Dall's Diaries, December 2, 1868, and May 17, 1869, Dall Papers.

work." In that the survey was to concentrate on hydrographic problems and was justified by commercial necessity, Dall played the game of nineteenth-century politics. Tucked away at the end of his proposal was a curt observation: "I have not considered it necessary to discuss the immense amount of information in regard to the volcanic phenomena, geology, and natural history, which would be obtained."[4] Dall's later evaluations of the work stressed the gain to science, not commerce.

Some politico-economic justification for the work was required. Benjamin Peirce, head of the USCS, estimated that the survey would cost about $10,000 for an outfit and $13,500 annually for three years.[5] The amount was barely 5 per cent of the total USCS appropriation for the West Coast, but when compared to the number of traders served and population benefited, it was a sizable grant. On the other hand, given the character and vast extent of the territorial coast line, it was a ridiculously small figure.

(The Coast Survey Alaskan appropriation estimates for 1881–1895, for which separate figures are readily available, fluctuated between $8,000 and $15,000, excluding wages and special expenses for boundary surveys, tidal observers, and so forth. With so little money available, it was remarkable that so much was accomplished. By 1885, the USCS had surveyed 1,000 miles of coast, or about 5½ per cent of the total, according to a Survey calculation. Three years later the Superintendent announced that forty-five charts of Alaskan harbors and anchorages had been published.[6] Even so, navigational problems remained serious throughout the century.)

The New York *Tribune* wrote of Dall's plan: "He proposes a hydrographic reconnaissance, and very hydrographic in that climate of fog and rain his labors are likely to be."[7] Actually, he worked during the winter too, when the skies were clearer and the determination of positions easier.[8]

---

4. Dall, "Survey of Alaska and the Aleutian Islands: General Plan of Operations," *House Executive Document 255, 41st Congress: 2d session* (1425), 2–4. Superintendent Peirce vetoed the police function.

5. Peirce to G. S. Boutwell, March 22, 1870, in ibid., p. 2. The actual allotment for fiscal year 1872–73 was $12,000. Davidson to Dall, October 1, 1872, Dall Papers.

6. Figures culled from USCS–USC&GS, *Annual Reports*. Allison et al., "Testimony before the Joint Commission," p. 456. F. M. Thorn, *Notes on Alaska from Recent Surveys* (USC&GS Bulletin No. 2, Washington, 1888), p. 3.

7. New York *Semi-Weekly Tribune*, June 10, 1870.

8. Dall, "Memoranda for My Grandchildren," p. 83.

With M. W. Harrington (who later became the first civilian head of the Weather Bureau) active as his technical assistant, Dall departed San Francisco aboard the USCS steamer *Humboldt*. Marcus Baker replaced Harrington on the later voyages. Among other duties Baker was given the job of checking whether, as Dall had noticed earlier, the culmination of easterly variation of the magnetic needle in the Aleutian region for that century had passed, and the easterly declination was annually diminishing.[9] Along with magnetic observation, the parties determined astronomical positions, took deep-sea soundings, and kept meteorological, current, and sea temperature records.[10]

Dall found himself nominally still in the telegraph business. "When you resume work at the Aleutian Islands," Superintendent Peirce wrote in 1873, "please keep in view the wishes of the Telegraph Cable Company for the survey of the proper landing place . . . for the cable which is intended to connect the Western Coast and . . . Japan"; the task would not "seriously interfere with your own plans for the development of the Coast of Alaska." Dall was authorized to correspond with Cyrus W. Field, whose Atlantic cable had put the Russian American Telegraph Expedition out of business.[11] Field's choice for a cable landing was Attu; after investigating this site, however, Dall decided that Kiska was more desirable.[12]

Dall's final season of the four spent on hydrography found him on the eastern coast. He triangulated the height of Mt. St. Elias from four stations, three on land and one at sea, and arrived at estimates that varied by 2,000 feet; in his reduced notes he settled on 19,500 feet, plus or minus 400.[13] Even subtracting the 400, he was about 1,000 feet too high. Dall had no illusions about the finality of the estimate. Later attempts by other parties to establish the height and location of the peak eventually consumed more energy, time, and money than was warranted by the general importance of the problem.

9. Dall, "Marcus Baker, 1849–1903," *Bulletin of the Philosophical Society of Washington*, *14* (1900–1904), 280. Henry Gannett also applied for the position held by Baker and Harrington; see Gannett to Dall, April 22, 1871, Dall Papers.

10. Dall, "Explorations on the Western Coast of North America," SI, *Annual Report*, *1873*, p. 417. Also, Dall to Joseph Henry, November 28, 1873, Dall Papers.

11. Peirce to Dall, February 10, 1873, Dall Papers.

12. USCS, *Annual Report*, *1874*, p. 60.

13. J. D. Dana, "Note on Mt. St. Elias," *American Journal of Science*, ser. 3, *11* (1876), 242. Dall, "Report on Mount Saint Elias, Mount Fairweather, and Some of the Adjacent Mountains," USCS, *Annual Report*, *1875*, p. 159.

To Dall the Coast Survey expeditions were a natural extension of his earlier field work. The collections he made in his leisure time were extensive. He sent seven boxes of dry shells, echinoderms, and fossils to Professor Agassiz at the Museum of Comparative Zoology. Plant specimens were mailed direct to the eminent American botanist, Asa Gray. In one year alone, Dall forwarded twenty-seven boxes and kegs of general zoological and ethnological materials to the Smithsonian. Altogether he secured, according to Joseph Henry, "a wonderfully complete series of specimens for the National Museum."[14] Dall's experience along the mountainous southern coast permitted him to extend his observations on Alaskan glaciation.

In anthropology, his study of Aleut village sites, shell heaps, and middens revealed (he claimed) a gradual cultural progress in the successive strata. To the Army Medical Museum he sent a large number of Aleut crania for study. In *Contributions to North American Ethnology*, he expressed doubt that the North American Eskimo came from Asia by way of the Aleutians. He made an issue of terminology in the same paper by noting that his 1869 term "Orarian" for the Aleuts and Eskimos had not received "the general recognition which it called for."[15] The paper tended to ignore established labels: he used "Innuit" rather than Eskimo, "Unungun" rather than Aleut, "Tinneh" rather than Athapaskan, applying the new names in an attempt to establish a more precise nomenclature. Another paper, "On Masks, Labrets, and Certain Aboriginal Customs," for the Bureau of Ethnology, speculated in a highly tentative manner on the distribution of specific native customs. In explaining its limitation, Dall chose an apt metaphor: "It will be avowedly a matter of sketching landmarks and indicating openings to possible harbors, rather than a survey with soundings and sailing directions."[16] Dall's work in ethnology illustrated a current American fascination with the character and culture of the American Indian.

With so much to be done in the interior and along the southern and

14. Dall to Agassiz, March 27, 1873, Dall Papers. SI, *Annual Report, 1873*, pp. 61, 39.

15. Dall, "Glaciation in Alaska," *Bulletin of the Philosophical Society of Washington*, 6 (1883), 33–36, published in *Smithsonian Miscellaneous Collections*, 33 (1888). Dall, "Alaska as It Was and Is," p. 141. Dall, with George Gibbs, "Tribes of the Extreme Northwest," *Contributions to North American Ethnology*, 1 (U.S. Geographical and Geological Survey of the Rocky Mountain Region, Washington, 1877), 63, 8, 97. Also, L. Jones, *A Study of the Thlingets of Alaska* (New York, 1914), p. 28.

16. Dall, in BE, *Third Annual Report, 1881–82*, p. 73.

western coasts, the reason for concentration on the Aleutian chain is difficult to isolate. It may have been purely economic. Whalers and fur traders passing through the Islands needed charts, and Davidson's *Coast Pilot of Alaska*, published in 1869, did not extend beyond Cook Inlet. Yet from a scientific standpoint the Islands were strategic. Like Seward Peninsula to the north, the Aleutians reached out toward Asia. Their position might hold a key to certain gross biogeographical questions. For example, after Dall's first tour of duty in the Aleutians, he was able to communicate a significant observation to Asa Gray, the great American botanist and champion of Darwin. Dall informed Gray that the Coast Survey party had met with a species known to exist in Asia and in the Atlantic regions of North America.[17] To Gray, this was a key fact in his explanation of disjunct species, that is, plants occurring in widely separated locales. Gray's theory postulated the existence of a circumboreal temperate flora continuous across Bering Strait during the Tertiary period, a flora that was pushed southward by glaciation in the Pleistocene epoch. A warm period after the Pleistocene permitted a second mingling of species across the Strait. Dall's notice of an intermediate station, in the Shumagin Islands, for one disjunct species thus provided Gray with evidence for his pattern of distribution—a pattern that gave powerful support to Darwin's concept of the descent of species from a common ancestor as opposed to Louis Agassiz' view that individual species were created separately and had no genetic connection.[18] It was largely due to the revolution in biologic and geologic theory that Dall, and before him Kennicott, sought floral, faunal, and physical evidence in Alaska that might be brought to bear on such big generalizations. The location of the Alaska Peninsula and Aleutian Islands was crucial to the search.

By 1873, Dall was homesick. "In the spring of 1875, under Providence, I hope to return to Washington, and settle quietly down to study, as I think that seven years of one's life are quite enough to be devoted to fieldwork in such an inaccessible region."[19] His personal hope corresponded with a reduction in the Coast Survey appropriation, and with the desire of

17. A. Gray, "Address," AAAS, *Proceedings*, 21 (1872), 30, 31. For Dall's concern about distribution see also Dall to Gray, November 18, 1873, Letterbooks, Dall Papers.

18. A. H. Dupree, "Asa Gray and American Geology," *Journal of the Washington Academy of Sciences*, 49 (1959), 227–30.

19. Dated November 28, 1873, Dall, "Explorations on the Western Coast," p. 418. SI, *Annual Report*, 1873, p. 418.

the Alaska Commercial Company. He had on one or two occasions been critical of the Company and had controverted some of its views on the territory. According to Dall, the Company lobbyist had approached the Chief Hydrographer of the Survey and threatened to use Company influence to reduce USCS appropriations if Dall were ordered to Alaska for another season.[20]

The Alaska Commercial Company, organized in 1868, was capitalized at two million dollars. In 1870 it obtained a federal lease to exploit the fur seal rookeries on the Pribilof Islands in Bering Sea. One of the stockholders, Hayward M. Hutchinson of Baltimore, had bought the ships, houses, and property of the Russian American Company. Louis Sloss and Company of San Francisco formed the financial nucleus of the firm, whose stockholders included General (later Senator) John F. Miller.[21] Cornelius Cole, who also became a senator, handled the legal work involved in obtaining the lease.[22] With such an array of talent, the Company probably did not wield the more vulgar forms of Congressional influence common in the century, though it could easily have afforded to suborn a Congressman or two. The Alaska fur business was a lucrative enterprise. For 1872–1874, the Company paid 7 to 10 per cent annual dividends on its capital stock; in 1875, 37½ per cent; in 1878, 45 per cent; and in 1880, a whopping 100 per cent, or two million dollars.[23] The Company's job was literally to "skin" Alaska.

By 1880, the firm had extended its fur trade to the Yukon, the Kuskokwim, and the Nushagak Rivers, and to the Aleutians. At one time or another it had posts on Cook Inlet and Prince William Sound.[24] The

20. Dall was told this, he said in a memoir, by Captain Patterson, the Chief Hydrographer. The Company agent was named. Dall, "Memoranda for My Grandchildren," p. 108.

21. S. P. Johnston, editor, *Alaska Commercial Company, 1868–1940* (San Francisco, 1940), pp. 5, 7.

22. Gruening, *The State of Alaska*, p. 67.

23. Alaska Commercial Company, Dividend Book, with Ledgers and Correspondence, MSS, Jackson Library, Stanford University, Palo Alto, California.

24. L. D. Kitchener, *Flag over the North* (Seattle, 1954), pp. 92, 155, 156, 163, 164. Testimony of Sheldon Jackson, 1880, U.S. Senate, Committee on Territories, "Civil Government for Southeastern Alaska," *Senate Report 457, 47th Congress: 1st session* (2006), 13. H. W. Seton-Karr, *Shores and Alps of Alaska* (London, 1887), p. 131.

Company hired former Russian subjects and former Hudson's Bay traders; Ferdinand Westdahl and Michael Lebarge of the Telegraph Expedition also worked for the firm. Here and there on the mainland the Company encountered competition. On the Yukon and the Kuskokwim it was challenged by the Western Fur and Trading Company, and only the Indians profited from the price war that followed.[25] When around 1882 the Company agreed to buy out Western Fur for $175,000,[26] the natives became surly. A government explorer reported: "such a hornet's nest was stirred up that ultimately the company was obliged to abandon nearly a half-dozen posts, all above Nukluklayet, for fear of the Indians, who required a Krupp steam-hammer to pound into their thick heads the reason why a man might sell them a pound of tobacco for ten cents to-day and to-morrow charge them ten dollars an ounce."[27] The Company continued its mainland operations after 1890, but that year it lost the twenty-year Seal Island lease to a new rival. By then open-sea, or pelagic, sealing had reduced the yield on the Islands.

The fur trade is naturally hostile to development, local and national governmental regulation, and settlement; it thrives in a vacant land unhindered by legal restrictions. It is not surprising that the Alaska Commercial Company looked with disfavor on attempts in Washington to create a territory of Alaska, but the Company was not consistently opposed to settlement; on the contrary, in 1874 it offered to transport 500 Icelanders for settlement in any part of Alaska. Though the firm seemed tacitly to approve antimissionary propaganda, the missionaries themselves often commented on the courtesy and cooperation of A.C. traders.[28] Exploration often precedes development, but the Company was not opposed to exploration; almost every explorer and scientist extended acknowledgment to the Company. The firm made a variety of contributions to scientific work. One of its agents took over meteorological observations

25. Kitchener, *Flag*, pp. 85–87, 89, 149.

26. Alaska Commercial Company, Minutes of Meetings, MSS (2 vols. California Historical Society Library, San Francisco), I, 113, 117.

27. F. Schwatka, *Exploring the Great Yukon* (no place, no date), p. 268; first published as *Along Alaska's Great River* (New York, 1885), then as *A Summer in Alaska* (St. Louis, Mo., 1893).

28. For example, A. Schwalbe, *Dayspring on the Kuskokwim* (Bethlehem, Pa., 1951), p. 51; P. de Schweinit, "The Moravian Mission on the Kuskokwim," *Missionary Review of the World*, 3 (1890), 116; P. C. Yorke, "The Sisters of Alaska," *Catholic World*, 56 (1893), 800, 801. Also, Kitchener, *Flag*, pp. 163, 148, 149.

for a federal scientist so that the latter could travel and collect in the vicinity. A.C. sent specimens to the Smithsonian Institution and acted as its San Francisco agency.[29] The Smithsonian reported of the firm: "It has not simply been the agent for the transmission or reception of packages between Washington and San Francisco, but has readily undertaken to purchase supplies and their transmission to the agents of the Institution, in many cases making large money advances." The entire business was done "cheerfully" and without "any consideration whatever."[30] At San Francisco, the Company maintained an ethnological museum, where learned papers were prepared.[31]

Obviously, it was not to science that the Alaska Commercial Company objected when it blocked another marine exploration by William Dall. The reasons are found elsewhere: Dall had publicly confuted the report and opinions of a friend of the Company, Henry Elliott.

Elliott was one of Kennicott's "Carcajous," assigned to the Canadian Division of the Telegraph Expedition. His failure to promote science while in that position prompted him to confess to Joseph Henry: "As month after month has passed by the mortifying thought of my failure to make, and send to the Smithsonian a Natural History Collection has caused me to burn several letters that have been written for my friends at the Smithsonian."[32] Dall extracted a promise from Bulkley that Elliott would be sent up to aid the Scientific Corps on the Yukon, but Elliott preferred to stay in the telegraph business further south.

His relatively small scientific contributions did not, however, prevent Spencer Baird from nominating him as assistant Treasury Agent for the Pribilofs. Elliott landed on St. George Island April 8, 1872.[33] The next month he wrote Baird: "This exhibition of seal life . . . is really a wonderful sight and it has thus far been touched by Dall and Bryant in the most superficial manner, especially Dall. That which Capt. Bryant has written is full of error from beginning to end. . . . Allen's paper is much in

29. SI, *Annual Report, 1875*, pp. 47, 48.

30. SI, *Annual Report, 1880*, p. 64. Also Johnston, *Alaska Commercial Company*, p. 22.

31. BE, *Annual Report, 1882–83*, p. 191. Ibid., *1888–89*, p. 519. W. J. Hoffman, "The Graphic Art of the Eskimos," USNM, *Report, 1894–95*, pp. 739–968.

32. Elliott to Henry, April 30, 1869, SI Archives.

33. Elliott's testimony. U.S. House of Representatives, Committee on Ways and Means, "The Alaska Commercial Company," *House Report 623, 44th Congress: 1st session* (1712), 76.

error."[34] A year later he was more outspoken in a letter to George Bout-well, Secretary of the Treasury: "I have to inform you that the report of Mr. Bryant, the Agent placed by you . . . in charge of these Islands, *is a perfect burlesque;* his description of the Islands is a caricature, and *every single paragraph* that he has given to you and to the scientific world, through Agassiz, relative to the fur seal is either totally wrong or simply ridiculous!"[35]

Elliott's impulsive exaggeration bespoke an artistic temperament. As early as 1872, he planned to resign and devote his full energies to paint-ing.[36] After a season on the Pribilofs he informed Baird that he had painted a gallery of over one hundred water colors. Elliott modestly ob-served, "these paintings are not only works of Art viewed alone as pic-tures . . . [but are also scientifically accurate;] they will I am sure give me an enviable name among Artists and win the hearty approbation and in-terest of men who loom up in the intellectual world."[37] He was no less enthusiastic about his manuscript on the Seal Islands and Alaska. The Secretary of the Treasury, he announced, would shortly publish the work "and make it one of the most interesting, valuable and elegant docu-ments ever issued by the Government for I have the materials for a mag-nificent book."[38]

The volume to which he referred involved William Healey Dall, and was a focal point in a controversy over the Alaska Commercial Company. Its publication corresponded with a Congressional investigation of charges against the Company. In 1875, General O. O. Howard, distinguished former head of the Freedman's Bureau, made a routine inspection of mili-tary establishments in Alaska. Attached to his report, as a matter of in-formation, was a document that indicted the A.C. Company for criminal neglect and the abuse of its privileged franchise. The document issued from the so-called Anti-Monopoly Association of the Pacific, in San Fran-cisco,[39] and was principally the work of Agapius Honcharenko. Hon-charenko's tabloid, the *Alaska Herald* of San Francisco, had for some time

34. May 1872, SI Archives.
35. July 13, 1873, SI Archives.
36. Elliott to Baird, May 1872, SI Archives.
37. Elliott to Baird, May 1873, SI Archives.
38. Elliott to Baird, September 29, 1873, SI Archives.
39. Howard, "Report of the Commanding General, Department of the Columbia, of His Tour in Alaska Territory, in June, 1875," *Senate Executive Document 12, 44th Congress: 1st session* (1664), 11–33.

been picking at the Company. The document and the *Herald* have both been rightly described as "scurrilous." The issue having been raised, however, Congress investigated, but the charges could not be substantiated.[40]

Henry Elliott's *Report upon the Condition of Affairs in the Territory of Alaska* took a benevolent view of Company activities;[41] at the same time, it left an impression that, aside from Company operations, Alaska had little value. It was altogether an excellent idea, Elliott thought, that the Pribilofs were leased to a single firm, and its profits were "a pure matter of business" about which the Company "should not be subjected to impertinent inquisition"; thanks to the lessees, the condition of the natives on the islands "has been wonderfully improved" and elsewhere, too, the natives were treated with "kindness" by Company traders. As for Dall's comment that New England contempt for Alaska betrayed the heritage of the former region, Elliott claimed that the agricultural value of Alaska was nil and the situation was therefore not comparable to conditions facing the Massachusetts pioneers: there were more arable acres still in wilderness within sight of a Pennsylvania road than could be found in all Alaska. Elliott had some hope for mineral development, but Alaska's cod banks were "greatly overrated."

His political recommendations for the territory corresponded almost exactly with the desires of the A.C. Company. He suggested that the troops stationed in Alaska be withdrawn, that a collector of customs be located at Kodiak, that an agent be appointed to keep the Government "well informed," that the jurisdiction of Washington or Oregon courts be extended, and that the mineral land laws be made applicable to Alaska. "Beyond the adoption of this plan . . . , nothing more is required by the Territory and its people. Any scheme of establishing Indian reservations or agencies in this country, with an idle and mischievous retinue of superintendents, chaplains, and school-teachers, seems to me entirely uncalled for." Education of the "better class of the natives" could be handled by the Russian Church.[42]

40. U.S. House of Representatives, Committee on Ways and Means, "Alaska Commercial Company," *House Report 623.*

41. Treasury Department, Washington, 1875. Also published with *House Executive Document 83, 44th Congress: 1st session* (1687). Another edition appeared as *Our Arctic Province* (New York, 1886). Still another version was published as "Report on the Seal Islands of Alaska—Tenth Census," *House Miscellaneous Document 42, 47th Congress: 2d session* (2136).

42. Ibid., pp. 97, 39, 19, 5, 6, 37, 38.

In an article written for *Harper's* two years later, Elliott retracted his hope for mineral development (which put him 100 per cent in current agreement with the Company), while he lauded the country as a great scientific laboratory: "It is a paradise for the naturalist, a happy hunting ground for the ethnologist, a new and boundless field for the geologist, and the physical phenomena of its climate are something wonderful to contemplate. It is, and will be for years to come, a perfect treasure-trove for these gentlemen; but alas! it bids fair, from what we now know, never to be a treasure-trove for the miner or the agriculturist."[43] Elliott's encouragement of science in the article was matched by his careful (if ebullient) report on the fur seal and his inclusion of a special chapter on the birdlife of the Islands by Elliott Coues, one of the nation's leading ornithologists.

Appended to Elliott's *Report* was a letter he had asked Dall to write, "to show the contrast" between the views of the two men. The idea seemed fair enough; but then Elliott added a special criticism of Dall's letter.[44] The appendage was ethically dubious, no matter how picayune some of Dall's comments.

Dall took to the newspapers. In the Boston *Daily Advertiser* for July 15, 1875, he answered Elliott's criticism. The following month, more exchanges appeared in the paper.[45] A scathing review of the Elliott book appeared in the New York *Evening Post*.[46] Reviewing the book anonymously for the *Nation*, Dall touched a sore point: "Mr. Elliott's ocular observation has not extended over more than one and a half per cent of the whole Territory; he has never touched the mainland of the Territory except at the Stickeen River; his actual residence has been confined to two little barren islands containing an area not over 150 square miles"; his statements mislead the reader into thinking otherwise.[47] In a letter to the editor of the *Nation*,[48] Dall also took issue with Elliott's *Harper's* article calling Charles Sumner's speech a "rich burlesque."[49] This letter called

43. "Ten Years' Acquaintance with Alaska: 1867–1877," *Harper's Monthly*, 55 (November 1877), 802.
44. *Report upon the Condition*, pp. 168–212; Dall's letter dated August 31, 1874, pp. 229–36; Elliott's rejoinder, pp. 236–40.
45. August 18 and 20, 1875.
46. July 9, 1875.
47. *Nation*, 21 (September 2, 1875), 154, 155.
48. *Nation*, 25 (November 15, 1877), 298.
49. Elliott, "Ten Years' Acquaintance," p. 812.

forth another from Elliott, and a response from Dall.[50] Both men affixed their signatures and the words "Smithsonian Institution," seeking to invoke the weighty prestige of that establishment; it must have embarrassed the Institution and confused the reader, who was confronted by conflicting testimony from two "experts." A Brooklyn woman wrote to the Smithsonian to inquire whether Elliott was entitled to the appellation "professor." Baird said no, but mentioned that Elliott had had "large experience" in exploring the Northwest.[51] The Sitka *Alaskan* charged Elliott with falsely representing himself as officially connected with the Institution.[52] In fact, neither Dall nor Elliott was on the Smithsonian payroll. The former worked over his collections there. Elliott occasionally occupied a sleeping cuddy in one of the towers[53] in exchange for voluntary services—a loose connection, as he readily admitted.[54]

The *Report* drew fire from other sources. William Gouverneur Morris, Special Treasury Agent for Alaska, set out to refute it in another government document: "No man of sane mind would ever pronounce Alaska an *agricultural country*, that is a simple *reductio ad absurdum*, and requires no demonstration, but that there are portions of the country where successful experiments have been made in raising hay, garden vegetables, and other produce, is as plain as a nose on a man's face."[55] The issue of Alaska's agricultural potential remained a windmill at which too many "experts" tried to tilt. Predictably, Elliott denounced Morris' report, terming it "an admirable example of what fools call sense, and wise men rigmarole."[56]

Henry Elliott's influence was pervasive, less because he claimed the respect due science than because he spoke unequivocally with a most unscientific lack of caution, and because he said what the Congress preferred to believe. He popped in and out of Washington, and was a pivotal

50. *Nation*, 25 (November 22, 1877), 316, 317. Ibid. (December 6, 1877), 349.

51. Baird to Mrs. Harriet M. Sutter, November 20, 1878, SI Archives.

52. July 17, 1886.

53. Elliott to Baird, August 26, 1881, SI Archives.

54. U.S. House of Representatives, Committee on Ways and Means, "Alaska Commercial Company," *House Report 623*, p. 85.

55. "Report upon the Customs District, Public Service, and Resources of Alaska Territory," *Senate Executive Document 59, 45th Congress: 3d Session* (1831), 89.

56. Elliott to "professor" (probably Baird), April 24, 1879, SI Archives.

witness at the hearings on civil government for southeastern Alaska. Testimony by Dall, who was far and away better informed on the subject, did little to counteract Elliott's words. Even Marcus Baker took the chair. Upon the fur seal, admitted Baker, Elliott is well informed;

> But for his knowledge of the remainder of the Territory, he knows as any one may know from conversation with people who have visited the ground, and from books and papers, and his statements are generally antagonized by people who have been on the ground; that is, the impressions he leaves are bad, whatever may be the intention. Saying nothing about the intention, if you desire to get an accurate knowledge of any particular region, the general statements which Mr. Elliott has made about it do not conduce to accurate knowledge. Mr. Elliott is on the ground every winter in Washington. I see him from time to time, and am personally acquainted with him. He is very kind to me; I have never had any quarrel with him; but it is my belief, saying nothing about his intentions, that he does not fairly represent the sentiment there; and it has been believed and charged that he does represent this company, whose interest it is to antagonize any legislation.[57]

Baker said a great deal when he said "nothing about intentions." The charge that Elliott was a paid lobbyist for the A.C. Company came up again and again. The Sitka *Alaskan* called him a "hireling" and a "newspaper stuffer" for the Company.[58] A recent student of Alaskan history also indicts him for mercenary complicity.[59] But the evidence is inconclusive. Dall, who should have known, and who would have had ample reason to

57. U.S. Senate Committee on Territories, "Civil Government," *Senate Report 457*, pp. 40, 41.

58. July 3 and 17, 1886.

59. Gruening, *State of Alaska*. Gruening claims Baker identified Elliott as an employee of the Company, but I found no specific identification in the source Dr. Gruening cites (p. 68). Gruening also says that Governor Swineford mentioned Elliott's admission before a committee that he was a "paid lobbyist" (p. 69). I could not confirm the admission in the time I allotted to the issue. The Company may have bought Elliott's outfit when he left Alaska in 1875, a not untoward practice: Elliott to Baird, March 30, 1875, SI Archives. Neither is it unreasonable to suppose that Company officials urged the publication of his work by the government. But the allegation that he was personally paid by the Company remains to be proved.

announce it if he had known, said later in his memoir only that Elliott "lent himself actively to the Company's campaign"—an observation that could be made by anyone.[60]

Termination of the hydrographic work did not end Dall's Alaskan activities for the Coast Survey. Employed in Washington, Dall and Baker prepared an Appendix to the *Coast Pilot*. It consisted of extensive meteorological tables and a long and remarkably thorough bibliography of Alaskan materials in several languages, including Russian.[61] The work was enriched by Dall's 1878 attendance, as a representative of the Survey and the Smithsonian, at an annual meeting in Dublin of the British Association for the Advancement of Science.[62] The Appendix must be reckoned one of the more notable contributions to knowledge of Alaska.

In 1880 Dall and Baker returned to Alaska for a season. Dall worked on a hydrographic survey in Bering Strait and the Arctic; Baker continued his magnetic observations.[63] Alaska's broad geographical extent and its location astride the auroral zone, combined with its accessibility, "affords a great natural laboratory" for the study of geomagnetism and the "vexing question of the magnetic pole or poles."[64] The results of studies in terrestrial magnetism are of vital importance to the navigator and surveyor. Baker's work in 1880, his observations while with the earlier hydrographic surveys, and his researches in Washington formed a solid foundation for the extensive and significant geomagnetic analyses of C. A. Schott.[65]

Baker and Dall's association with the Coast Survey culminated in a revision of Davidson's *Coast Pilot*. The Dall-Baker volume was published in 1883. In addition to their own work, they added information from H. E. Nichols' two tours in southern waters, together with the observations of

60. "Memoranda for My Grandchildren," p. 108.

61. Dall and Baker, *Pacific Coast Pilot, Coasts and Islands of Alaska*, Appendix I, "Meteorology and Bibliography" (USC&GS, Washington, 1879).

62. Bartsch et al., *Bibliography and Short Biographical Sketch*, p. 8.

63. Dall, "Notes on Alaska," *American Journal of Science*, ser. 3, 21 (1881), 104–11. L. A. Beardslee, "Report Relative to Affairs in Alaska," *Senate Executive Document 71, 47th Congress: 1st session* (1989), 64.

64. D. G. Knapp and E. B. Roberts, "Geomagnetism—Cosmic and Prosaic," in H. B. Collins, *Science in Alaska* (Arctic Institute of North America, 1952), pp. 163, 164.

65. Dall, "Marcus Baker, September 23, 1849—December 12, 1903," *NGM*, 15 (January 1904), 42. C. A. Schott, *Historical Review of the Work of the Coast and Geodetic Survey in Connection with Terrestrial Magnetism*, USC&GS, Bulletin No. 7, (Washington, 1888), pp. 35–40.

navigators and travelers familiar with the coast. It was a useful if "imperfect" work.[66]

In 1884 Dall transferred to the Geological Survey as a paleontologist, working at the U.S. National Museum with the title "Honorary Curator of Mollusks and Tertiary Fossils." The move reflected a crisis in the Coast Survey. The USCS suffered from old age, partisan politics, and interagency rivalry. In 1871 Survey field operations were extended to include a geodetic connection of the Atlantic and Pacific systems. Seven years later a change of names, from United States Coast Survey to United States Coast and Geodetic Survey, was public confirmation of the bureau's new role, but its jurisdiction was still in doubt. In 1882 the Secretary of the Navy recommended that the agency be transferred from the Treasury Department to the Navy Department.[67]

The idea raised the troublesome issue of civilian versus military control. In Alaska during the '80s, cooperative surveys by the Navy and Coast Survey irked the Naval Hydrographic Office. Naval officers took USC&GS titles, and naval vessels surveyed the coast; results went to the Coast and Geodetic Survey.[68] Despite such jurisdictional complexities, the National Academy of Sciences, and even civilian scientists with the Navy, urged against military control of the Coast Survey. A Senate committee investigating the bureaucratic organization of federal scientific operations felt that coast surveys would soon be unnecessary, and it recommended consolidation of hydrography in the Naval Office when USC&GS activities were confined to the interior.[69] (At that point, 95 per cent of the Alaskan coast, linearly greater than the combined Pacific and Atlantic coasts of the United States, had not yet been surveyed.)

The controversy was sharpened by an investigating committee from the Treasury Department, staffed by political friends of the new Democratic Administration. F. M. Thorn of the committee found in the Coast Survey an easy subject for a political exposé. J. E. Hilgard, Superintendent of the Coast Survey, was an old scientist with little appreciation of modern accounting methods. For example, the reduced USC&GS appropria-

66. Dall and Baker, *Pacific Coast Pilot, Alaska, Dixon Entrance to Yakutat Bay* (USC&GS, Washington, 1883), **page iv.**

67. G. A. Weber, *The Coast and Geodetic Survey,* Service Monograph of the U.S. Government No. 16 (Baltimore, 1923), pp. 8–10. Dupree, *Science in the Federal Government,* pp. 202, 203.

68. Allison et al., "Testimony before the Joint Commission," p. 80.

69. Dupree, *Science in the Federal Government,* pp. 216, 219.

tion had omitted a salary for the tidal observer at Kodiak. Hilgard discovered that he could pay this legitimate expense with a voucher from
another division of the agency. It was illegal but a common practice,[70]
and making an issue of it was an example of the sort of thing the Treasury
committee resorted to in its attack on the Survey. Against such charges,
and others even less substantial, the bureau was not permitted to defend
itself. Hilgard resigned. The morale of the Coast Survey, once the pride
of American science, was severely shaken.[71] Baker quit in 1885. Dall,
having feared Naval control and transferred to the Geological Survey the
year before, was glad he had read the portents accurately.

Although Dall's move to the Geological Survey gave him an opportunity to pursue his specialty, he by no means doffed his mortarboard of
Alaskan expertise. Of the 2,000 molluskan species and subspecies known
in 1921 from Alaska to the southern Pacific border of the United States,
roughly half bear his name. Between 1870 and 1884, he published some
400 papers.[72] His name was attached by other investigators to numerous
animals, from the regal mountain sheep, *Ovis dalli*, to the blackfish, *Dallia
pectoralis*, a main winter staple of the natives along the Yukon and Kuskokwim deltas. A naturalist reported on the blackfish: "The vitality of
these fish is astounding. They will remain in . . . grass-baskets for weeks,
and when brought into the house and thawed out they will be as lively as
ever."[73]

Dall's vitality in and out of science was unusual. If his Washington
testimony was occasionally rendered unavailing by the impulsive pes-
simism of Henry Elliott, it was no fault of William Dall. Neither did it
discourage him from saying what he thought was relevant and right in the
political realm of territorial affairs. In 1869 he believed that "Emigration
[to Alaska] is not likely to take place in large numbers, and it would be
folly to establish a territorial government at present." But the country was
valuable.[74] In 1872 in an article ingenious for its manipulation of quan-
titative data, Dall assayed "the absurdity of the demand . . . that Alaska

70. Dall, "Memoranda for My Grandchildren," pp. 124, 125.
71. Dupree, *Science in the Federal Government*, p. 222.
72. Woodring, "William Healey Dall," p. 103. Bartsch et al., *Bibliography and Short Biographical Sketch*, p. 8.
73. L. M. Turner, "Contributions to the Natural History of Alaska," *Senate Miscellaneous Document 155, 49th Congress: 1st session* (2349).
74. Dall, "General Thomas' Alaskan Report," Boston *Daily Advertiser*, October 18, 1869.

should return . . . a good commercial interest on its cost."[75] Five years later, his political plan for Alaska did not differ materially from Elliott's.[76]

All the time Dall cautiously emphasized the inherent worth of the territory in the face of uninformed critics. In an 1886 review of *Our New Alaska* by Charles Hallock, Dall wrote: "If his [Hallock's] hopes for the future of the Territory may seem in some particulars a trifle too sanguine, it must be said that the popular view for a long time was too far the other way, and the reaction against obvious injustice is apt to be energetic in one who has the courage of his convictions."[77] By 1895, on the eve of the Gold Rush, Dall was vigorously pushing political reform.[78] That year his presidential address before the Philosophical Society of Washington appeared in print. "I was rash enough twenty-five years ago to indulge in prophecy as to the future of the territory. I did not count on the inertia of Congress or the stupidity of officials, as I might now."[79]

Similar comments later in the century formed the theme of political histories to come. Alaska's economic status, so the "neglect" interpretation goes, was a result of political inactivity in Washington, of the "stupidity of officials." In short, Alaska was underdeveloped because Congress decreed it so. The idea was not unique with Dall. Appointed officials, like Governor A. P. Swineford, underlined the cause. Dall's testimony was the more acceptable because where Swineford, for example, spoke irritably because of restraints on his power as Governor of Alaska,[80] Dall was interested mainly in overcoming obstacles to the pursuit of science in the territory. As applied to the nineteenth century, the "neglect" interpretation of Alaskan history ignores American social and economic realities and the true extent of federal activity in Alaska. Attention to civil legis-

75. Dall, "Is Alaska a Paying Investment?" *Harper's*, 44 (January 1872), 253.

76. Reprint of a New York *Herald* article for May 10, in the San Francisco *Post*, May 24, 1879.

77. *Nation*, 43 (October 28, 1886), 360.

78. "Alaska Revisited," *Nation*, 61 (September 26, 1895), 221. The article appeared in installments: July 4, July 11, August 14, August 22, September 12, and September 26, 1895.

79. Dall, "Alaska as It Was and Is," 142, 143.

80. For example, Swineford thought every government official in Alaska should heel to his authority. He made ridiculous charges against officers of the Naval ship *Pinta* when they would not put their vessel at his disposal. When later the ship was ordered to accommodate him, he complained about its inadequacy. He also thought the USCS ship *Hassler*, then working on the Oregon coast, should make a special trip to Sitka in order to carry him home. Swineford to Secretary of the Interior, January 4 and April 3, 1886, NA, RG 48.

lation for the handful of citizens in Alaska would have been more consistent with the professed ideals of the United States but whether it would have induced speedier economic and social growth is doubtful.

The theme of conspiratorial neglect originated in southeastern Alaska, the only area even slightly populated by whites. The idea thrived on the absence of property laws and legal authority and by 1890 it had reached paranoic proportions. To cite an example, Dall recommended that the Sitkans erect a fireproof library building, and promised to provide a couple of hundred volumes himself—a large donation by nineteenth-century standards. The editor of the Sitka *Alaskan* thought the liberal offer would probably be indefinitely postponed, and added, moreover, that the "solidly built public buildings . . . are decaying so fast that they will be nothing but heaps of ruins, through sheer neglect on the part of the Government."[81] Just what the latter observation had to do with Dall's offer is obscure, but illustrative. When military explorations of the interior were projected in 1890, and numerous American newspapers expressed approval, the Sitka *Alaskan* objected on the ground that the money should be expended nearer home—the precise position taken by Congress vis-à-vis Alaska in general and about which the newspaper complained.[82]

In his efforts to promote exploration and development, William Healey Dall had to contend with provincialism in and out of Alaska. Countless elements conspired to test his expertise: monopoly influence, exuberant but lightly informed week-end "authorities," local officialdom, Congressional apathy, interagency rivalry, and pseudo-scientists.

In the last category was a curious character named Ivan Petroff, who never directly challenged Dall's pre-eminence but who should probably be ranked second only to Dall as an expert on the territory during the nineteenth century. He was no scientist but he assumed the cloak of scientific language. He sought no publicity (for good reason) and received little; his name is hardly known in Alaska even today. He had one advantage over Dall: he was fluent in the Russian language. As a facile and highly imaginative writer he was a formidable power in general Alaskan history and in the history of science in Alaska.

81. March 1, 1890.
82. U.S. House of Representatives, Committee on Military Affairs, "Exploration and Survey of Alaska," *House Report 3760, 51st Congress: 2d session* (2888) 4–7. Sitka *Alaskan*, September 20, 1890.

4. The Enigmatic Ivan Petroff

OF THE THREE most influential books on Alaska published in the nineteenth century, Ivan Petroff was largely responsible for one and wholly responsible for a second.[1] Few would disagree that the first volume, H. H. Bancroft's *History of Alaska,*[2] has been the single most important history of the northland, and Petroff's report for the Tenth Census of 1880 was,[3] according to Brooks, a "most notable contribution to the knowledge of Alaska's geography and resources.[4] Despite his influence, very little is known about Ivan Petroff personally. He was willing enough to gather, order, and disseminate information about Alaska, its history, its people, and its resources, but he was deliberately reluctant to distribute any great amount of information about himself. His own life is shrouded in a dozen minor mysteries. Any evaluation of his contribution to the accumulation of knowledge on the Far Northwest must account for the enigma of Ivan Petroff—his background, qualifications, and motivation. On the last score, more will be left unsaid than said.

The Tenth Census of the United States was more than a mere head count. It was a general-purpose scientific organization, with the emphasis on natural resources. A large force of enumerators having only census duty

1. Petroff's name in print is variously spelled "Petroff," "Petrof," "Petrov." The latter is the modern transliteration. His work is carded in Bancroft Library with a terminal "v." In 1871 he signed his name on an official document with two "ff's."

2. San Francisco, 1886.

3. Petroff's preliminary census report appeared as "Population and Resources of Alaska," *House Executive Document 40, 46th Congress: 3d session* (1968). The compendium appeared as "Compendium of the Tenth Census—Alaska," in *Compendium of the Tenth Census,* Vol. 2, and as *House Miscellaneous Document 64, 47th Congress: 1st session,* Pt. 2 (2060), 1419–1429. The complete report is in Vol. 8 of the same work, which also appeared as "Tenth Census—Alaska," *House Miscellaneous Document 42, Part 8, 47th Congress: 2d session* (2136). The source I cite most of the time is identical with the complete census except that the map, lists, index, and illustrations have been omitted: "Report on the Population, Resources, etc., of Alaska," in *Compilation of Narratives of Explorations in Alaska, Senate Report 1023, 56th Congress: 1st session* (3896), 53–281.

4. *The Geography and Geology of Alaska,* p. 121.

were enlisted and closely supervised by the Superintendent, who was also empowered by law to employ special agents. The specialists could "investigate in their economic relations the manufacturing, railroad, fishing and mining, and other industries of the country, and the statistics of telegraph, express, transportation, and insurance companies," in addition to collecting the usual social statistics.[5] Thus the Tenth Census was an expansion of the national government's welfare function and an important landmark in the history of science, particularly the social sciences, in America.

Ivan Petroff qualified as an Alaskan expert. He was "perhaps, the most competent person in all respects who could have been selected for the work," according to Governor A. P. Swineford.[6] Petroff was born in Russia and handled written English expertly. He spent time in the Kenai and Kodiak areas prior to 1871. Sometime during the first few years of that decade he joined the staff of Hubert Howe Bancroft, the energetic historian of the West. For Bancroft he collected, examined, and translated Russian sources in Alaskan history. In 1878, he journeyed to Alaska, where he conducted interviews and examined local records in Sitka, Kodiak, and Unalaska. Petroff edited the small semimonthly *Alaska Appeal*, published in San Francisco. The paper dealt with Alaskan affairs and was laced with the lively wit of its editor.

Petroff's census report was a general guide to Alaska's history, geography and resources. The enumeration was of doubtful accuracy, though it was probably as exact as the circumstances permitted. As Swineford put it, the report was, considering the obstacles, "fully as complete and reliable as could have been expected."[7] It embraced education, health, climatology, the fish and fur industries, timber, minerals, geography, volcanism, and ethnography. Included were partial translations of Doroshin, Veniaminov, and Grewingk.

En route to Alaska in 1878 Petroff had met Treasury Agent William Morris, then engaged in the compilation of a report on territorial resources. Said Petroff of Morris: "The Major entertains the most extravagant ideas concerning the resources of Alaska and falls into the common error of applying what he has seen at Sitka and Wrangell to the whole

5. Dupree, *Science in the Federal Government*, pp. 277, 278. W. S. Holt, *The Bureau of the Census* (Washington, 1929), pp. 21–24.

6. Governor of Alaska, *Reports to the Secretary of the Interior, 1884–1896, 1897–1905* (2 vols. Washington), *1*, 5. The reports are paginated individually.

7. Ibid., *1*, 5.

country."[8] Petroff avoided generalization about the whole from one or two of its parts by dividing the territory into districts in an attempt to distinguish the several physical and climatic provinces. Petroff was aided by what Brooks calls the first example of any "clear conception of the distribution of mountain ranges in Alaska."[9]

Petroff reported on Alaska's resources with measured reserve. He noted some little success in the cultivation of potatoes and turnips, and in cattle and sheep raising on Kodiak Island. Climate in many parts of the territory precluded extensive agricultural development, and in any event it would be difficult to find a market for the garden variety of agricultural products that could be grown in Alaska. In 1880 there was not much he could say about mineral resources. The fisheries promised to become an industry of value, but at the moment there was again the problem of available markets. Trees, Petroff admitted, clothed a large area, but by Oregon and Washington standards of that day the valuable varieties were sparse.[10] A later expert called the data on Alaskan timber "extremely vague, and in light of new information, faulty; but it attempts at least to designate the species found."[11] Fur, asserted Petroff, was the real wealth of Alaska. As then managed, the fur business paid all the expenses of Alaskan government and left a large surplus. The extinction of fur-bearing animals, he claimed, was unlikely.[12]

Petroff walked an imprecise middle ground between the pro–Alaska Commercial Company opinions of Henry Elliott and the anti-Company bias of Governor Swineford. After the Governor admitted the difficulties involved in Alaskan census taking, he observed "some glaring inconsistencies in his [Petroff's] report which . . . are calculated to retard rather than promote the advancement" of territorial interests. Swineford took particular exception to the population figures for southeastern Alaska.[13] These were collected by Southeasterners—a businessman and some missionaries[14]—and the count for the area was probably inaccurate, though

8. Petroff, "Journal of a Trip to Alaska in Search of Information for the Bancroft Library," MS (Bancroft Library), p. 73.

9. *The Geography and Geology of Alaska*, p. 121.

10. Petroff, in *Compilation of Narratives*, pp. 61, 83, 84, 108, 109, 147, 148.

11. B. E. Fernow, in *Harriman Alaska Expedition*, 2, 239.

12. Petroff, "Population and Resources," p. 70.

13. Governor of Alaska, *Reports*, 1, 5.

14. Dall, "Native Tribes of Alaska," AAAS, *Proceedings*, 34 (1885), 375. S. H. Young, *Hall Young of Alaska* (New York, 1927), p. 191. Also Petroff, "Population and Resources," p. 3.

not enough to render Petroff's political conclusion fallacious. The population, he thought, was about sufficient for "a small county organization." He went on: "The main difficulty of organizing or legislating for Alaska lies in the utter impossibility of reconciling the widely diverging interests and wants of two sections, entirely separate geographically, and having no one feature alike, besides being very unequal in size. . . . The only practical solution of the question will be to treat each portion separately."[15] The solution was a reasonable one for the time. For the country as a whole, Petroff's recommendation resembled Elliott's:

> It must be a source of much satisfaction to the Government of the United States to know that . . . the native population . . . is not at all likely in the future . . . to appeal for food and raiment at the cost of the public Treasury; that it is not at all necessary to send a retinue of Indian agents, with their costly supplies and dubious machinery, into this country; that the protection of the traders and the conservation of law and order in that region will not require the presence of an extravagant civilized government, nor the movement and disposition of soldiery and sloops of war. The simple needs of the people there to-day are embraced substantially in the establishment of courts of justice and record, with their inexpensive accessories.[16]

Of the Pribilof lease, Petroff wrote: "No better plan could be devised by experienced political economists to provide in a just and equitable manner for all the members of an isolated community cut off from all the means of support but the one secured for them by the government."[17]

He was not in unalloyed agreement with Elliott and the Company. Petroff thought competition on the Kuskokwim would afford two firms "a moderate profit," and he took exception to Elliott's confidence in the ability of the Russian Church to educate the natives. Petroff pointed to the need for more missionary and educational work generally.[18] Withal, the A.C. Company was not unhappy about the Tenth Census for Alaska. The firm's Washington lobbyist did Petroff a great personal favor in 1883.

It was only natural that Petroff, the census taker, should discourse at

15. Petroff, in *Compilation of Narratives*, p. 107.
16. Petroff, "Population and Resources," p. 70.
17. Petroff, in *Compilation of Narratives*, p. 119.
18. Ibid., pp. 71, 103.

length on the natives. He relied on the old authorities and on Dall, whose ethnological work he credited as the most valuable since acquisition of the territory by the United States. The implication of Petroff's language, however, is that his own labor was an original study by an expert. The differences between his ethnographic map and Dall's were slight, he felt, "and give evidence only of an extension of the field of investigation. This result is all the more gratifying because Mr. Dall and myself have arrived at very similar conclusions through entirely different channels and without consultation upon the subject." The language must have infuriated Dall. At several points, Petroff seems even to paraphrase the "Dean": "All that can be done at present in the way of classifying the natives of Alaska is to divide them into four distinct families or tribes. . . . The numerous subdivisions of each family . . . can only be vaguely indicated, in the hope of furnishing to future investigators a framework upon which to build a more satisfactory structure." The "four distinct families," Petroff fails to mention, had been suggested by Holmberg and outlined by Dall. Petroff used different labels than Dall. The former explained: "I have adopted the terms Eskimo and Athabaskan, in lieu of the Innuit and Tinneh of recent writers, purely in the interest of uniformity, and in deference to the action of both the American and British science associations, which have decided that priority must prevail.[19] In a later article, Petroff said he retained the older terms on the advice of Otis T. Mason of the National Museum, and of Powell and Baird.[20] Further, Petroff "agreed" with Dall that the Aleutians were peopled from the east, not Asia, but probably not before the invention of the kayak.[21] Snorted Dall: The Tenth Census report on the Alaska Peninsula "is retrograde in many particulars rather than an advance, being the work of a person unqualified for the task."[22]

Ivan Petroff, though well qualified as a regional specialist, was no ethnologist or for that matter a scientist. He was a journalist, and occasionally a pretentious one at that. His ingenious composition employed techniques he probably derived from Dall, techniques that implied he was at least the equal of Dall as an anthropologist. The implied expertise in

19. Ibid., pp. 209, 210.

20. Petroff, "Geographical and Ethnographical Notes on Alaska," *Transactions and Proceedings of the Geographical Society of the Pacific,* 2 (1891), 8.

21. Petroff, "The Limits of the Innuit Tribes on the Alaska Coast," *American Naturalist,* 16 (1882), 571. Petroff, in *Compilation of Narratives,* p. 240.

22. "Native Tribes of Alaska," p. 372.

turn disguised his reliance on old sources and his wholesale use of Dall's own material. Though a good general treatment of the subject, there was nothing scientifically new in Petroff's ethnographical report. His writing was chiefly the result of bookish research and casual travel and not the result of original investigations.

Petroff's census itinerary is vague. According to his official account, he went from San Francisco to Unalaska, then eastward to the Shumagin Islands and westward to Atka; then he sailed north to the Pribilofs and St. Michael. From the latter place he ascended the Yukon in a kayak, probably with a trading party, to the Nowitna River. From there he drifted downstream, perhaps to Kaltag, portaged to the Kuskokwim, and ascended that stream to Lukeen's old post. From the mouth of the Kuskokwim he coasted to Naknek, then cut across the Alaska Peninsula to Katmai on Shelikof Strait, which he crossed to Kodiak. He took passage from Kodiak to San Francisco. The journey was apparently made in 1880. The round trip, according to Petroff's calculations, was 8,700 miles, 2,500 of them by canoe.[23] If indeed he traveled the route he claimed, it was a considerable achievement; even so, he covered no ground not already visited by Russian or American traders and explorers, despite his hints to the contrary.[24]

A number of puzzling questions arise about Petroff's journey or journeys. What was the extent of his work in the Alexander Archipelago? Where did he go on a second trip he seems to have made in 1881? A missionary in the southeastern section reported him at Wrangell late in 1880: "He stayed for several weeks at our town and enjoyed the hospitality of one of the merchants. He was known at Wrangell by the name of 'Hollow Legs,' because of his unlimited capacity of absorbing whiskey and rum without the usual effects of such potations being visible."[25] Petroff claimed to have put in two seasons in the Yukon and Kuskokwim districts,[26] but when he could have found time for a second investigation is a mystery.

23. Petroff, "Population and Resources," p. 86, and map. New York *Herald*, January 11, 1881. C. L. Hooper, *Report of the Cruise of the U.S. Revenue-Steamer Corwin in the Arctic Ocean, Nov. 1, 1880* (Treasury Department, Washington, 1881), p. 19.

24. C. L. Hooper, *Cruise of the Corwin*, 1880, p. 19. New York *Herald*, January 11, 1881. J. E. Spurr, "A Reconnaissance in Southwestern Alaska in 1898," USGS, *Twentieth Annual Report, 1898–99*, Pt. 7, p. 95.

25. Young, *Hall Young*, p. 191.

26. In *Compilation of Narratives*, p. 110.

The Sitka *Alaskan* reported his alleged capture in 1881 by Indians around the Copper River. The natives reportedly held him prisoner all summer, thus preventing a more complete execution of his census duties. The newspaper rightfully thought the story too thin.[27] Petroff's biography before and after the Tenth Census is checkered with discrepancies, some of which were intentional.

In February of 1880, Petroff testified at the hearings on civil government for southeastern Alaska. For 1886 he was reported at Kodiak as a deputy customs collector. He was chosen again in 1890 to direct the Census of Alaska, and again it is difficult to determine the precise extent of his travels. He allegedly covered 12,000 miles.[28] Petroff himself said he ascended the Nushagak, and went some distance up the Kuskokwim and the Yukon rivers.[29] As in 1880, Ivan Petroff relied once more on the help of missionaries for enumeration. The second report also contains many articles by recognized specialists on the different regions of Alaska.

According to the Superintendent of the Eleventh Census, sometime between 1880 and 1890 the American frontier disappeared. The announcement was of considerable moment to the historian Frederick Jackson Turner, who postulated the close of a great historic movement.[30] The American frontier had not, of course, vanished; the coast line of all Alaska was still a frontier. As the Superintendent also observed, "This remote portion of our territory presents difficulties in the way of enumeration scarcely conceivable in the older portion of the country. On an estimated area greater than that of all the states north of Tennessee and east of the Mississippi there is a population less than in most single counties of the populous east."[31]

Petroff's contribution to Bancroft's *History of Alaska* was more significant than his work on the Eleventh Census. The *History* traces the be-

27. May 8, 1886. Also A. P. Swineford in Governor of Alaska, *Reports, 1,* 6.

28. Petroff's testimony, U.S. Senate, Committee on Territories, "Civil Government for Southeastern Alaska," *Senate Report 457,* pp. 17–21. Seton-Karr, *Shores and Alps of Alaska,* pp. 231, 232. I. C. Russell, "Mount St. Elias Expedition," *JAGS,* 22 (1890), 666.

29. "Geographical and Ethnographical Notes on Alaska," pp. 1–15.

30. "The Significance of the Frontier in American History," in *The Frontier in American History* (New York, 1950; originally published in 1893), p. 1.

31. R. P. Porter to J. W. Noble, February 9, 1893, in U.S. Census Office, *Report on Population and Resources of Alaska at the Eleventh Census: 1890* (Washington, 1893), page viii.

ginning of Russian interest in America, the Russian eastward movement, the discovery and exploration of Alaska, and management of the country by the Russian American Company. The American period necessarily receives brief treatment; only a few years of American rule had passed when the book was published in 1886. There is, however, a section on resources that remained an important source on the subject in the nineteenth century.

The *History* was one of many on the West produced by Hubert Howe Bancroft. "Produced" rather than "written" is the more accurate word for Bancroft's method: he employed a staff of collaborators who researched and to some extent wrote the histories. Where individual authorship for the Alaskan volume began and ended is speculative. One student credits Bancroft with one-half authorship, Alfred Bates with one-third, and Petroff with one-fourth; the total is an improper fraction, and illustrates the difficulty in assigning responsibility for the finished work.[32] Petroff translated the major Russian sources and wrote a good part of the volume.[33] He also searched Russian records in Alaska and Washington, and collected statements in Alaska. Because Bancroft's *History of Alaska* is essentially a history of the Russian period, it is safe to assume that Petroff's work was the foundation if not all of the superstructure.

According to Bancroft's *Literary Industries*,[34] Ivan Petroff had a moderately exciting life prior to his arrival in San Francisco. He was born in 1842 in St. Petersburg. A speech impediment forced him to abandon his schooling as a military interpreter, and he took employment with a scholar studying Sanskrit. From that position he transferred to another academician who was engaged in the investigation of Armenian antiquities and literature. After a scientific exploration into Armenia, Petroff was sent to Paris. He decided in 1861 to sail for America. He worked for the *Courier des Etats Unis* until his enlistment in the Union Army; he fought in all of General Butler's campaigns, eventually rising from the ranks to a com-

32. J. W. Caughey, *Hubert Howe Bancroft* (Berkeley and Los Angeles, 1946), pp. 262, 263.
33. Some of Petroff's translations, of Tikhmenev and Zagoskin, for example, are with the Pacific Manuscripts in Bancroft Library. I have spot-checked his translations by comparison with other unpublished English translations, and with published German translations, and found no sharp departures from fact. Petroff's translation of Zagoskin is far superior to the one usually used by anthropologists and historians.
34. (San Francisco, 1890), pp. 270–72.

mission as lieutenant, and was twice wounded. Upon his discharge in 1865 he contracted in New York for five years with the Russian American Company to act as an English and German correspondent in Sitka. En route west, he traveled by horseback and was wounded in the arm by Shoshones. By the time he arrived in Sitka, the place had been filled; so he was made chief trader of a post on Cook Inlet, a job he held until the sale of Alaska to the United States. He left Alaska for San Francisco in 1870 and entered the service of Hubert Howe Bancroft. This story of Petroff's life before 1870, as reported in *Literary Industries*, has been taken at face value by historians. The facts were probably supplied to Bancroft by Petroff himself, and unfortunately, at least part of the story is untrue. On June 4th, 1868, Battery "F" of the Second U.S. Army Artillery departed Fort Vancouver, Washington Territory, for Kenai, Alaska, and occupation duty.[35] The unit was at least one man shy—Private Ivan Petroff, who had enlisted in July 1867, at Fort Colville, W.T.[36] Soon after the company arrived in Alaska, the commander wrote to his superior asking for the wayward trooper: "I have the honor to make application that Private Ivan Petroff . . . who is now in confinement at Fort Vancouver W.T. for desertion, be forwarded to his Battery at the earliest practicable opportunity, as his services will be valuable as an interpreter."[37] Sometime thereafter Petroff arrived, and in July 1870 he was discharged at Fort Kenai.[38] Petroff, it would seem, became an Alaskan expert reluctantly.

In January 1871, Petroff re-enlisted as a private at Sacramento, this time for five years.[39] His new unit was assigned to Angel Island in San Francisco Bay, where he deserted a second time. It was the last of the Army for Ivan Petroff. He worked in San Francisco for the *Bulletin* and the *Chronicle* until about 1874, when he was employed by Bancroft. While in Washington, D.C., examining Alaskan archives in the State Department, he was picked for the Census job.[40] In the meantime, he had written

35. McGilvray to McIntyre, August 7, 1868, Department of Alaska, NA, RG 98.

36. Muster Role, April 30–June 30, 1870, AGO Records, NA, RG 94.

37. McGilvray to Campbell, September 23, 1868, Department of Alaska, NA, RG 98.

38. Muster Roll, June 30–August 31, 1870, AGO Records, NA, RG 94.

39. Oath of enlistment, January 4, 1871, AGO Records, NA, RG 94.

40. H. M. Hutchinson to Secretary of War R. T. Lincoln, February 1833, AGO Records, NA, RG 94.

and worked—and even edited the *Appeal*—under his own name.

Petroff's record was finally cleared in 1883, when Hayward M. Hutchinson, agent of the Alaska Commercial Company in Washington, wrote to the Secretary of War outlining Petroff's activities between 1871 and 1883—probably from details furnished by Petroff. Ivan, according to the letter, had taken employment with an Arizona newspaper that went bankrupt, and financial distress forced him to re-enlist in order to support his wife and child. Hutchinson's main point was well taken: Petroff had used his own name in San Francisco, and he had subsequently made valuable contributions to the nation as an employee of Bancroft and the Tenth Census. It was clearly a case for executive clemency, thought Hutchinson. Accordingly, Petroff was officially discharged in compliance with Special Order 45 of the Adjutant General's Office, Washington.[41] Hutchinson's argument was probably less telling than his political influence. One cannot help wondering whether he learned that Petroff was a runaway before or after the Census reports were submitted.

It is understandable that Petroff would seek to cover his background for Bancroft's *Literary Industries,* and that—insofar as his own life is concerned—he was led into falsehood. Just how much fabrication was necessary is another question. His testimony in February 1880, before the Congressional hearings on civil government for Alaska, is a case in point. He testified that prior to the Alaskan purchase he was ordered by the Russian company to find a direct route between Cook Inlet and the Yukon River.

> Q. Have you ever been in the interior?—A. Yes sir; I have been in the interior from Cook's Inlet north across the Yukon, and on the Atna or Copper River.
>
> Q. How far have you gone up the Yukon River?—A. I only crossed it about 600 miles above its mouth.
>
> Q. How did you cross that country from Cook's Inlet to Yukon River; what was your mode of conveyance?—A. Partly in canoes up the Suchitno River [sic]—in canoes for about 100 miles, then made portages from one lake to another until I crossed the mountain range and got on the tributaries of the Yukon southward, and then

41. Adjutant General to M. M. Hutchinson [sic], April 4, 1883, AGO Records, NA, RG 94.

took the canoes again. We had to carry our canoes all the way. The canoes which I used were made out of skin, and were very light.[42]

Petroff claimed that he left Cook Inlet on June 2d and returned by the same route September 23d. If he had made the journey, it would have to be recorded as one of the most notable accomplishments in the exploration of the Far Northwest. Of course, he did not. In his own Census report he wrote:

> What the country north of Cook Inlet is like no civilized man can tell, as in all the years of occupation of the coast by the Caucasian race it has remained a sealed book. The Indians tell us that the rivers lead into lakes and that the lakes are connected by rivers with other lakes again, until finally the waters flow into the basins of the Tanana and the Yukon; but conflicting with this intermingling of the waters are stories of mountains of immense altitude visible for hundreds of miles. The natives living north of this terra incognita give, however, a similar description, which may be accepted until reliable explorers are enabled to penetrate this region.[43]

While stationed on Cook Inlet in the Army, Petroff may have journeyed up the Kenai River to the lakes, he may have climbed the volcano Iliamna, and he may have traveled from the head of Resurrection Bay to Cook Inlet, then crossed the portage from Turnagain Arm to Prince William Sound. The Kenai River and Mt. Iliamna adventures appear in the San Francisco *Chronicle*. It is reasonable to assume that Petroff wrote the accounts. But the assumption that he actually made the excursions is something else again.[44]

Now and then, Ivan Petroff was given to flights of pure fancy that had no bearing on his personal reputation and fortune. During his researches he came across the tragedy of Father Juvenal, a Russian monk who near the end of the eighteenth century was dispatched to the Lake Iliamna re-

42. U.S. Senate Committee on Territories, "Civil Government for Southeastern Alaska," *Senate Report 457*, pp. 17–20.

43. Petroff, in *Compilation of Narratives*, p. 160.

44. H. W. Seton-Karr, "A Fresh Field for the Sportsman," *Fortnightly Review*, 47 (March 1, 1887), 404. Seton-Karr, *Shores and Alps of Alaska*, p. 239. Polaris, "Sketches of Alaska," San Francisco *Sunday Chronicle*, December 26, 1875. "Alaska's Great Volcano," Washington, D.C., *Evening Star*, January 22, 1876, reprinted from the San Francisco *Chronicle*.

gion and murdered there by the Indians. The dramatic possibilities were a temptation to Petroff. He "translated" Juvenal's "Journal," which he "found" on one of his Alaskan trips; it is a remarkable story, and is almost certainly a fraud.[45] It contains all the elements of high drama—a caricature of Alexander Baranof, the conflict between rival Russian traders on Cook Inlet, bad Indians and better Indians, a seduction, and a murder. It foreshadowed Somerset Maugham's "Rain." There appears to be no good reason for the forgery, unless it was Petroff's way of attacking the Russian Church, for which he had little affection.

A similar incident had more serious consequences. In 1892, after Petroff's pardon and after he had organized and collected data for the Eleventh Census, he was engaged by the State Department to translate Russian documents pertinent to the British-American dispute over sealing in the Bering Sea. The Department was preparing its case for an international tribunal established to mediate the dispute. Petroff interpolated into his translations whatever might be of assistance to the American case, and he forged other statements not in the original documents. The discrepancies were discovered, and the British were notified by Secretary John Foster.[46] When confronted, Petroff confessed. He was released by the State Department. He was also discharged by the Superintendent of the Census;[47] the report of 1890 was prepared for the press by another man, and Petroff's name was expunged. After this incident, Ivan Petroff drifted into obscurity.

Petroff's reasons for fabricating were often defensible. He sought to hide a portion of his background which if exposed could jeopardize his livelihood; and his motives in 1892 were apparently patriotic. On the other hand, it was hardly necessary to tarnish the name of Father Juvenal or lay claim to an original exploration of the Susitna valley. (It is to Petroff's credit that he in effect withdrew the latter claim.)

He is a likable character for all his delinquencies. As an authority on Alaska, only William Healey Dall could claim wider experience in the

45. I am indebted to Dr. Helen A. Shenitz of Auke Bay, Alaska, for her analysis of Juvenal's "Journal." The MS is in Bancroft Library as Father Juvenal, "A Daily Journal" (1796), translated by Ivan Petroff from the original manuscript. In H. H. Bancroft's *History of Alaska* (San Francisco, 1886), the story appears on pp. 365–74.

46. S. F. Bemis, *The American Secretaries of State and Their Diplomacy* (10 vols. New York, 1937), 8, 197.

47. R. Porter to Secretary of Interior, November 16, 1892, NA, RG 48.

field, in the library, and in print. A few writers have tried to make Petroff out as an enemy of Alaskan development, but this opinion does not square with the evidence in his published work. Petroff's writing is balanced and calm, if occasionally flippant and inconsistent, and by nineteenth-century standards it is usually reliable. The influence of his two monuments—the Tenth Census report and Bancroft's *History of Alaska*—on subsequent investigations is incalculable.[48] As recently as 1950, the "Report on Population" was used in a government document to help determine the legal status of Alaskan natives.[49]

48. For example see F. Schwatka, *Exploring the Great Yukon*, p. 378, and W. R. Abercrombie, "Supplementary Expedition into the Copper River Valley, Alaska," in *Compilation of Narratives*, p. 392.

49. V. Gsovski, "Russian Administration of Alaska and the Status of the Alaskan Natives," *Senate Document 152, 81st Congress: 2d session* (11401), 22, 60, 61.

5. Briskly Venture, Briskly Roam

Keep not standing fix'd and rooted,
Briskly venture, briskly roam:
Head and hand, where 'er thou foot it,
And stout heart, are still at home.

GOETHE, *Wilhelm Meister*

THE VARIETIES of tourism, commented an Englishman, have been lateral and vertical, "the ordinary traveller who tried to get as far as possible from his fellows, and was, therefore, something of a misanthrope, and the mountaineer whose endeavour was to get a little nearer to the angels, and who might be called a philangelist."[1] Alaska had both types, though few of its "lateral" travelers were misanthropes and not all of its "vertical" travelers were "philangelists." To tourism Alaska owes a large measure of the publicity it received before the Gold Rush. Interest in the territory generated by the tourist business explains many of the microgeographical investigations of the country. Visitors, lay and scientific, added to the growing bibliography of Alaskana. And the transportation facilities that were developed to accommodate tourists provided scientists and explorers with means of easy access to parts of an unexplored wilderness.

There was a peculiar element to early Alaskan tourism. While the great bulk of the Far Northwest was left unexplored, money and time in great quantity were devoted to overrunning the southeastern section. Expedition after expedition assaulted Mt. St. Elias but the regions beyond its inland slope were largely ignored. Every season, beginning in the early 1880s, luxury steamers threaded the quiet fiords of the Alexander Archipelago, while to the west the interior lay vacant and apparently uninviting.

A variety of reasons help to explain the sporadic, unco-ordinated, miniscule investigations of southeastern Alaska, but most explanations may be subsumed conveniently under one general heading: the coexistence

1. Comments of D. W. Freshfield, after a paper read by H. W. Seton-Karr, "Alpine Regions of Alaska," RGS, *Proceedings*, n.s. 9 (1887), 280.

of two disparate philosophical positions—lingering traces of the American romantic spirit and the rise of the scientific attitude. To many Americans, life in the United States during the final quarter of the century—at least until 1898—lacked the heroic dimensions of earlier eras. With the disappearance of the frontier, Americans sought adventure at first hand in travel or vicariously in travel stories, and mountaineering was an exciting substitute for wilderness exploration. Growth of the life sciences and geology gave a special meaning and pleasure to travel. The tourists who came to southeastern Alaska were amateur natural historians, and the scientists who came were amateur tourists. John Muir was both naturalist and travel writer. Israel C. Russell was above all a scientist, but his expeditions were billed as Alpine adventures. The symbiosis of tourism and science along the Alaskan Panhandle gave geologists an opportunity to study in the greatest glacial laboratory in America, to test and elaborate on Louis Agassiz' revolutionary hypothesis of 1834, which explained how ice fields helped chisel the earth's profile. Glaciers are special objects of both aesthetic and scientific curiosity, and in southeastern Alaska all extant types exist and are easily reached by water transportation.

Lateral tourism flourished in the Panhandle because the Inside Passage was a quiet, comfortable way to touch a fringe of wilderness, with spectacular mountains, dramatic glaciers, and lush evergreen forests. By the time the ship reached Glacier Bay the tourist was sated with glorious scenery, which according to one globe-trotter was "so continuously magnificent, it becomes monotonous."[2] A scientist urged the old to visit Alaska, but the young to stay away: "The scenery of Alaska is so much grander than anything else of the kind in the world that, once beheld all other scenery becomes flat and insipid. It is not well to dull one's capacity for . . . enjoyment by seeing the finest first."[3] Between 1884 and 1890 over 25,000 passengers, at $100 a head, came to marvel at the area's marine Alps.[4] The Northwest Coast Indians were an extra attraction. By 1885, Tlingit relics had already been replaced by curios.[5] Another thrill was

2. R. W. Meade, "Alaska," *Appleton's Journal*, 6 (1871), 126.

3. Henry Gannett, "The General Geography of Alaska," *NGM*, *12* (May 1901), 196.

4. U.S. Census, *Report on . . . Alaska at the Eleventh Census*, pp. 250, 251.

5. Dall, "Native Tribes of Alaska," p. 368.

the side trip to Glacier Bay. As a point of interest its natural beauty was enhanced by tales of a "silent city" in the icy expanse of Muir Glacier. The mirage was not seen by all. One enthusiast "photographed" the "silent city" in 1889. It was later identified as Bristol, England.[6]

Others came to the region to fish and to hunt. Alaska was early boosted by travelers and officials as a sportsman's paradise. The virtual ruler of Alaska during the Navy's tenure wrote under a pseudonym for *Forest and Stream*,[7] and in the same magazine another author is applauded for dispelling, "once and for all, the old superstition that Alaskan trout will not rise to a fly."[8] One popular writer, impressed with the country's piscatorial wealth, recommended that on Alaska's coat of arms a fish be emblazoned, "either natant, torqued, or salient."[9]

A few of the visitors were dignitaries. There were the inevitable Congressional junkets; "head and stout heart" were usually left at home. One senator, according to an Alaskan newspaper, stopped in Sitka for a day and in Juneau long enough to take a bath.[10] Obviously the effect of brief Congressional vacations in southeastern Alaska could be deleterious: when the reports of explorers, scientists, and regional experts were read in the House or Senate, any individual congressman who had taken a bath in Juneau or spent a few hours gazing intently at Muir Glacier in hope of seeing the "silent city" might rise and insert his personal—though inexpert—opinion.[11]

Daniel Coit Gilman and Nicholas Murray Butler headed a list of prominent educators who accompanied one political tour. Gilman and Butler instigated the foundation of the Alaskan Society of Natural History and Ethnology, designed to collect and preserve information on Indians, resources, climate, and flora and fauna.[12] In addition to its collection activities, the organization enlisted a string of distinguished corresponding

6. Alex Badlam, *Wonders of Alaska* (San Francisco, 1890), pp. 127–37.

7. For example, L. A. Beardslee, or "Piseco," July 8, 1880.

8. November 18, 1886. Reported in Sitka *Alaskan*, March 19, 1887.

9. E. R. Scidmore, "Alaska Fish and Game," *Harper's Weekly*, 37 (September 2, 1893), 838.

10. Gruening, *The State of Alaska*, p. 84.

11. Nichols, *Alaska*, p. 128.

12. Anon., "The Alaskan Society of Sitka," *Science*, 10 (December 9, 1887), 280, 281. Sitka *Alaskan*, October 8, 1887.

members, aided A. P. Niblack in his ethnological researches,[13] and sponsored at least one learned paper.[14]

Alaska's lateral travelers, celebrated and ordinary, were induced northward by an outpouring of articles, books, and pamphlets, some promoted by the transportation companies, others written by explorers with a literary flair, and still others authored by individual tourists. The man most responsible was the poet-naturalist John Muir.

Said Muir: "I care to live only to entice people to look at Nature's loveliness."[15] In the pursuit of that goal he met with huge success. Articles about his Alaskan travels were printed and reprinted in American newspapers.[16] A charming story of his glacier adventures with a canine companion has been called "one of the finest studies of dogliness in all literature."[17] Of the Inside Passage, he said: "No other excursion that I know of can be made into any of the wild portions of America where so much fine and grand and novel scenery is brought to view at so cheap and easy a price."[18] His own travels were inspired by Goethe's admonition to "briskly venture, briskly roam,"[19] and by Wordsworth on the lessons of a vernal wood:

> One impulse from a vernal wood
> May teach you more of man,
> Of moral evil and of good,
> Than all the sages can.[20]

13. Alaskan Society of Natural History and Ethnology, Minute Book, November 30, 1887–February 10, 1896, MSS, Sheldon Jackson Junior College, Sitka, Alaska. I am indebted to Mr. George Hall, Park Historian, of Sitka, for his examination of and report on these materials, which I did not have the opportunity to inspect during my Sitka visit.

14. G. F. Wright, *The Muir Glacier* (Sitka, n.d.).

15. Muir, *Travels in Alaska* (Boston, 1915), page v.

16. See C. B. Bradley, "A Reference List to John Muir's Newspaper Articles," *Sierra Club Bulletin*, 10 (1916), 53–59.

17. R. U. Johnson, "John Muir as I Knew Him," ibid., p. 11. The story appeared in article form as "An Adventure with a Dog and a Glacier," *Century*, 54 (September 1897), 769–76, and was enlarged later in book form as *Stickeen* (Boston, 1909).

18. "The Alaska Trip," *Century*, 54 (August 1897), 514.

19. H. F. Osborn, "John Muir," *Sierra Club Bulletin*, 10 (1916), 29.

20. S. H. Young, *Alaska Days with John Muir* (New York, 1915), p. 97. The stanza is from "The Tables Turned." Young, in quoting Muir's recitation, fittingly substitutes the word "will" for "may" teach.

Muir was a nineteenth-century romantic in every dimension including his science. A friend of great men in science—Arnold Guyot, the LeConte brothers, Sir Joseph Hooker, Asa Gray—Muir declined all teaching offers with the comment that "there were already plenty of professors in the colleges and few observers in the wilderness."[21] His Romanticism made his science aesthetic and spiritual: he was a Nature-alist rather than a naturalist in the nineteenth-century scientific sense, but he knew his glaciers and he knew his botany and the knowledge helped him understand the beauty in Nature's great and small manifestations. After describing the island forests of the Alexander Archipelago, Muir wrote: "The harmonious tree relations are so constant that they evidently are the result of design, as much so as the arrangement of the feathers of birds or the scales of fishes."[22] He hated tampering with the design; he had an aversion to killing animals, and cheerfully rocked the canoe when his Alaskan Indian companions were sighting in on a flock of ducks or a deer on shore. He thought the Gold Rush "crowd" was on a "sordid" mission and would "be spoiling our grand Alaska."[23] Eventually John Muir became high priest of what historians have called the "aesthetic" branch of the American conservation movement, and the wilderness conservation crusade gained momentum in the decade following his first visit to Alaska.

In the summer of 1879, along with the energetic young Presbyterian missionary S. Hall Young and a party of Stikeen Indians, and with a volume by Thoreau under his arm, Muir set off by canoe to investigate the natural wonders of the Alexander Archipelago. He carried a pocket compass, a barometer, and Vancouver's ancient chart.[24] Young was an amiable companion. He was, said Muir, "one of those fearless and adventurous evangelists who in seeking to save others save themselves."[25] The forms of religion did cause some good-natured friction. When Young insisted that the party camp on Sunday, Muir objected, saying the Lord's Day would be better kept by flying before the winds He sent, in order to hear what He had to say. Muir wanted always to see what was beyond. On

21. J. Swett, "John Muir," *Century*, 46 (May 1893), 122.
22. *Travels in Alaska*, p. 18.
23. Young, *Alaska Days*, pp. 171, 172, 211.
24. Ibid., p. 67. Young, *Hall Young of Alaska*, pp. 184, 185, 198.
25. Muir, "The Discovery of Glacier Bay," *Century*, 50 (June 1895), 234.

one occasion he demanded that the Indians paddle across a reef during a storm. The Indians complied, under protest, and the canoe was almost dashed on the rocks. The chief, heretofore silenced by Muir's seemingly bottomless wisdom, scolded the naturalist severely, and from then on the Indian captained his canoe.[26]

The "beyond" that Muir found was Glacier Bay. His explorations of the Bay and his glowing description of its crystal wonderland brought a flood of tourists and a stream of scientists to the area. Regular excursions to the Bay began in 1883, before the inlet was charted by the government.[27]

The opportunity to study glacial phenomena was eagerly taken. In 1883 one visitor theorized grandly about the effects of glaciers on climate, after studying the ice fields of the Bay from the deck of a steamer.[28] The area was visited in 1886 by G. Frederick Wright, who spent a month studying the glaciers and collecting specimens. An account of his work appeared in the *American Journal of Science*[29] and in *The Ice Age in North America, and Its Bearings Upon the Antiquity of Man.*[30]

Wright was followed in 1890 by Harry Fielding Reid of Cleveland's Case School of Applied Science.[31] Reid, accompanied by a party of students, brought cameras and a complete set of instruments, some furnished by the Coast and Geodetic Survey. Attracted by Wright's report of a forty- to seventy-foot daily motion of Muir Glacier,[32] Reid determined to measure the ice field's movement, and also to map the area, take magnetic readings and meteorological observations, and study the geology and biology. He concluded that, although the ice undoubtedly had moved more rapidly in 1886, Wright's figures were in error—seven feet per day was more like it. Reid's observation that one hundred years earlier the glaciers might have filled a greater part of the Bay went far to explain why Van-

26. Young, *Hall Young of Alaska*, pp. 200, 218.

27. E. R. Scidmore, "Discovery of Glacier Bay, Alaska," *NGM*, 7 (April 1896), 144.

28. T. Meehan, "Glaciers of Alaska," *Proceedings of the Academy of Natural Sciences of Philadelphia*, 35 (1883), 249–55.

29. "The Muir Glacier," ser. 3, *33* (1887), 1–18.

30. (New York, 1889), Chapter 3.

31. Muir, *Travels in Alaska*, p. 286.

32. See Wright, *Ice Age*, p. 51.

couver did not "discover" the fiord. In 1892 Reid returned to extend his work.[33] His method included photography and detailed instrumental observations, and set the pattern for modern glacier studies.[34]

John Muir's great contribution was the publicity he gave to the Far Northwest as a field for scientific and aesthetic investigation. But his trips did more than attract public and scientific attention to Alaska. The crude chart he and Young made of Glacier Bay remained for several years the only one in existence. He helped Young enumerate the Tlingit Indians, and the figures were used by Ivan Petroff in the Tenth Census.[35] Muir's investigations also permitted him to explain certain large problems associated with glacial action.[36] And there were new wonders to describe— the strange self-emptying glacial lakes, for example.[37] Toward the end of the century, Muir accompanied members of the National Forest Commission to Alaska and concluded, as had Dall and Petroff, that Alaskan timber would not compete with lumber from the Pacific Northwest because, with one exception, of inferior quality and distance from a market.[38]

Muir was not the first to see Glacier Bay, the great glaciological laboratory that he and Young put on the map; another American had observed it before him. Lieutenant C. E. S. Wood of the Army, with one companion, had made a private journey to Alaska in 1877 in the hope of climbing Mt. St. Elias, which was believed by some to be the highest peak on the continent. The ascent was abandoned, however, when an Indian crew refused to carry the party to Yakutat. The Indians balked at making a dangerous canoe voyage just to give a couple of eccentric white men the opportunity to climb Mt. St. Elias. With logic that would have devastated

33. H. P. Cushing, "Notes on the Muir Glacier Region, Alaska, and Its Geology," *American Geologist*, 8 (1891), 216. H. F. Reid, "Studies of Muir Glacier, Alaska," *NGM*, 4 (March 21, 1892), 21, 44. Reid, "Report of an Expedition to Muir Glacier, Alaska . . . ," USC&GS, *Annual Report, 1891*, Pt. 2, Appendix 14, p. 494. Reid, "Glacier Bay and Its Glaciers," USGS, *Sixteenth Annual Report, 1894–95*, Pt. 1, pp. 415–61.

34. W. O. Field, "Glaciological Research in Alaska," in Collins, *Science in Alaska*, p. 124.

35. Young, *Hall Young of Alaska*, p. 190.

36. For example see Muir, *John of the Mountains*, edited by L. M. Wolfe (Boston, 1938), pp. 266–69.

37. Muir, *Travels in Alaska*, p. 101.

38. Muir, "Alaska Forests," San Francisco *Bulletin*, October 30, 1879. See also W. F. Badè, *The Life and Letters of John Muir* (2 vols. Boston, 1924), 2, 304, 305, 398, 399.

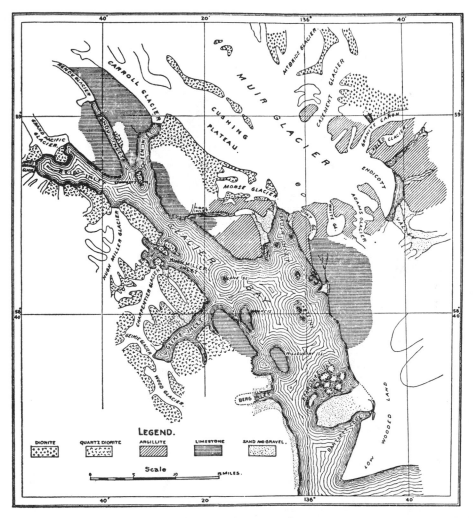

3. Glacier Bay, from Reid's report

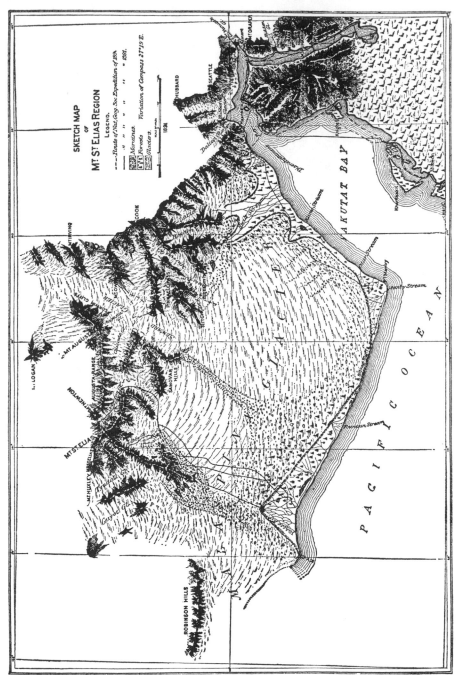

4. Mt. St. Elias, from Russell's report

almost anyone but an Alpine enthusiast, the Indians told Wood: "One mountain is as good as another. There is a very high one. Go climb that if you want to."[39] His hopes frustrated, Wood nevertheless stayed on, to accompany an Indian hunting expedition behind Mt. Fairweather—and it was in the course of this journey that he caught a glimpse of Glacier Bay.[40] When later there was a minor flurry over who discovered the Bay—one of many such controversies—Wood disclaimed the honor,[41] and rightfully, because he had not realized in 1877 that the Bay was a new discovery, and because he reported the observation much later in a popular magazine.

A new mountaineering expedition in 1886 was led by Frederick Schwatka, who had already made a reputation in Arctic and Northwest exploration. Born in Illinois, Schwatka had worked as a printer and attended Willamette University in Oregon. He graduated from West Point in 1871. Schwatka's wanderlust was both intellectual and geographical. While serving at different Army posts, he studied law and medicine; eventually he was admitted to the Nebraska bar and received a medical degree from New York's Bellevue Hospital Medical College. In 1879–1880, he led a belated search in the Canadian Arctic for evidence of the long-lost Sir John Franklin expedition. Schwatka's journey received considerable publicity and won him a reputation as an Arctic explorer.[42]

Sponsored by George Jones and the New York *Times*, the 1886 venture promised if nothing else to provide exciting fare for the newspaper's public. Schwatka was accompanied by William Libbey, a professor of physical geography at the College of New Jersey. Specimen collections were to go to Libbey's college and to the National Museum.[43] At Sitka the men were joined by Heywood W. Seton-Karr, an English traveler, apparently the only member of the party with any Alpine experience. For Seton-Karr to guide Schwatka, "of eighteen stone," up a 19,000-foot mountain, an English geographer pointed out, would be a "Quixotic enterprise,"[44] and so it turned out: the Schwatka party spent only nine or

39. Wood, "Among the Thlinkets in Alaska," *Century, 24* (July 1882), 332.
40. Ibid., pp. 323, 324, 332, 333. Chicago *Tribune*, June 13, 1877.
41. Scidmore, "Discovery of Glacier Bay," pp. 141, 142.
42. *DAB*, *16*, 481, 482.
43. Libbey, "Some of the Geographical Features of Southeastern Alaska," *JAGS, 18* (1886), 279. Buffalo *Sunday Express*, August 29, 1886.
44. Comments of D. W. Freshfield in Seton-Karr, "Alpine Regions," p. 282.

ten days away from the beach.[45] (Seton-Karr later published a light and amusing travel book on his adventures, which stimulated interest in Alaska both in England and in the United States; in 1888 an English Alpine expedition to Mt. St. Elias reached 11,400 feet.)[46]

The Schwatka expedition mapped, collected ethnologic materials, and took a couple of hundred photographs. In addition, Schwatka used the opportunity to indulge a favorite pastime—naming the physical features of the area. Many of his names honored men of science, but to what Schwatka thought "geographically was one of the most important discoveries" he assigned the name of the expedition's sponsor: the Yahtse River became the Jones River.[47] The temptation to poke fun at this new name was irresistible. The New York *Sun* and the *Tribune* made merry over it, and the *World* offered new lyrics for the tune "Swanee River":

> Way up upon de Geojones ribber
> Far, far away,
> Dere's where de mud am running ebber,
> Into de Icy Bay.

> All de mouth am wide and muddy,
> Eberywhere am stones;
> Oh darkies how we smile at Schwatka,
> An dat funny ribber Jones.[48]

When a French geographer called the name "trivial," Schwatka was defended in an American journal: "can any name be more trivial and more out of place than that of the 'Ferdinand de Lesseps Mountains,' superfluously given [by a Frenchman] . . . to the Sierra Parima?"[49] William

45. W. Williams, "Climbing Mount St. Elias," *Scribner's Magazine*, 5 (April 1889), 387.

46. G. Broke, *With Sack and Stock in Alaska* (London, 1891), pp. 1, 2. H. W. Topham, "An Expedition to Mount St. Elias, Alaska," *Alpine Journal*, 14 (August 1889), 366. Also Topham, "A Visit to the Glaciers of Alaska and Mount St. Elias," RGS, *Proceedings*, 2 (1889), 424–35.

47. Schwatka, "Mountaineering in Alaska," *Alpine Journal*, 13 (November 1886), 90–93.

48. Reprinted in the Sitka *Alaskan*, November 20, 1886.

49. G. C. Hurlburt, "Geographical Note on the Topography of Mt. St. Elias," *JAGS*, 22 (1890), 287.

Healey Dall agreed that Schwatka had every right to name the stream, but the scarcely more euphonious Indian name "Yahtse" won the day.

Dall felt Schwatka's geographic work would be a solid gain for science; but then, he went on to note, a conscientious explorer could hardly fail to return with valuable information.[50] Schwatka's scientific achievement was, like his Alpine accomplishment, insignificant.[51] He returned with some black sand from Yakutat, but the discovery was not new, since the area had been prospected in 1880.[52] The real accomplishment, as with Muir, was in public relations. Government reports, explained the *Times*, had failed to bring Alaska's wealth to the attention of people interested in commercial opportunity, and the results of an expedition undertaken by a newspaper were sure to be more widely known. "In this sense the expedition of Lieut. Schwatka may be said to have done more to realize the expectation which Mr. Seward founded upon his purchase of Alaska than any other event that has happened since the purchase itself."[53] The *Times* overvalued its own contribution, but the main point was legitimate.

In the summer of 1890, an impressive expedition was organized to renew the assault on Mt. St. Elias. Its leader was the scholarly and productive geologist Israel C. Russell. Russell had traveled the Yukon's course on a reconnaissance for the Geological Survey, and even before the *Times* expedition he had his eye on the St. Elias region as a field for the study of glacial phenomena. He was more interested in geology than in the thrill of conquering what was thought to be the highest peak on the continent. Science was the main object of the expedition; if "practicable," an attempt to climb the mountain would be made. The party was jointly sponsored by the National Geographic Society and the Geological Survey; the latter furnished instruments and $1,000 from its current appropriation and was personally represented in the expedition by Mark Kerr, who went along as topographer. Among the individuals who subscribed to the exploration were Henry Gannett, John Wesley Powell, Alexander Graham Bell, and Adolphus W. Greely.

50. Sitka *Alaskan*, December 4, 1886.
51. Schwatka, "New York Times Exploring Expedition to Mount St. Elias," New York *Times*, September 20, 1886.
52. A. P. Swineford, "Report," dated October 1, 1887, in Governor of Alaska, *Reports*, 1, 16.
53. Editorial, New York *Times*, September 20, 1886.

The party did not achieve the summit, because of insufficient supplies.[54] But Russell returned the following year, under the same auspices, to continue his work. Seton-Karr, in a footnote in his travel book, had advised that "further explorers . . . should land either at Cape Yagtag or Yakutat Bay," warning that the surf at Icy Bay was too treacherous.[55] Russell's second expedition failed to heed this advice, and when they sought to land at Icy Bay, an officer and four seamen from the Revenue Cutter *Bear*, along with a member of Russell's party, were lost in the pounding sea.[56] It was one of the few tragedies in the history of American exploration in the Far Northwest.

Russell's glacial investigation was extensive and methodical. In addition to glaciers of the usual Alpine type, he examined the giant Malaspina, a piedmont glacier sprawled over 1,500 square miles. The Russell party discovered a feasible route by which the summit of Mt. St. Elias could be reached, and mapped topographically an area more than 1,000 miles in extent. His researches led to specific and general articles and books.[57] Also, in response to existing doubts about the precise location of the peak, Russell urged a precise survey of the boundary line.[58]

Two international questions were being asked about Mt. St. Elias by geographers. First, was it higher than Orizaba in Mexico? And second, was it in Canada or Alaska?

The mountain moved up and down in print.[59] Alaska's discoverer, Vitus

54. Russell, "Yukon River," *JAGS*, 22 (1890), 139–43. Russell, "Existing Glaciers of the United States, *USGS, Fifth Annual Report, 1883–84*, p. 353. Russell, "Mount St. Elias and Its Glaciers," *American Journal of Science*, ser. 3, 43 (1892), 169. Russell, "An Expedition to Mount St. Elias, Alaska," *NGM, 3* (May 29, 1891), 75, 192. Russell, "Mt. St. Elias and the Malaspina Glacier," *Appalacia, 7* (March 1894), 274. Also Russell, "Mount St. Elias Expedition," *JAGS* (1890), pp. 661, 662.

55. *Shores and Alps of Alaska*, pp. 66, 67.

56. Russell, "Second Expedition to Mount St. Elias in 1891," USGS, *Thirteenth Annual Report, 1891–92*, Pt. 2, p. 10. Russell, "Mount St. Elias Revisited," *Century, 44* (June 1892), 190.

57. For example, "The influence of Debris on the Flow of Glaciers," *JG, 3* (1895), 823–32; and *Glaciers of North America* (Boston, 1897).

58. Russell, "Mount St. Elias Expedition," p. 664. Russell, "Alaska: Its Physical Geography," *Scottish Geographical Magazine* (Edinburgh), *10* (1894), 395.

59. Heilprin, "The Culminating Point of the North American Continent," *Science, 16* (November 7, 1890), 260–61, and *16* (November 21, 1890), 289, 290. Dall, "Mount St. Elias," *Science, 16* (November 14, 1890), 275, 276, and *16* (November 28, 1890), 303.

Bering, had been content merely to estimate the mountain's height, but others were more precise. The French expedition under Laperouse (1786) calculated it at 12,672 feet. Alejandro Malaspina came close in 1791 with an estimate of 17,851 feet. The Russian Michael Tebenkov gave the elevation as 17,000 feet in his atlas.[60] Dall's calculation (19,000), though it was a thousand feet too high, at least called the world's attention to a spectacular peak so far unscaled. Then came the Russell expeditions: the first estimated it at 15,350 feet, and the second, at 18,100 feet, plus or minus a hundred.[61] The actual elevation, as ultimately established by the precise triangulation of a Coast and Geodetic team, was 18,010 feet. Orizaba thus lost out, not only to Mt. St. Elias, but also to Mt. Logan, in Canada, estimated by the same Coast and Geodetic team as higher than 19,000.[62]

The location of the peak aroused equal interest. At a Fourth of July celebration in Sitka, Seton-Karr had managed to pluck up "sufficient spirit" to suggest that the mountain might be entirely, and must be at least partially, in British territory.[63] When he landed at San Francisco on the way home, he was told by representatives of the newspaper that any statement questioning the United States' claim to Mt. St. Elias "would adversely affect their circulation and inflict injury upon their reputation," as the *Times* expedition was represented as an all-American enterprise; accordingly, Seton-Karr remained quiet for the moment.[64] Dall, meanwhile, agreed with Seton-Karr that the location was in doubt, while Dall's former colleague, George Davidson, inclined to the view that the mountain was American.[65] Eventually the nationality of the peak was settled by the same United States party that determined its height: Mt. St. Elias was on the border.

Ironically, neither Britisher nor American ever achieved its eventual

---

60. Brooks, *Blazing Alaska's Trails*, pp. 278, 270.

61. M. B. Kerr, "Mount St. Elias and Its Glaciers," *Scribner's Magazine*, 9 (March 1891), 369. Russell, "Height and Position of Mount St. Elias," *NGM*, 3 (January 28, 1892), 231.

62. Anon., "Measurements of St. Elias and of Orizaba," *Alpine Journal*, 17 (February 1894), 68. Anon., "Note on Mount Logan," *American Geologist*, 13 (1894), 292.

63. *Shores and Alps of Alaska*, p. 63.

64. Letter from Seton-Karr, inTopham, "A Visit to the Glaciers," p. 434.

65. RGS, *Proceedings*, n.s. 2 (1889), 611.

conquest. It was successfully climbed in 1897 by the Italian party of Prince Luigi Amadeo di Savoia, Duke of the Abruzzi.[66]

While federal agencies tried (usually without success) to get support for systematic lateral exploration, private groups spent heavily on novel and news-making vertical expeditions that contributed little to geographical knowledge. The expeditions of 1890 and 1891 led by two government geologists, were scientifically successful, though confined to a tiny district. The sponsorship of gross geographical discovery, rather than detailed investigation of a relatively small area, would have been wiser. To Dall and Petroff,[67] who recommended carefully planned exploration of the whole country, the Mt. St. Elias junkets must have seemed like endless fidgeting. Yet Dall himself was reconciled to the fact that Alaska would be explored "piecemeal."[68]

Even before any Englishman or Italian amused himself with Alpine adventure in Alaska, two German lateral expeditions, or series of expeditions, had made important contributions to the ethnography of the territory. The Geographical Society of Bremen had sent the brothers Arthur and Aurel Krause to the Chukotsk Peninsula in Siberia, and after they completed their work there, a trading company invited them to stay on at the firm's Chilkat post in southeastern Alaska. They arrived on Christmas Day, 1881, to make intensive studies of the Tlingit Indians. Aurel returned to Europe in April 1882, but his brother remained through the summer and traveled twice into Canada. The first trip took him over the Chilkoot Pass to Lake Lindemann (named the following year by Schwatka after the Secretary of the Bremen society). On the second trip, Krause ascended the Chilkat River, went over the pass, and turned back after sighting Kusawa Lake.[69]

Arthur Krause was the first scientific explorer to traverse the famous southern Gold Rush trails. Both he and his brother were meticulous investigators. Their contribution to all branches of science was immense.

66. F. de Filippi, *The Ascent of Mount St. Elias*, translated by L. Villari (Westminster, 1900).

67. Petroff, "Alaska as It Is," *International Review*, 12 (1882), 122.

68. Sitka *Alaskan*, December 4, 1886.

69. E. Gunther, "Introduction," in Aurel Krause, *The Tlingit Indians*, translated by E. Gunther (Seattle, 1956) page iii (originally published as *Die Tlinkit Indianer*, Jena, 1885). Krause, pp. 1–6. See also Arthur Krause, "Das Chilcat-Gebiet in Alaska," *Zeitschrift der Gesselschaft für Erdkunde zu Berlin*, 18 (1883), 344–68, with map.

Their collections were divided among well over a dozen European scientists.[70] Until recently, their study of the Tlingits, which was translated into English in 1956,[71] was not superseded by any comprehensive modern ethnography.

At the time the Krause brothers were making their intensive study of the Tlingits, another foreign ethnological investigator roamed along the coasts and rivers to the westward. Captain J. Adrian Jacobsen was a Norwegian collector sponsored by the Museum für Völkerkunde in Berlin. He visited the British Columbian coast, Prince William Sound, and Kodiak. At Unalaska, he met H. D. Wolfe, a correspondent of the New York *Herald*, who accompanied him on later journeys. From St. Michael, Jacobsen traveled up the Yukon in 1882 with a party of prospectors. He drifted downstream from Tanana, studying the Ingaliks along the way. That winter he bisected the neck of Seward Peninsula on a trip to Kotzebue Sound, and also visited Bering Strait. On these travels he collected 7,000 ethnological items for the Berlin museum.[72] Jacobsen eventually touched the Kuskokwim, Togiak, and Nushagak delta regions, and negotiated the Iliamna Lake portage between Cook Inlet and Bristol Bay. He made the first archaeological excavations on Cook Inlet, where he discovered pottery. According to Professor Cornelius Osgood, Jacobsen's studies of the Tanaina Athapaskans were more important than the work of either Petroff or Dall.[73] Thanks to the labor of Jacobsen and the brothers Krause, Germany by 1883 had Alaskan ethnological collections second only to those at the Smithsonian Institution.

The Telegraph explorers had mapped the Yukon in Alaska and begun the systematic study of Alaska's natural history. William Dall, in addition to the wide application of his regional expertise, helped to meet the need for coastal charts and for more precise knowledge of the Alaskan natives. Petroff compiled existing information on Alaska's resources and population for the Tenth Census. Some gains for ethnography and geology came

70. Dall, "Explorations in Alaska," *Science*, 1 (February 9, 1883), 19.

71. Gunther, "Introduction," *The Tlingit Indians*, page iii.

72. Woldt, editor, *Capitain Jacobsen's Reise an der Nordwestküste Amerikas, 1881–1883*, pp. 151, 152, 319.

73. Osgood, *The Ethnography of the Tanaina*, Yale University Publications in Anthropology No. 16 (New Haven, 1937), p. 20. Another foreign investigator, the Frenchman Alphonse Pinart, made anthropological studies along the southern Alaskan coast in the early 1870s. See Bancroft, *Literary Industries*, pp. 622, 623.

from lateral foreign collectors, and from foreign and domestic tourism and Alpinism in southeastern Alaska. Muir and the mountain climbers called attention to the territory in the nation's press. It remained for the Army, long the chief instrument of American scientific exploration, to undertake overland reconnaissance. The story of scientific exploration in the Far Northwest, as a chronologically and institutionally coherent narrative, began with the awakening of Army interest in the territory.

6. The Inspecting Generals and the Generals' Inspectors

Year by year we shall add still further to our knowledge of this once distant country. We shall find the sources of its mighty rivers; we shall follow the shore of the wondrous northern sea; on every hand we shall make acquisition of new and abundant treasures of science, which shall continue to enrich mankind when our lost millions have been long forgotten. If these are to be the results of the acquisition of Alaska, I am confident that, whatever may be the doubts of statesmen or the lamentations of economists, there will be consolation and satisfaction in the Hall of the Geographical Society.

CHARLES RAYMOND[1]

THE INSTITUTIONAL PATTERN of Alaskan exploration is strikingly similar in general outline to the whole experience of American westward expansion, but it is an anachronism. Everything that happened south of the forty-ninth parallel occurred in roughly the same order "north of fifty-three," but twenty-five to fifty years later. It could not have occurred earlier because of Russian ownership. While to the south the main institutions of United States' scientific exploration were undergoing a metamorphosis in function and duty, in Alaska they were playing their old roles in the opening of a new land.

The Coast Survey and the Army, which had dominated pre-Civil War governmental science through exploration-centered activities, began a period of decline after the war. The Coast Survey's dry land operations shifted to geodesy, and the Army, with the disappearance of the wilderness and the Indian, found that its excuse for pre-eminence in Western exploration had vanished. Then when the opportunity for exploration presented itself in Alaska, the Coast Survey took the initiative; leadership was assumed by the Army later, in the 1880s. When the Coast and Geodetic Survey appeared in the interior of the Far Northwest in 1889, its activities were chiefly geodetic.

Establishment of the Geological Survey in 1879 did not interrupt the

1. "The Yukon River Region, Alaska," *JAGS*, 3 (1872), 192.

progression. The USGS was a modern civilian scientific bureau designed to carry on where the old general-purpose military survey left off. Despite a clear mandate to handle inland exploration, the USGS took little organized interest in Alaskan exploration until 1895. By then, the Coast and Geodetic Survey and the Army had engaged in northern exploratory activities remarkably similar to their pre-Civil War operations to the south. Two unusual inland expeditions of the Revenue Marine and the Navy fail to fit the pattern. As in the States, a constant factor was the continuing interest of the Smithsonian Institution, acting as a central agency for pure science to which all departments referred.

The time lag between institutional activity south of the forty-ninth parallel and activity in Alaska can be clarified by a look at some of the demands made upon technical and fiscal resources of the United States during the nineteenth century. Public land subdivision surveys by the Interior Department, made in response to population pressures, cost the government $25½ million between 1802 and 1885. The Coast Survey, from 1806 to 1818 and from 1832 to 1885, expended $20 million, principally for coastal charts to serve the booming maritime commerce of the nation. The State Department was given nearly $3 million between 1798 and 1885 for international boundary surveys connected with pressing diplomatic problems. The Interior Department spent about $1¼ million for various geological and mineral examinations, mostly west of the Mississippi, between 1834 and 1879, and the Geological Survey in a six-year period before 1885 spent $2 million on similar investigations. War Department surveys—geographical and military, for railroads, roads, rivers, harbors, and lakes—were supported by appropriations of over $10 million.

From the birth of the Republic to July 1886, Congress spent approximately $68 million for surveys.[2] Of that figure Alaska's share was infinitesimal, but so was Alaska's claim measured in relation to the nation's total population, industry, commerce, and resources. Commerce of the Atlantic and Pacific coasts called for reliable charts prepared by the Coast Survey; the Army's transportation surveys helped bind the nation together and facilitate social and economic unity between population centers; min-

2. G. M. Wheeler, *Report upon the Third International Geographical Congress and Exhibition at Venice, Italy, 1881* (Washington, 1885), pp. 473, 474. Dupree, *Science in the Federal Government*, pp. 184, 194, 195.

eral investigations by the Interior Department were designed to answer urgent questions raised nearby. By contrast, Alaska was remote and unpopulated, its resources unknown and virtually untapped. The Republic had problems to solve near its center before it could attack peripheral affairs vigorously. And the concept of federal science to serve the nation's welfare was little developed outside the plans of pioneer science administrators like John Wesley Powell. On balance, seen as a matter of priority, what the federal government did in fact achieve in Alaskan exploration was progressive when viewed against the complex character of American life in the nineteenth century, although Alaskan activity, illustrated by the Army's early experience, was seldom initiated with welfare development as its justification.

The Army's role in Alaskan scientific exploration before 1886 may be divided into three phases. The first was between 1867 and 1877, when the Army ruled the territory of Alaska, with headquarters at Sitka and posts scattered along the southern coast. This period was, strangely, the least productive for military exploration, and was marked only by tours of inspecting generals and one reconnaissance along the Yukon River. The second phase, dominated by the Signal Service, began before Army evacuation of Alaska and ended in the early 1880s. Army meteorological observations made during this time in the Aleutians and the Yukon-Kuskokwim deltas contributed chiefly to background research rather than to gross geographical discovery. The third phase resembled the organized, pre-Civil War explorations of the trans-Mississippi West, except that in Alaska there was no specialized Corps of Topographical Engineers. Original overland reconnaissance was the result principally of one departmental commander's curiosity about an unknown wilderness combined with the ambition of his energetic aides. The third phase ended with Henry Allen's exploration of the Copper, Tanana, and Koyukuk rivers.

In the first period of Army activity in Alaska, between 1867 and 1877, the Army was *de facto* ruler of the country, but its influence was limited to the area immediately adjacent to a few small garrisons. As a source of information on the country, military reports from the Department of Alaska were woefully inadequate. Few serious attempts were made to gather data, scientific or otherwise, and no important explorations were undertaken.

The situation did not prevent military men from making policy recom-

mendations. In 1868 General Halleck of the Division of the Pacific, passing along the suggestions of his Alaskan commander, included a recommendation that lands on Kenai Peninsula be surveyed and brought into the
market;[3] but nothing came of the idea. Halleck believed that no civil government was necessary beyond the establishment of courts at Kodiak and
Sitka. Reflecting the unhappy past relationship of the Army and the Indian Bureau, he strongly urged against the use of Indian agents in the
country. Halleck's observation that military posts in the territory would be
able to raise all the vegetables they needed was an unusual note in the
perpetual nineteenth-century bickering over Alaska's agricultural potential.[4]

Of the inspecting generals who toured the remote northern protec-
torate, the most thorough was George H. Thomas, "the Rock of Chicka-
mauga." Even his trip was only a summer excursion. He touched at Sitka,
Kenai, Kodiak, Unalaska, and the Pribilofs. For the exploitation of fur
seals at the latter place, he recommended a lease system like the one that
was eventually adopted. If Thomas had succeeded in persuading William
Dall to accompany him, the trip might have proved more valuable to
science,[5] but as it was, neither scientist nor scientific equipment was on
hand to make direct scientific observations of the solar eclipse on August
7, 1869.[6] Thomas's only notable scientific contribution was an examination of the coal seams on Kachemak Bay; he forwarded a box of the fuel
to the Smithsonian.[7] The General concluded that there was "no immediate
prospect of the country being settled up," for suitable agricultural land
was at a premium; like so many commentators after him, he coupled settlement inseparably with agricultural development.[8] His aide, even less

3. O. H. Browning, "Lands in Alaska," *House Executive Document 80, 40th Congress: 2d session* (1332).

4. Halleck, "Report of General Halleck, Military Division of the Pacific; the Department of Alaska," in "Report of the Secretary of War," *House Executive Document 1,
40th Congress: 3d session* (1367), 41, 42.

5. Dall's Diaries, March 27, 1869, Dall Papers.

6. A. L. Hough, in R. G. Athearn, editor, "An Army Officer's Trip to Alaska in
1869," *PNQ*, 40 (1949), p. 55.

7. SI, *Annual Report, 1869*, pp. 29, 57.

8. Thomas, "Report, dated San Francisco, September 7, 1869," in "Report of the
Secretary of War," *House Executive Document 1, 41st Congress: 2d session*, Pt. 2
(1412), 115–19.

enthusiastic, thought the country's acquisition important only if it might
lead to the annexation of British Columbia.[9]

Dall felt obliged to take exception to a few "very gross errors" in the
telegraphic summary of Thomas' report. Calling attention to the rich Seal
Islands, Dall took issue with the General's charge that revenue officers
were a useless expense. Tempted like so many others to enlarge on the agricultural question, Dall—while admitting that grain probably would not
be grown in Alaska—suggested that some garden vegetables could be cul-
tivated.[10]

A summer tour in 1875 by General O. O. Howard, though not significant scientifically, had important social and political ramifications that im-
pinged on the history of Alaskan development generally. First, Howard
recommended that Alaska be attached as a county to Washington Territory, or at least that some form of civil government be furnished immediately. Second, he attached to his report a pamphlet sharply critical of
the Alaska Commercial Company—a pamphlet that helped agitate for an
investigation of the Company.[11] Third, and more important, Howard
urged promotion of religious and secular teaching among the Alaskan
Indians. (Howard met with Presbyterian leaders in Oregon who eventually initiated a missionary program that led to the establishment of mission schools in the territory.) In addition, the General, anticipating difficulties over the Alaska-Canada boundary, recommended that the line be
definitely fixed. If the last suggestion had been immediately followed,
much subsequent international grief might have been avoided.[12]

The first official inland expedition was designed to settle an old problem concerning the location of Fort Yukon, a Hudson's Bay Company post
founded by Alexander Hunter Murray in 1847 at the confluence of the
Porcupine and Yukon rivers, well west of the 141st meridian that di-

9. A. L. Hough to Mary Hough, July 23, 1869, cited in Athearn, "An Army Officer's Trip," p. 46 n.

10. Dall, "General Thomas's Alaskan Report," Boston *Daily Advertiser*, October
18, 1869.

11. See above, page 47.

12. Howard, "Report of the Commanding General, *Senate Executive Document 12*,
pp. 5, 11. Howard, "Report of a Visit to Alaska in June 1875," in *Compilation of Narratives*, pp. 46, 48. W. S. Holt, "Beginning of Mission Work in Alaska by the Presbyterian Church," *Washington Historical Quarterly*, 11 (1920), 90, 91. W. G. Morris,
"Report upon the . . . Resources," *Senate Executive Document 59*, p. 77.

vides Canada and Alaska. Another Hudson's Bay trader, John Bell, had preceded him, exploring north and west from the Peel River to the Rat and, in 1842, over to the Bell and Porcupine.[13] Still earlier another Britisher, Robert Campbell, approaching from the south, had discovered the Yukon system from inland in 1840, at the time when he named the Pelly River. In 1848 Campbell established Fort Selkirk at the Pelly-Yukon junction and in 1850 he descended the Yukon to the Porcupine.[14]

Alexander Murray knew when he established Fort Yukon that he was in Russian territory.[15] Sir George Simpson, chief of the "Honourable" Hudson's Bay Company, must have known it too, but Sir George wanted to be certain. "It is very desirable we should know the precise situation of that post, both as regards latitude & longitude," he wrote in 1848 to a Company official. "I should therefore, be glad if you could instruct Mr. Murray, or some one else, in the use of the sextant, so as to remove any doubt on that point." In the meantime, Sir George was "not anxious" about Campbell pushing the discovery of the Pelly to the sea; in 1850 he is still on record as "uncertain" about the location of Fort Yukon. "As regards our Post on the Youcon [sic]," he advised, "we should carry on our operations there without reference to the movements of the Russians, until we ascertain to a certainty that we are upon their territory and are warned off by them, which will of course be done by the authorities in St. Petersburg."[16]

Sir George's successors in the Hudson's Bay Company adopted his attitude toward the trading post: the Company should remain until ordered to move. But independent American traders on the Yukon, unlike their Russian predecessors, would not tolerate poaching. When during the summer of 1868 Yankee traders on the river were confronted at Nukluklayet

13. Bell to James Hargrave, August 22, 1842, in G. P. de T. Glazebrook, editor, *The Hargrave Correspondence, 1821–1843* (Toronto, 1938), pp. 407, 408. A. K. Isbister, "Some Account of the Peel River, N. America," RGS, *Journal, 15* (1845), 332–43.

14. Campbell, "The Discovery and Exploration of the Pelly (Yukon) River," *Royal Readers: Fifth Book of Reading Lessons* (Toronto, 1883), pp. 435–43. L. J. Burpee, "Campbell of the Yukon," *Canadian Geographical Journal, 30* (1945), 200, 201.

15. A. H. Murray, *Journal of the Yukon, 1847–48,* edited by L. J. Burpee (Ottawa, 1910), p. 54.

16. Simpson to Rae, November 21, 1848, and Simpson to Rae, December 10, 1850, in E. E. Rich, editor, *John Rae's Correspondence with the Hudson's Bay Company on Arctic Exploration, 1844–1855* (London, 1953), pp. 326, 331.

5. Alaska

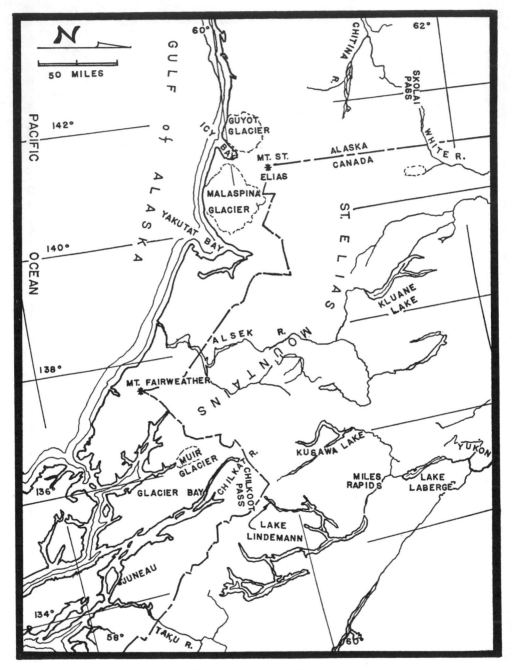

6. Southeastern Alaska

by Hudson's Bay Company rivalry, the Americans threatened to use force to protect their territory from British encroachment.[17] Complaints came to Secretary of State Seward by way of the War Department. Seward thought existing treaty provisions were sufficient legal excuse to halt English activity, but he put the burden of execution on the Army. He told the Secretary of War: "Of the practical difficulties in the execution of these provisions you have better means of judging than has this department."[18] Accordingly, General Halleck directed Captain Charles Raymond of the Corps of Engineers to determine the latitude and longitude of Fort Yukon, and to report on Hudson's Bay Company trade in Alaska. Raymond was authorized to represent the Treasury Department temporarily, to declare importation of British goods illegal, to take official possession, and to order the Honourable Company to vacate the post.[19]

Raymond left St. Michael on July 4 aboard the Alaska Commercial Company river steamer *Yukon*, which had been hauled north from San Francisco to service Company agents along the river. The steamer caused much excitement among the natives. "Our little steamer," Raymond reported, "which, puffing about the bay of San Francisco, had seemed a mere toy, appeared to them a huge monster, breathing fire and smoke." The vessel reached Fort Yukon at the end of the month, and Raymond began immediate preparations to determine the Fort's location. Two large wall tents pitched end to end opened into each other and contained two observation slits at the top. A Zenith telescope was erected on a spruce log. The transit was set on two logs fastened together, and the log mount was planted three feet deep. Unfavorable weather prevented any suitable observations during the first week, but on August 7th, a good shot of the solar eclipse permitted computation of an approximate longitude. Raymond was able to inform the Hudson's Bay Company that its post was well within United States' territory.[20]

For the downstream voyage, Raymond and his two assistants were left

17. C. W. Raymond, "Report of a Reconnaissance of the Yukon River," *Senate Executive Document 12, 42d Congress: 1st session* (1466), 9.

18. Seward to Secretary of War, January 30, 1869, in Seward, "The Encroachments of the Agents of the Hudson's Bay Company . . . ," *Senate Executive Document 42, 40th Congress: 3d session* (1360) 4.

19. R. N. Scott to Raymond, April 2, 1869, in Raymond, *Senate Executive Document 12*, pp. 6, 16.

20. Ibid., pp. 5, 14, 44, 16.

to their own devices. There were no bark canoes available, so a small skiff was made of spruce drift logs, caulked with rags, coated with pitch, and christened the *Eclipse*. The boat was launched, then tethered to shore with a strip of moose hide. Next morning the party discovered that hungry sled dogs had eaten the fastening, and the skiff had begun an independent journey to the coast. "In excuse for the dogs," Raymond wrote, "it should be added that they are fed once a week during the summer." The *Eclipse* was recovered and on August 28, with a piece of bacon, a ham, a little hardtack, and about twenty-five pounds of moose pemmican, the Raymond party left Fort Yukon.[21]

The downriver trip was monotonous. Frequent landings were necessary to repair the unlucky *Eclipse*, and at Anvik the skiff was abandoned. In the company of the post trader the party began an ascent of the Anvik River, intending to portage at its head to Norton Sound. After considerable hardship the men arrived at St. Michael, and on September 27 Raymond sailed for San Francisco.[22]

Raymond's report dealt with familiar topics. He described the river and adjacent country, the natives and the resources. The timber of the Yukon, he thought, would not become a commercial article for many years because of large supplies elsewhere nearer the market. He concluded emphatically that the Yukon fur trade could support only one company.[23] In a paper read before the American Geographical Society of New York, he "set to rest" the question of agricultural development along the river with "a simple statement": "In the month of August, we ascertained, by digging at Fort Yukon, that the earth was frozen at a distance of less than two feet below the surface." A few plots on the Kenai Peninsula far to the south might be productive, he allowed, but there was not quite enough acreage for a single farm. Raymond noted that the lower Yukon natives lived almost exclusively on fish, and he went on, "I failed, however, to notice the intellectual development which, according to recent theories, should accompany this phosphoric diet." Like General Thomas' aide, Raymond thought the value of Alaska was geopolitical: United States' posses-

21. Ibid., p. 16.
22. Ibid., pp. 17–26.
23. Ibid., p. 39. Also "Yukon River and Island of St. Paul," *House Executive Document 112, 41st Congress: 2d session* (1417) 112.

sion of Alaska enclosed Western Canada in a vise and rendered the possibility of American continental union more likely.[24]

The goal of the 1869 expedition—to settle officially the nationality of Fort Yukon—seems in retrospect a silly reason for so long a voyage, especially when other geographical problems begged for solution. Between the Yukon and the southern coast, and between the river and the Arctic Ocean, Alaska was a blank on the world map. Equally inappropriate was the choice of an Army officer who took no advantage of the opportunity for making original contributions to science or discovery; Raymond himself felt the reconnaissance could scarcely "be dignified by the title of an exploration." In extenuation, the season was short and Raymond's chart of the river was an improvement over the old maps.

The second phase of Army activity in Alaska before the Gold Rush was more productive, but unrelated to the accident of Army occupation. The Army, seeking employment for the Signal Service, assumed the functions of a federal meteorological agency. When General William B. Hazen became Chief Signal Officer, he faced the need for basic research squarely.[25] A close working relationship was established with the Smithsonian. The Institution nominated meteorological observers who were— not incidentally—trained naturalists. Weather was a practical concern.

By 1874 the Signal Service appropriation had risen spectacularly and an observer was assigned to Alaska, where the immediate economic aspects of meteorological observation could have little relevance because of slow communication with the States. Lucien McShan Turner of the Signal Service arrived at St. Michael in May. Before long he had an ethnological collection described by Joseph Henry as "one of the most striking of its kind ever contributed to the [Smithsonian] museum."[26] In 1877 Turner was replaced at St. Michael by Private Edward W. Nelson. Returning in the summer of 1878 to the Aleutians, Turner trained voluntary observers and traveled about collecting additional specimens until he was relieved in 1881.[27]

24. Raymond, "Yukon River Region," *JAGS* (1872) 186–88, 170, 191.

25. Dupree, *Science in the Federal Government*, pp. 188, 189.

26. SI, *Annual Report, 1876*, pp. 39, 40.

27. Turner, "Contributions to the Natural History of Alaska, 1874–1881," *Senate Miscellaneous Document 155, 49th Congress: 1st session* (2349), 5–7. SI, *Annual Report, 1879*, 44.

In the history of scientific exploration in the Far Northwest, Edward Nelson, Turner's replacement, is in a direct line from Kennicott and Dall. Nelson came to the Yukon delta region of Alaska by way of Chicago and the Smithsonian Institution. When his first application for government work, promoted by a senator, was rejected by the Smithsonian, he wrote to Spencer Baird outlining his experience in ornithology.[28] The direct approach must have worked, for he embarked in 1877 with instructions from the Chief Signal Officer to obtain an unbroken series of weather observations in Alaska and to obtain data on the geography, ethnology, and zoology of the area surrounding his station at St. Michael.[29] In each category Nelson's application and zeal produced remarkable results. Petroff used his enumeration of the Indians for the Tenth Census. Nelson's collections were even larger than those of his predecessor:[30] his efforts, combined with previous work by Kennicott, Dall, and Turner, made the Lower Yukon by 1881 the most thoroughly biologized part of Alaskan territory. The marsh and muskeg of the region were favorite breeding grounds for bird species from as far away as Tahiti. Ornithology was Nelson's private forte, and altogether he submitted to the Smithsonian over 2,000 bird skins and 1,500 egg specimens. Through the cooperation of the Yukon trader L. N. McQuesten, Nelson obtained rare mammalian species from upriver, including types of mountain sheep which Nelson named after William Healey Dall. The bulk of Nelson's published report was devoted to ornithology. The volume, number three of the Signal Service's Arctic series, was beautifully illustrated with color plates. Joint articles on mammals, fishes, and diurnal Lepidoptera were appended. Nelson's report was by far the most valuable contribution to Alaskan natural history yet made.[31]

Edward Nelson was an energetic ornithologist but no bird-watcher of

28. Nelson to Baird, January 11, 1876, SI Archives.

29. Nelson, "Report upon the Natural History Collections Made in Alaska, 1877–1881," *Senate Miscellaneous Document 156, 49th Congress: 1st session* (2349), 11.

30. For examples see ibid., pp. 21, 300; SI, *Annual Report, 1879,* p. 44, and *1880,* p. 47.

31. Nelson, "Report," p. 230. Nelson, "Description of a New Species of *Lagomys* from Alaska," *Proceedings of the Biological Society of Washington,* 8 (1893), 117. W. H. Osgood and L. B. Bishop, *Results of a Biological Reconnaissance of the Yukon River Region,* Biological Survey, North American Fauna No. 19 (Washington, 1900), p. 19. M. Lantis, "Edward William Nelson," *Anthropological Papers of the University of Alaska,* 3 (1954), 4–16.

the aesthetic John Muir variety; his interest in fowl during the Alaskan adventure was more scientific, sporting, and gastronomic than it was artistic. In 1881 he recommended May as the sportsman's time for hunting black brant, observing that "a double discharge . . . will often bring down four to ten birds." For sport and succulence, he preferred the brant in springtime.[32] Fresh wildlife was a relief from the tiresome diet of fish on which he lived during the long and lonely winter. As long afterward as 1898, in an article directed at the Gold Rush crowd and containing advice on how to hunt Alaska's game, he still remembered "the hearty zest with which we put an extra edge on our knives and attacked the pioneer old gander that fell to our guns." Feeling at the same time that it would be a pity if Alaskan animals were rendered extinct before a series of skins and skulls were in the National Museum, Nelson encouraged the preservation of specimens as a patriotic duty.[33] In 1913 he congratulated Theodore Roosevelt on the establishment of a bird reservation in the Yukon Delta, and by 1916, when Nelson became Chief of the Biological Survey, he was regretting the "wanton waste" of wildlife on the North American continent.[34] Thirty-five years after his Alaskan experience Nelson had become a conservationist, though a somewhat ambivalent one: as head of the Biological Survey, his qualified conservationism resulted in vacillation over strong measures designed to curb hunting, especially of birds.[35]

Undoubtedly, personal factors are behind Nelson's own view, but the fact remains that nineteenth-century Alaska was no more a seed ground of conservationism than the Old West had been. Muir's experience is no exception; he carried his philosophy with him to the country. Conservationism flourishes when the period of abundance has nearly passed, when the need for total or wilderness conservation is imperative if nature is to be preserved at all. It was no historical accident that in the United States the drive to exploit natural resources was gradually replaced by preserva-

32. Nelson, "Habits of the Black Brant in the Vicinity of St. Michael's, Alaska," *Bulletin of the Nuttall Ornithology Club*, 6 (1881), 133, 134.

33. Nelson, "Notes on the Wild Fowl and Game Animals of Alaska," *NGM*, 9 (April 1898), 122, 132.

34. Nelson, "The Emperor Goose," *Bird Lore*, 15 (1913), 132. Nelson, "The Larger North American Mammals," *NGM*, 30 (November 1916), 385–472.

35. D. C. Swain, "The Role of the Federal Government in the Conservation of Natural Resources, 1921–1933," typescript PhD Dissertation in History, University of California, Berkeley (1961), pp. 63–65.

tion sentiment during a decade marked by the closing of a frontier. But in the Far Northwest of 1880 the wilderness was not threatened or even much explored. It is safe to assume that Edward Nelson carried away from Alaska an impression of natural abundance that was later to influence his attitude on the thorny political issue of conservation.

The cooperation of Alaska Commercial Company agents at St. Michael, who tended Nelson's barometer and thermometer, permitted the naturalist to roam. On his first expedition in December 1878 and January 1879, accompanied by the trader Charles Peterson, Nelson examined the area between the Yukon and Kuskokwim deltas, and inland just short of Anvik.[36] The trip, covering over 1,000 miles, was Nelson's baptism in the discomfort of winter exploration in the Far North. He adopted a number of novel expedients. For example, to begin each day with dry clothes, he parceled out his gloves, socks, and a few outer garments to the native families with whom he spent the night; for a small gift of tobacco, the Eskimos slept in the wet garments and dried them with body heat.[37] Nelson's sketch map resulting from this expedition was the only geographical information available on part of the region at the end of the century.[38]

In the first quarter of 1880, Nelson sledded up the coast of Norton Sound past Golovin Bay, and between November 1880 and January 19, 1881, he went overland to the Anvik River, down it to the Yukon, and up the Yukon. He explored the head of the Innoko River, then returned to St. Michael.[39] During the summer of 1881, Nelson and John Muir cruised Bering Sea and the Arctic Ocean aboard the Revenue Cutter *Corwin*. The voyage resulted in important additions to knowledge of the Arctic Eskimo and to natural history.[40]

Turner and Nelson were followed by other Army meteorological observers at St. Michael, in the Aleutians, and on the Nushagak River at

36. Nelson, "A Sledge Journey in the Delta of the Yukon, Northern Alaska," RGS, *Proceedings*, n.s. 4 (1882), 661.

37. Nelson, "Report," *Senate Miscellaneous Document 156*, p. 14.

38. Brooks, *Blazing Alaska's Trails*, p. 273.

39. Nelson, "Report," pp. 15, 16.

40. Nelson, "The Eskimo about Bering Strait," BE, *Annual Report*, 1896–97, pp. 1–518. Muir, Nelson, and I. C. Rosse, *Cruise of the Revenue-steamer Corwin in Alaska and the N. W. Arctic Ocean in 1881, Notes and Memoranda: Medical and Anthropological; Botanical; Ornithological* (Treasury Department, Washington, 1883; also printed as *House Executive Document 105, 47th Congress: 2d session*).

Bristol Bay. Some were diligent collectors and investigators but none came close to the achievement of Nelson or Turner.[41]

The era of Signal Service background research ended in the middle 80s. The so-called Allison Commission, which also aimed at the Coast and Geodetic Survey, focused on the Signal Service as a prime object of interest. The issue of civilian versus military control of federal scientific activity was tackled directly. There was internal as well as external opposition to the Army civilian scientists. As one scholar has noted: "The Army wanted science no more than science wanted the Army. Whatever internal dissensions brought it about, [General] Hazen, the enlightened reformer, stood almost alone for a lost cause."[42]

Scandal complicated the situation, as it had for the Coast Survey.[43] The public inquiries meant two things for Alaskan science. First, objection was raised to publication of the Turner and Nelson reports. They were eventually printed anyway, on the advice of Spencer Baird and on the admonition of a senator that certain other persons were deliberately dispensing erroneous information about the territory.[44] More important, Congress virtually ordered the abandonment of Alaskan weather stations as useless.[45] Simultaneous meteorological and geomagnetic observations during the First International Polar Year, undertaken in Alaska at Point Barrow by the Army, had yielded important results to science[46] that might have been enhanced by the continued operation of the climatic posts, but Congress would not consider it. A. W. Greely, Hazen's successor as Chief Signal Officer, emphasized the importance of agricultural meteorology and immediate practical results from weather observations. However, with almost no agricultural activity and in the absence of swift communication

41. SI, *Annual Report, 1883*, p. 16, and *1886*, pp. 6, 7. F. W. True, "An Annotated List of Mammals Collected by the Late Mr. Charles L. McKay in the Vicinity of Bristol Bay, Alaska," USNM, *Proceedings*, 9 (1886), 221–24.

42. Dupree, *Science in the Federal Government*, pp. 190–92.

43. D. R. Whitnah, *A History of the United States Weather Bureau* (Urbana, Ill., 1961), pp. 46–60.

44. W. J. Rhees, *The Smithsonian Institution: Documents Relative to Its Origin and History, 1835–1899*, Smithsonian Miscellaneous Collections, 42 (Washington, 1901), 923, 924, 982–86.

45. Greely, *Handbook of Alaska*, p. 37.

46. P. H. Ray and John Murdoch, "Report of the International Polar Expedition to Point Barrow, Alaska," *House Executive Document 44, 48th Congress: 2d session* (2298).

with the outside, Alaskan observation was relegated to the category of a
scientific luxury with no immediate application. Protests from Alaskans,
who stressed the utility of climatic information to potential industrial in-
vestors, were of no avail.[47]

The era of the Signal Service brought spectacular gains for background
research in natural history, but almost no original geographic discovery.
The third phase of Army interest in the Far Northwest before the Gold
Rush saw major achievement in geographic discovery, but little progress
in natural history. The character and extent of Army activity in both
periods broadly reflected the changing pattern of federal scientific institutions.

The champion of old-style Army exploration in Alaska was General
Nelson A. Miles. As commandant of the Northwestern Department of
Columbia, Division of the Pacific, Miles stubbornly refused to ignore the
simple fact that "according to the official maps, orders, and army register,"
Alaska was the military responsibility of his department; neither did he
overlook the lack of knowledge on Alaska's interior and its indigenes.
Officially at least, every move he made to gather information on the territory was motivated by the twin threat of the Indian and the unexplored
wilderness. Miles typified the classic situation leading to Army domi-
nance in the trans-Mississippi West, brought into play when the wilderness
Indian was rapidly disappearing in the States, when specialized civilian
scientific bureaus were rising to assume hegemony in western exploration.
Miles' desire to explore the interior of Alaska systematically met the combined opposition of a Congress reluctant to spend public money in a region that supported almost no whites, vociferous proponents of civilian
as opposed to military science, rival ambitions of scientific bureaus and
military agencies, and deliberate obstructionism from the War Department and his own Army superiors. It is hard to understand how anything
was accomplished. In a word, the Army explorations of 1883–1885 resulted from the persistence of Nelson A. Miles and a handful of energetic
junior officers. As an institutional phenomenon in the history of American
science and exploration, they may be viewed as the dying gasp of original
geographical discovery by the Army.

Miles' struggles began in 1881, when he recommended a special appro-

47. Sitka *Alaskan*, October 29, 1887.

priation of $68,000 to explore the country. A bill was introduced in the Senate but failed to become law.[48] The following year, in the face of difficulties imposed by his superior, he made a personal visit to the southeastern section. At the time, Alaska had no civil government; since 1877, when the Army ended its occupation of the country, Treasury Department revenue cutters had policed the western and northern coast, and the Navy ruled the southeastern coast with a man-of-war at Sitka. Miles was forced to explain that he understood clearly General Order Number One of 1877, which directed the Army withdrawal from Alaska. "Have no intention of exercising any control of matters in Alaska," he telegraphed; he merely wanted to inspect a region for which he was militarily responsible. He felt obliged to ask whether it was necessary to take leave in order to visit the territory. Officers who accompanied him at their own expense had the time charged against their leave allotment.[49]

The trip only reinforced Miles' determination to learn more about the country. In April of 1883, he ordered First Lieutenant Frederick Schwatka, then acting as his aide in Washington Territory, to Alaska, "in view of the frequent reports of the disturbance of peace between the whites and Indians in Alaska, and the indications that the present condition of affairs must lead to serious hostilities . . . in the near future." Indian disturbances had occurred in southeastern Alaska, where the natives were controlled by an official gunboat, and Schwatka was to investigate the interior. The only hint of hostility in the North was word of Indian discontent after trading competition was ended along the Yukon, just prior to Schwatka's visit.

The immediate threat of Indian hostility, no matter how dubious, provided Miles with an excuse for exploration. Schwatka was instructed to determine the number, character, and disposition of "all natives" in the country, their weapons, their relations with each other, their attitude toward the encroachment of whites, and the means of using and sustaining a military force should one be necessary.[50] He was accompanied by Assistant Surgeon George Wilson, Army topographical assistant Charles A.

48. Miles to Division HQ, May 15, 1884, in F. Schwatka, "Report of a Military Reconnaissance in Alaska, Made in 1883," *Senate Executive Document 2, 48th Congress: 2d session* (2261), 121.

49. Miles to Assistant Adjutant General, telegrams, July 26, 1882, and August 4, 1882, Department of Columbia, NA, RG 98.

50. Miles to Schwatka, in *Senate Executive Document 2*, p. 119.

Homan, three enlisted men, and a civilian.[51] Because of opposition to the venture inside as well as outside the Army, the party was financed by the local command. Schwatka was enjoined to exercise "strict economy" and to "consider this duty especial and confidential."[52] The little expedition, Schwatka later wrote, "stole away like a thief in the night" with less money than was afterward spent to publish its report.[53]

Schwatka chose to examine the Yukon River and to enter its watershed via the Chilkoot Pass of southeastern Alaska.[54] The decision to intercept the Yukon's head in Canada was unfortunate; it added another element of friction to Miles' future plans. The Yukon's course in Alaska was fairly well known from the work of Raymond and the Russian American Telegraph Expedition, while the other major rivers of the country were unexplored. Congress wondered why an American Army expedition should explore British territory, and an English diplomat later noted that though "Her Majesty's Government do not attach any importance to . . . [the] fact," Schwatka had "traversed British territory for a considerable distance without any intimation having been given to the British authorities of his intention of so doing."[55] Miles assumed personal responsibility for the move; he explained, "That part of the report which embraces a survey of a portion of British America, with description of same, was not called for by the letter of instructions."[56] The long-range significance of Schwatka's Canadian reconnaissance was that it provided the first survey of a main route to the Klondike gold fields.

Schwatka reached Lake Lindemann, the upper limits of Krause's exploration, by climbing over Chilkoot Pass, to which he gave another name. On June 13, 1883, his party began the construction of a raft about fifteen by forty feet, with decks built up fore and aft. Spaces were left at the ends for bow and stern oars. The means of locomotion, in addition to the current, were side oars and a sail fashioned from a wall tent. The

51. Schwatka, "Report of a Military Reconnaissance Made in Alaska in 1883," in *Compilation of Narratives*, p. 283; this version is substantially the same as *Senate Executive Document 2*, with some omissions and slight alterations.

52. Miles to Schwatka, *Senate Executive Document 2*, pp. 119, 120.

53. Schwatka, *Exploring the Great Yukon*, p. 11.

54. Schwatka, in *Compilation of Narratives*, p. 291.

55. L. S. Sackville-West to Bayard, September 14, 1887, in U.S. Department of State, *Papers Relating to the Foreign Relations of the United States, 1888*, p. 768.

56. Miles to Division HQ, May 15, 1884, in *Senate Executive Document 2*, p. 121.

craft, christened *Resolute,* drew twenty inches of water. It plowed un-
daunted through submerged snags, but hung up on sand and gravel bars.
More dangerous were the large and lethal "sweepers," trees toppled over
on the banks, leaning straight out over the river; if observed too late, they
could "sweep" the decks clean of passengers. The raft shot the rapids in
Miles Canyon on July 2 with only minor damage. The cumbersome and
colorful *Resolute* carried the party all the way from Lake Lindemann to
Nukluklayet by August 6th—about 1,300 miles (according to Schwatka).
At Nukluklayet, Schwatka obtained a small-decked schooner that trans-
ported him to Anvik, where the A.C. Company steamer *Yukon* took the
party in tow to St. Michael.[57]

En route down the Yukon Schwatka distributed new geographic names
with liberality and a frequent disregard for priority and usage. Whether as
a service to travelers or as an attempt to magnify the importance of his
own work, he also made disparaging comments about prior mapping of
the route.[58] The two practices drew barbed criticism from the geological
survey bureaus of both Canada and the United States. The great Canadian
geologist and explorer George M. Dawson decided that Schwatka's pre-
dilection for naming anew every topographical feature he saw required
sharp comment, as "he is not sparing in his condemnation of the inac-
curacy of the compilers of the maps made before the results of his journey
were available." Dawson thought strict justice demanded the exclusion of
the new names, but decided to retain as many as possible in order to avoid
arbitrary action and "more especially in view of the scientific eminence of
some of the names which he [Schwatka] has selected."[59] Dall was equally
severe. Schwatka, "like many military men," said Dall, preferred "to ignore or affect contempt of any work outside of military circles." Schwatka

57. Schwatka, "The Great River of Alaska," *Century,* 30 (September 1885), 741–
43. Schwatka, "Exploration of the Yukon River in 1883," *JAGS,* 16 (1884), 352.
Schwatka, "The Great River of Alaska," *Century,* 30 (October 1885), 823. Schwatka,
in *Compilation of Narratives,* pp. 303, 319, 320, 323. Schwatka, "The Alaska Military
Reconnaissance of 1883," *Science,* 3 (February 29, 1884), 252.

58. See Schwatka, in *Compilation of Narratives,* pp. 300, 301, 303; *Exploring the
Great Yukon,* pp. 180, 181; "Great River of Alaska," *Century,* 30 (September 1885),
p. 739; and "The Alaska Military Reconnaissance of 1883," *Science,* 3 (February 22,
1884), 220.

59. Dawson, "Report of an Exploration in the Yukon District, N.W.T., and Adjacent Northern British Columbia, 1887," *Annual Report of the Geological and Natural
History Survey of Canada,* 1887–88, n.s. 3, Pt. 1, 143B.

had contributed to the knowledge of the Yukon valley, but so had others before him: "The credit due to each cannot be monopolized by any man or set of men, and it does not impair any man's reputation to do justly by his forerunners."[60]

Schwatka made no great contribution to scientific knowledge. His map, however, in addition to correcting the work of other explorers above Fort Selkirk, represented the first survey of the river between Lake Lindemann and Selkirk, a distance of 500 miles, all in Canada. The Canadian surveyor William Ogilvie found the chart reasonably accurate in its main features.[61] Credit for the map must go to topographer Charles Homan, whose error in dead reckoning between Chilkat Inlet and Fort Yukon was less than one per cent, or about ten miles.[62] Homan also acted as photographer of the expedition, and was largely responsible for the design and construction of the raft. Schwatka wrote: "I feel confident that these charts, . . . although in no way claiming perfection, will render unnecessary any more minute surveys until some industry may open up this section, should that event ever come to pass."[63]

In other fields, results were skimpy. The ethnographical information on Alaskan Indians was not new, and was directed toward military considerations; moreover, it could have been gathered at less expense. The Indian report was due "almost wholly" to Surgeon Wilson.[64] Schwatka undertook no detailed mineral investigations, but along the Yukon in Canada he encountered miners. The route had been prospected since 1880. Schwatka reported: "From the D'Abbadie [Big Salmon River] to the very mouth of the great Yukon, a panful of 'dirt' taken from almost any bar or bank with any discretion will, when washed, give several 'colors.' "[65]

The information reached a large audience, because Schwatka published accounts of his reconnaissance in newspapers and magazines even before the official report was issued. Miles disapproved,[66] but apparently the

60. Dall, "Schwatka's Along Alaska's Great River," *Science*, 7 (April 2, 1886), 308.
61. Dawson, "Report of an Exploration," p. 143B.
62. Brooks, *Blazing Alaska's Trails*, p. 275. Schwatka, *Exploring the Great Yukon*, pp. 150, 151, 278.
63. Schwatka, in *Compilation of Narratives*, pp. 295, 297, 306.
64. Ibid., p. 323.
65. "The Alaska Military Reconnaissance of 1883," *Science*, 3 (February 29, 1884), p. 249. Also, "Great River of Alaska," *Century*, 30 (September 1885), p. 750.
66. Miles to Division HQ, May 15, 1884, *Senate Executive Document 2*, p. 121.

public did not; articles that streamed from the explorer's pen were eagerly accepted by journals and popular periodicals. In *Century*, Schwatka shared billing with William Dean Howells, George Washington Cable, and Henry James. The report, slightly altered, appeared as a book that went through several editions. The adventure was called by one commentator "more tropical than boreal in its coloring."[67]

Though Schwatka's journey brought publicity to Alaska and its resources, and advertised the need for exploration, it neither increased the likelihood of additional federal expeditions nor decreased the opposition to Miles' plan. The following year, the General was still pushing a claim for expenses incurred by Private Homan. The Commissary General thought compensation would violate regulations, and recommended that Miles reimburse Homan. Miles retorted, "The theory that an enlisted man sitting at a comfortable desk at Department Headquarters is entitled to more than he would be when traveling on important duty through an unknown country, packing his blankets, or on a raft drenched with water from above and below, seems too preposterous to merit consideration."[68] Miles refused to be discouraged. While he haggled over the Homan claim, he busily prepared to renew the assault on Alaska's wilderness.

The plan in 1884 was two-pronged. A military detachment led by Miles' aide, William R. Abercrombie, was to enter the interior through the Copper River Valley. A civilian scout, Willis E. Everette, was sent along Schwatka's route to the White River. From the White headwaters, Everette, at a salary of $75 per month for two months,[69] was to explore the eastern portion of Alaska south of the Yukon by crossing to the headwaters of the Copper.

Everette apparently did no more than travel the Yukon's length. His plan to cross from the head of the White to the Copper River, he claimed,

67. C. Hallock, *Peerless Alaska* (New York, 1908), p. 75.

68. Miles to Adjutant General, U.S.A., 4th endorsement of Commissary General, April 14, 1884, and 7th endorsement, June 27, 1884, Department of Columbia, NA, RG 98.

69. Aide de Camp to Chief Quartermaster, April 7, 1883; Assistant Adjutant General to W. S. Patten, March 4, 1884, Department of Columbia, NA, RG 98. Dall, "Notes and News," *Science*, 6 (September 25, 1885), 278. Miles also apparently hired a Chris Gilsen as scout, possibly to explore the region south of the Yukon and west of the Copper. Gilsen was seen at Nukluklayet on the way down the Yukon "back where he came from." H. T. Allen's Diary, 1883–84, p. 68, Henry T. Allen Papers, Manuscript Division, Library of Congress.

was frustrated by the reluctance of anyone either white or native, to accompany him.[70] There is evidence that Everette was something less than the courageous investigator Miles thought he had hired and Everette later represented himself to be. According to a group of miners, Everette remained a month at old Fort Reliance south of Dawson near the mouth of the White River, with a native interpreter, who by chance was a woman. The miners volunteered to go with him to the Copper, but Everette was unwilling. To add to the derogatory evidence, one of Miles' officers examined a letter from a civilian who had been with Everette, and who had towed the Army scout upriver a distance. The letter questioned: "Friends, I will ask you why does the Govt. send in such men to explore this country when they are not able to help themselves."[71]

Everette remained on the Yukon all winter, collecting data. According to newspaper articles, he stated that his report, although largely second-hand, was extensive and valuable.[72] The report may never have been submitted. It was certainly never published, perhaps because of the evidence of Everette's questionable behavior. In 1887 he tried without success to sell to the Smithsonian Institution an ethnological collection that included sketches and jade implements, and during the Gold Rush he was reported in "various remote districts of Alaska" collecting linguistic data for the Bureau of Ethnology, incidental to "his vocation as a mining engineer."[73]

A second attempt to explore the Far Northwest in 1884, led by Abercrombie, was no more successful. Though Abercrombie called his expedition "supplementary" to that of Schwatka in 1883, the Copper River Valley had never been traversed, even by prospectors, and Abercrombie commanded a relatively large, well-equipped party. Charles Homan was topographer. Abercrombie probed the Copper Delta, but the water was too high and the glaciers too soft. He decided that a summer journey north from the delta was not feasible, and that a small party would not be safe on the Copper during the winter, when game was scarce.[74] He did manage

70. Dall, "Notes and News," p. 278.

71. Allen's Diary, 1883–84, pp. 67, 68, 73.

72. Dall, "Notes and News," p. 279. Bancroft, *History of Alaska,* pp. 735, 736 (San Francisco *Chronicle,* August 30, 1885, cited). Also, Sitka *Alaskan,* November 7, 1885.

73. Baird to Everette, February 2, 1887, SI Archives. BE, *Annual Report, 1899–1900,* page xii, and *1898–99,* page xi.

74. Abercrombie, "Supplementary Expedition into the Copper River Valley, Alaska," in *Compilation of Narratives,* pp. 383, 384, 389, 391, 405. Wood to Miles, March 1, 1885, Department of Columbia, NA, RG 98.

to learn about a short-cut portage to the river by way of Port Valdez, which his party surveyed roughly. Abercrombie did not even advance to Taral, at the confluence of the Copper and Chitina rivers. Despite a lively report of the endeavor, the "supplementary" expedition was a failure.[75] To his superior's demand for a full explanation, Abercrombie replied that the Copper River route was impractical; he had turned back, he explained, for want of assistance from interior natives, and because of glaciers, rapids, and other natural obstacles.[76] To a fellow junior officer, Lieutenant Henry T. Allen, he confided that he would never return to the country.[77]

75. Abercrombie, "The Copper River Country, Alaska," *Journal of the Franklin Institute*, *158* (1904), 300.

76. Wood to Abercrombie, February 27, 1885; and Wood to Miles, March 1, 1885, Department of Columbia, NA, RG 98.

77. Allen's Diary, 1883–84, Allen Papers.

7. The Remarkable Journey of Henry Allen

THE FAILURE OF ABERCROMBIE to penetrate the Copper River Valley in 1884 marked the end of a long and tragic history of attempts to explore and exploit the region, a history that had begun soon after discovery of the river's mouth by Russian traders in the late 1700s. Two or three attempts to ascend the river before the close of the eighteenth century were apparently frustrated by native hostility,[1] and another party was similarly turned back in 1803.[2] In 1819 the Creole Klimovsky reached Taral at the junction of the Chitina River, where he erected a trading cabin. His map was a rude approximation of his route.[3]

The next attempt to investigate the area, in 1843, resulted from the growing concern of the Russian American Company over the loss of fur to Indian middlemen trading with the English.[4] An expedition led by Grigoriev left Nuchek on Prince William Sound and reached the mouth of the Tazlina River above Taral. The party went east up the Tazlina to

1. Dall, *Alaska and Its Resources*, p. 317. H. T. Allen, *Report of an Expedition to the Copper, Tanana, and Koyukuk Rivers in the Territory of Alaska, 1885*, p. 19. Allen's report was also published as *Senate Executive Document 125, 49th Congress: 2d session* (2449) and as "Report of a Military Reconnaissance in Alaska, made in 1885," *Compilation of Narratives*, pp. 409–94. The last version differs slightly from the original report.

2. Allen, *Report of an Expedition*, p. 19. See also U. Lisiansky, *A Voyage Round the World in the Years 1803, 4, 5, & 6* (London, 1814), p. 188.

3. F. von Wrangell, *Statistische und ethnographische Nachrichten*, pp. 161, 162. Brooks, *Blazing Alaska's Trails*, p. 235.

4. Russian-American Company, "Report, 1846," copied in Russian by A. Pinart, MS, Bancroft Library. Translated for the author by Ayesha Andersen. The paragraph is based largely on this short document. The report, to my knowledge, has never before been used by American scholars. It was correlated with the following standard sources: C. Grewingk, *Beitrag zur Kenntniss der orographischen und geognostischen Beschaffenheit der nord-west-küste Amerikas* (St. Petersburg, 1850), p. 347; Golovin, "Ueber die russischen Colonien," *Archiv für wissenschaftliche Kunde von Russland*, p. 58; and Pinart, "Sur les Atnahs," *Revue de Philogie et d'Ethnographie*, 2 (1875), 1, 2; P. A. Tikhmenev, *Historical Review of the Formation of the Russian-American Company and Its Activity to the Present Time*, translation of Vol. 2 by Dimitri Krenov (WPA, Seattle, 1940), microfilm of a translation in University of Washington Library (originally published St. Petersburg, 1863), pp. 232, 233.

Tazlina Lake, scouting the country as they traveled, and received a friendly welcome by the Indians. Their reconnaissance confirmed the suspected loss of trade.

The report of cooperative natives and lost business opportunity induced the Company to send another expedition up the Copper in 1847. Rufus Serebrenikov, with eleven men, arrived in September at Taral, where he wintered. In May of 1848 Serebrenikov proceeded upriver to the Tazlina, repeated the previous investigation of that river and the lake at its head, and returned to the Copper on June 5 to continue the exploration. There are no records of his movement thereafter except a latitudinal observation of 62° 48′ North. Some time after his return to the Copper, Serebrenikov and his entire party were massacred by the Indians. His journal was carried by natives to the Russian post at Nuchek. The cause of the tragedy, and whether he actually reached 62° 48′, are moot points.

After 1848 the Russians made no serious attempt to explore the Copper River, despite the lure of peltry and the stories of rich copper deposits.[5] Except for an occasional American prospector or trader, the region lay untouched until the arrival in 1884 of Abercrombie, who took precautions lest the natives be as quarrelsome as they had been thirty-five years earlier.

In 1885 the Copper River Indians shared their reputation in Alaska for warlike behavior with the Tananas and the Koyukons. In the face of reported native hostility in the Copper, Tanana, and Koyukuk River valleys, an exploration of all three regions was made within a single season by Henry Tureman Allen.

Henry Allen was born April 13, 1859, in Sharpsburg, Kentucky. He attended Peekskill Military Academy before going to West Point. As a cadet officer, he was neither blunt nor sharp-tongued, and the seeming lack of stern qualities made other officers doubt that he possessed command ability. Moreover, he was tall, erect, handsome, and meticulous in his dress, with a pleasant manner and distinguished military bearing that made him a favorite with the ladies; in an earlier generation he would have been competition for Jeb Stuart.

Despite his social aptitude and fondness for parties, dances, and the amenities of civilization, Allen actively sought an Alaskan assignment. He

5. Tikhmenev, *Historical Review*, 233–35. Allen, *Report of an Expedition*, pp. 19–21. Brooks, *Blazing Alaska's Trails*, p. 236.

fixed his eye on the opportunity for exploration soon after his arrival in the Far West. In January of 1883, he wrote to the girl he later married: "I am willing to forgo almost any benefit that I might receive by going East for an attempt at exploration in Alaska."[6] Schwatka got the job in 1883 and Abercrombie in 1884, but Allen was patient: he was determined to write a chapter in the story of North American discovery. His position as aide to General Miles, in Abercrombie's absence, brought him half a loaf in 1884. He was ordered to Sitka, there to tranship to a chartered vessel bound for Nuchek where he was to await Abercrombie. En route Allen interrogated everyone he met who knew anything at all about the territory, and he eagerly read reference material on the subject.[7] By the end of 1884, when he returned from Alaska, he had formulated a plan of exploration, which he presented to the Department of Columbia. Colonel H. Clay Wood, Adjutant of the Department, forwarded Allen's report to Miles, who approved the plan and obtained authorization for the reconnaissance from the Commanding General of the Army.[8]

From Allen's research in the printed sources on Alaska, and out of the information he gleaned from talks with prospectors and traders, he was convinced that he could reach the head of Copper River in one season. A start must be made in the spring before ice on the river moved. Reports of Indian hostility, Allen felt, were exaggerated. He further suggested that the expedition must be a small, three-man party, one of whom should be Private Frederick W. Fickett of the Signal Corps, recently at Sitka, who had volunteered for the duty. Miles recommended not less than four nor more than ten men, including a medical officer, but Allen insisted that he needed no medical officer, and that two companions were sufficient—the large, unwieldy Abercrombie expedition argued for a small party.[9] The problem was ultimately solved not by force of argument but by the refusal of General P. H. Sheridan to permit an expedition composed of more than three men.[10]

6. Biographical data, Allen Papers. Allen to Dora Johnston, January 10, 1883, Allen Papers.

7. Allen's Diary, 1883–84, pp. 54, 56, 57–59, 61, Allen Papers.

8. Instructions by H. C. Wood, January 27, 1885, in Allen, *Report of an Expedition*, p. 10.

9. Wood to Miles, telegram, December 19, 1884, Department of Columbia, NA, RG 98. Allen's Diary, 1883–84, pp. 104, 105, Allen Papers.

10. Sheridan to Pope, January 24, 1885, Allen Papers.

The decision of Sheridan reflected current political controversies over the role of the Army in American exploration. In addition, there had been criticism of Abercrombie's failure and of the value of Schwatka's reconnaissance. A series of conflicting dispatches at various levels of command threatened to delay Allen's departure. At one time, the Division of the Pacific refused to authorize funds, and ordered that subsistence be provided from stores on hand in the Department of Columbia.[11] A few days before, $1,000 for Army transportation and $500 for subsistence had been the limit of support set for Allen's use.[12] Eventually the sum of $2,000 from the public funds of the Department was transferred to Allen, "as an advance to pay yourself and members of your detachment."[13] It was enough for Allen. He also got Fickett, and Sergeant Cady Robertson.[14] At Nuchek he added Peder Johnson to the party and later on, at Taral, John Bremner—both prospectors.[15] Allen's instructions, like Schwatka's, called for acquisition of knowledge about the Indians and the country in which they lived.

Lieutenant Allen arrived at the Copper River delta in March 1885. For map-making he had a sextant and artificial horizon, a Howard-movement watch, a camera with plates and chemicals, a barometer, a pocket sextant, aneroid barometer, psychrometer, and prismatic and pocket compasses. To one thousand food rations he added extract of beef. The sleeping bags were of linen sailcloth waterproofed with beeswax and linseed oil.[16] The best equipment of this young officer barely three years out of West Point was confidence and determination.

As for native hostility, Allen was one step ahead before he began his inland journey. He was carried to the river by the *Pinta*, a fourth-rate man-of-war with small armament. As Allen ascended the river, Indian stories quickly enlarged the vessel: "At one place its length, as estimated by a . . . [native], was equal to the distance between two islands, approximately half a mile, and the bore of the guns was expressed by the greatest

11. Wood to Miles, January 30, 1885, Department of Columbia, NA, RG 98.

12. Wood to Adjutant General, Division of Pacific, January 24, 1885, Department of Columbia, NA, RG 98.

13. Wood's Instructions, January 27, 1885, in Allen, *Report of an Expedition*, p. 12.

14. Special Orders No. 16, January 27, 1885, in ibid., p. 9.

15. Allen's letter of transmittal, April 9, 1886, in ibid., p. 13.

16. Allen, in *Compilation of Narratives*, p. 419. Quotations on the following pages are from this work.

partial inclosure formed by the arms, tips of fingers widely separated"
(p. 420). The Indians were nevertheless reluctant to accompany the expedition as packers and guides, until Allen hit upon an expedient worthy
of Tom Sawyer: "These [Indians] promised one hour to go, the next refused all connection with the expedition. In order to persuade them that
it was a great privilege I was extending, I decided to take only five, and
had them draw lots to determine the one that was to remain. This had the
desired effect, though I would gladly have employed ten instead of five"
(p. 423). Eventually, he employed seven.

Fickett was left with most of the stores and instructed to join the party
later. On March 29, Allen, Robertson, and Johnson, with the natives in
five canoes, began the ascent. Fickett was soon called up. The rains, soft
snow, shallow channels, and floating ice forced the party to crisscross the
river, using now canoes, now sleds. Equipment and supplies were gradually
pared down: "On the morning of the 30th of March we abandoned about
one-half of our ammunition, cooking outfit, food, clothing, etc. A few
hours later we abandoned our tent and more clothing and food, and then
had with us about 150 pounds of flour, 100 pounds of beans, 40 pounds of
rice, 2 sides of bacon, 15 pounds of tea, some Liebig's extract of beef,
deviled ham, and chocolate. . . . A pack of 50 pounds on the back was, under the circumstances, as much as the strongest man could carry" (p. 424).
Very shortly Allen reached the upper limits of Abercrombie's investigation, where Childs and Miles glaciers frame the river on either side. A
dangerous passage by the glaciers was quickly made, to a canyon named
after Spencer F. Baird; the date was April 4, and the sun shone for the
first time since leaving Nuchek. Allen was pleased to learn that sufficient
snow remained for a dash to Taral. The season was well advanced. Had
Allen been delayed a week, he might have had to winter in the interior.

The party was welcomed to Taral by John Bremner, who had come up
the previous season to prospect for copper and been trapped by the
weather and terrain. Allen thought Bremner was

> certainly the most uncouth specimen of manhood that I had, up to
> that time, ever seen. He was a picture of wretchedness, destitution,
> and despair, suddenly rendered happy. John was reduced to a single
> round of powder, which he fired in answer to us. . . . In the meantime,
> he had been living on rabbits which he snared, with occasionally a

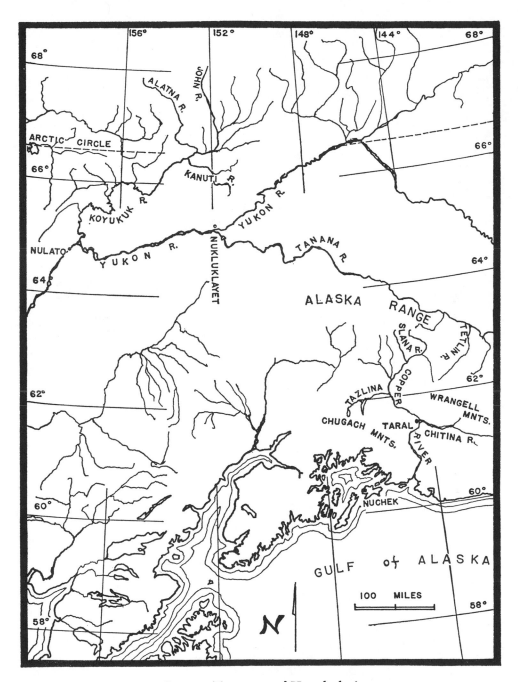

7. Copper, Tanana, and Koyukuk rivers

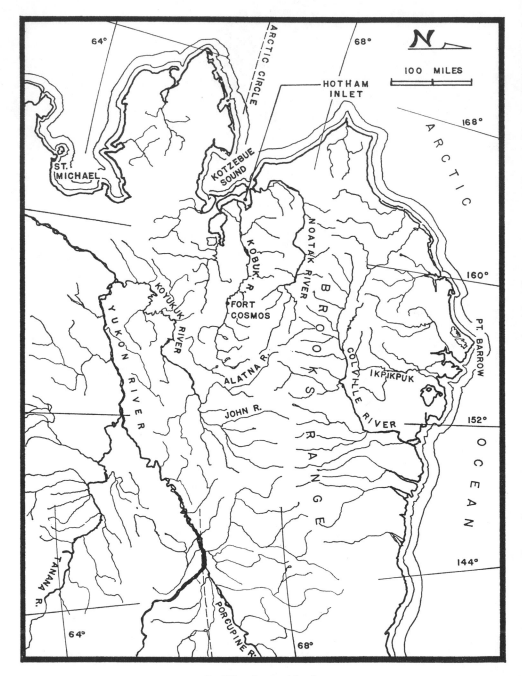

8. Northern Alaska

piece of dried salmon as a luxury. He was shortening his belt one hole every other day. . . . Nowhere did I receive such a warm greeting as at Taral from this naturally heroic specimen of manhood, then so depressed with hunger and destitution (p. 421).

The native women and children at Taral, deserted temporarily by their men, were also destitute, and Allen thoughtfully provided them with whatever he could spare.

At Taral, Allen postponed his upriver journey for an investigation of the Chitina River, which flows into the Copper from the East. He explained: "I was unwilling to pass such an important tributary . . . without learning something about it and the supposed stores of minerals existing thereon." The side trip was taken by all five white men, including Bremner, and one native. Baggage, together with 180 pounds of provisions, were cached at Taral. They carried rations for four days, and "from this time we began to realize the true meaning of the much-used expression 'living upon the country.' . . . Our main dependence was on rabbits, the broth of which was thickened with a handful of flour" (p. 429). On April 13, an Indian came in with the remaining scraps of a moose killed by wolves. Henry Allen celebrated his twenty-sixth birthday by eating rotten moose meat. A few days later, the explorers would have been delighted to have even tainted moose.

Allen decided to portage north and west to the head of the Chitistone and the village of Nikolai, a head chief (*tyone*) of the Copper-Chitina river Indians, in the hope of obtaining food. The party staggered in to a loud reception by the Indians. "On occasions of this kind a Midnooski will fire his last charge of powder though hunger stare him in the face. It is a courtesy that each shot be answered, and the number of shots with them, as with more civilized people, indicates the rank of the tyone. . . . We were so delighted to arrive at a settlement that a celebration of some sort seemed very appropriate; moreover, it was claimed the greater the demonstration we made the more food we would obtain" (p. 431). The famished white men rested on April 20 and gorged themselves on moose, beaver, lynx, and rabbit, prepared native fashion, which meant the animals were cooked whole, entrails and all.

At Nikolai's camp a twenty-seven-foot boat was built of untanned moose skins. It was made with no tools other than native axes and knives, and was assembled with rawhide strips and willow sprouts. By April 26, Nikolai's larder was empty. Two days later the adventurers, accompanied by Nikolai, proceeded downstream to Taral, where they rested for a day, took observations and photographs, and recuperated on "white man's food."

Resuming their journey up the Copper River, the laborious procedure of "cordelling," or tracking, was adopted. Nikolai served as steersman and one member of the group remained in the bow with a long pole. The rest of the party pulled on a 150-foot rope. Nikolai, comfortable in the less strenuous occupation of pilot, could not understand why if Allen were a genuine "tyone" he condescended to work and even carried his own pack. The sense of rank among the native chiefs was oppressive, and Nikolai, for all the prestige he added to the expedition, was "equal to or worse" than any of the other Indian noblemen. Allen reported: "None of the natives would sell us food of any kind without consulting . . . [Nikolai], and he advised prices that would make a commissary in civilization shudder. They realized full well our dependence" (p. 436). Allen had not time or authority to attempt a reform of native social customs. "On one occasion, when I attempted to snub a lazy chief by making a much-prized present to one of his vassals, and a splendid worker, rather than to himself, he pocketed the article and took all credit to himself for possessing so valuable a worker" (p. 435).

At the mouth of the Tazlina River, on May 15, Nikolai left the expedition in the neutral territory above his domain. Hereafter, Allen was traversing country which not only had probably never been visited by white men before, but about which the indigenes to the south knew little. The natives between the Tazlina and the headwaters of the Copper were the most destitute and miserable creatures Allen encountered on his journey (p. 437).

The party pushed—or, more appropriately, pulled—on up the river. Cordelling probably slowed the expedition. But the party was ahead of schedule. On May 27, the boat was redesigned and reduced in size under the direction of Robertson and Bremner. During the process, a crippled and hungry native came into camp and offered his services, which were rejected for lack of adequate provisions to feed the present members of the group. The native followed along, always appearing at mealtime. He was finally adopted, and by digging roots he proved to be a valuable assistant. Fickett recorded in his journal for May 30: "Temperature of water 43. Course northeast by east. Arrived at an Indian house at 11 A.M. hungry. Decided to abandon boat. Indian gave us a dinner of boiled meat, from which he scraped the maggots by handfuls before cutting it up. It tasted good, maggots and all" (p. 439).

A few miles above the mouth of the Slana River, Allen decided to cut north through the Slana valley to a mountain pass, which he named after Nelson Miles. At Lake Suslota, on the south side of the pass, salmon were at last found, and the men ate until satisfied for the first time in days (p. 443). During the early morning of June 9, Allen recorded one of the most memorable moments of the trip.

> At 1.30 a.m., after the steepest ascent made by the expedition, we were on a very short and narrow 'divide,' 4,500 feet above sea level, with bold, barren bluffs on each side. From this the most grateful sight it has ever been my fortune to witness was presented. The sun was rising, but not in the east; in fact, just two points east of north. We had nearly reached the 'land of the midnight sun' to find in our front the 'promised land.' The views in advance and in rear were both grand, the former showing the extensive Tanana Valley with numerous lakes and the low, unbroken range of mountains between the Tanana and Yukon rivers. On this pass, with both white and yellow buttercups around me and snow within a few feet, I sat proud of the grand sight which no visitor save an Atnatana or Tanana had ever seen. Fatigue and hunger were for the time forgotten in the great joy at finding our greatest obstacles overcome (p. 444).

Tetling's village on the Tetlin River, a tributary of the Tanana above Tok River, was reached on June 12, and construction of a new boat from three caribou hides was begun immediately. Members of the expedition were now displaying evidence of the hardships they had endured. Bremner's ankle, sprained during the trip on the Chitina, had swollen to an unusual size, and the trials to which he had long been exposed were affecting him mentally as well as physically. Robertson's body was covered with black spots.

Allen decided to run for the Yukon. He quickly attained the muddy

Tanana and proceeded down it by runs of as many as fifty miles a day. Observations along the river were occasionally obstructed by the smoke from forest fires set by Indian signal fires announcing Allen's presence in the country. The party arrived at the Yukon on June 25, and in Nukluklayet, though supplies were short, the explorers were invited to dine on fish fried in machine oil, until the arrival of one of the two small steamers then operating on the river (pp. 446–52).

Frederick Schwatka had reported the Koyukons as having the worst reputation of any Indians from Fort Yukon to the sea. "I do not believe, however," he continued, "that they would resist a force of 20 or 25 well-armed men attempting to explore and investigate their country."[17] Allen knew the rumors of Koyukon treachery, but he no longer put much faith in such stories. With amazing audacity and unbelievable energy, he decided to explore the Koyukuk River accompanied only by Fickett. Bremner and Johnson remained on the Yukon to prospect, and Robertson was sent to St. Michael.[18]

After a round trip to Nulato, Allen engaged some Koyukon guides and carriers and bought five pack dogs. To reach the Koyukuk, he chose an overland portage that commenced six miles downriver from Nukluklayet and extended due north to the Kanuti River, which he planned to descend to the Koyukuk. The tiny expedition left the Yukon on July 28. A march of six and a half days to Kanuti village was, Allen estimated, eighty-seven miles as the crow flies and 120 miles as the trail wound. Once again Allen displayed skill in handling the natives. He announced in advance that rations would be issued at the end of the period he thought necessary to reach a given destination. The Indians obligingly conformed to his schedule. During the ten-day run down the Tanana, Allen had been without footgear of any kind; at Kanuti village, on the Arctic Circle, he noted that nearly all the natives were barefoot.[19]

Two birch canoes were acquired for the speedy trip down the Kanuti to the Koyukuk, and then, instead of taking the easy way by continuing down the Koyukuk, Allen and Fickett began an ascent of the stream. Indulging a moment of vanity, Allen named the first river they encountered *Allenkakat* (his own name with a native suffix), but the name did

17. Schwatka, in *Compilation of Narratives*, p. 322.
18. Allen, in ibid., p. 454.
19. Ibid., pp. 455–57.

not stick.[20] Farther upstream the men came upon a main fork of the Koyukuk which they named the Fickett River; this name also did not remain on the map.[21] After ascending the "Fickett" a few miles, Allen and his partner decided on August 9 to head for home. They traveled down the Koyukuk to the Yukon, which they intersected on August 21. They then drifted down the Yukon beyond Nulato and made the Unalakleet River portage to St. Michael on Norton Sound, where they took ship for the States.

By Allen's own calculations, in round figures, he had traveled 160 miles from Nuchek to Taral, ninety miles from Taral to Nikolai's village on the Chitistone, 240 miles from Taral to Lake Suslota, across the pass, then 550 miles to the junction of the Tanana and Yukon. He estimated the distance from Nukluklayet to the confluence of the Kanuti and Koyukuk at 125 miles. From there, he traveled ninety miles up the Koyukuk, then downstream 530 miles again to the Yukon.[22] Assuming an error of 300 miles in his calculations, he had successfully completed an original exploration of about 1,500 miles, an exploration that crossed the Alaska Range and took him from below the sixty-first parallel to the Arctic Circle. Three major river systems were charted for the first time. It was an incredible achievement that deserves to be ranked with the great explorations of North America.

General Nelson Miles was pleased. He wrote to Allen: "I was more than gratified to hear of your success and safe return. For more . . . [than] four years I have tried to have that unknown region explored and I should have been pretty disappointed had you failed—as it was my last effort."[23] Dall credited Allen with a journey comparable to that of the celebrated Robert Campbell.[24] Walter C. Mendenhall, explorer and later chief of the Geological Survey, said: "No one geographer in recent years has made greater contributions to our knowledge of the Territory in so limited a time in the face of such obstacles."[25] Wrote Alfred Hulse Brooks: "No man through his own individual explorations has added more to our knowledge

20. The stream is now called the Alatna.

21. It is now known as the John River.

22. Allen, in *Compilation of Narratives*, pp. 467–69.

23. Miles to Allen, October 24, 1885, Allen Papers.

24. "Geographical Notes," *Science*, 6 (October 30, 1885), 380.

25. "A Reconnaissance from Resurrection Bay to the Tanana River, Alaska, in 1898," *Twentieth Annual Report, USGS*, 1898–99, Pt. 7, p. 297.

of Alaska than has Lieutenant Allen."[26] Brooks called Allen's journey "remarkable,"[27] and the adjective has been adopted by historians of Alaska.

Henry Allen's accomplishment was geographical: he recorded for future explorers and wanderers approximately 1,500 miles of virgin wilderness. His scientific contribution, under the circumstances, was of necessity scant. He had no time to collect, preserve, and carry natural history specimens, and his geologic notes were slim and of doubtful accuracy. Yet even without special scientific instruction he noted the absence of glacial evidence north of the Alaska Range,[28] confirming the observations of Dall, and he remarked on the "astonishing" similarity of the Copper River Indian language to that of the Apache, without being aware that both were Athapaskan.[29] He was a keen and intelligent observer. His maps, for which he claimed no special precision, remained for a dozen years the only source of topographical information on the regions he investigated and were found "marvelously correct" by an explorer who followed (to some extent) in his footsteps.[30]

Though all the experts applauded Allen, his triumph failed to capture the public imagination. For one thing, he lacked the literary flair of Schwatka, or even Abercrombie, and unlike the former Allen did not leap into print until after the results of the expedition were published in an official report. The report competed with Schwatka's book about a journey that by comparison was a schoolboy's summer excursion. Schwatka's expedition to St. Elias also vied for public recognition. Another explanation is the relative brevity (twelve years) of the period before the country covered by Allen was examined in more detail. To gain public admiration, an exploratory venture not only must be new but should retain its novelty for a period sufficient to permit the priority of discovery to

26. "A Reconnaissance in the White and Tanana River Basins, Alaska, in 1898," in ibid., p. 438.

27. *The Geography and Geology of Alaska*, p. 122.

28. Allen, "Copper River, Alaska, Glacial Action," *Science*, 8 (August 31, 1886), 145, 146.

29. Allen, "Atnatanas; Natives of Copper River, Alaska," SI, *Annual Report, 1886*, pp. 264, 265.

30. J. C. Castner, in E. F. Glenn and W. R. Abercrombie, *Report of Explorations in the Territory of Alaska . . . 1898*, p. 234.

permeate public consciousness. In this connection, and perhaps most important, Americans in the late nineteenth century could not realize that such a journey of geographical discovery was actually possible in North America. Their attention had been diverted to exploration in Africa, and that so large a segment of their own continent had just been explored for the first time was to many inconceivable. Alaska was an anachronism that the popular mind never fully understood.

But geographical discovery, like scientific advance, frequently has an internal history exclusive of timely recognition. Progress exists when experts use the findings of their predecessors, whether or not the result receives wide and immediate public acceptance. The contribution of Allen served as a useful framework on which later explorer-scientists could build. General Miles was on target when he viewed the remarkable journey of Henry Allen as the major exploration on the continent since Lewis and Clark.[31]

Allen's career following the exploration of 1885 has overshadowed the significance of his geographical contributions in the Far Northwest. For two years, beginning in 1888, he was an instructor in modern languages at West Point. The assignment was followed in 1890 by an appointment as military attaché in Russia for five years and in Berlin for two. He fought in Cuba and in the Philippines, where he organized and commanded the Philippine Constabulary. He was detailed as an observer of the Russo-Japanese War. Ironically, his only notable failure was as commandant of cavalry in Yellowstone Park, a position from which he was removed when he failed to capture some highwaymen. After a period as cavalry assistant to the Chief of Staff in Washington, he served with Pershing on the Mexican Punitive Expedition. Allen distinguished himself as commander of the 90th Division in World War I. His record won him the post of Corps commander, and later, commandant of United States occupation forces in Germany. In 1928, he was suggested as a possible vice-presidential running mate for Al Smith. Allen's northern adventure must have seemed

31. Sitka *Alaskan*, November 28, 1885. The *Alaskan's* words were: "Gen. Miles thinks Lieut Allen's trip excelled all explorations on the American continent since Lewis and Clarke, and the world's record since Livingstone." If the newspaper was laughing up its sleeve, then the last laugh must be on the *Alaskan*.

dim and distant and almost unreal as he sat at the councils of Europe, or during his brush with national politics afterwards.[32] Though the first episode of a memorable career, the Alaskan exploration was perhaps Allen's most important single accomplishment. It ranks with the earlier investigations of Alexander Mackenzie and Robert Campbell in the Far Northwest and was certainly the most spectacular individual achievement in the history of Alaskan inland exploration.

32. R. L. Bullard, *Fighting Generals* (Ann Arbor, 1944), pp. 87–92. New York *Times* book review, "When General Allen was King," November 18, 1923. Charleston, South Carolina, *Evening Post*, May 7, 1928, with Allen Papers.

8. Navy and Revenue Marine on the Kobuk

The Revenue Cutter 'Corwin' is here, and I learn from some of them, they are going to leave a party at Hotham Inlet, to explore the River I reported. I do not think they will take any honor from the Navy Department.

> GEORGE M. STONEY (USN) to the Secretary of the Navy, May 26, 1884[1]

We are the pioneers on the river, and I believe the report of Lieutenant Cantwell will be read with interest.

> M. A. HEALY (USRM) to Secretary of the Treasury, November 10, 1884[2]

BEFORE THE GOLD RUSH, interagency competition on the ground for priority of discovery in the Far Northwest was rarely obstreperous. The Navy and the Coast and Geodetic Survey on the one hand and the Army and the Geological Survey on the other usually confined their rivalry to the nation's capital. In the field, bureau cooperation was the rule. The most striking exception occurred not between civilian and military agencies but between the Navy and the semimilitary Revenue Marine (or Coast Guard, as it is now called). In that instance, despite the seeming duplication of effort, the cause of scientific exploration did not suffer. By 1886 competition on the Kobuk River between Lieutenant George M. Stoney, USN, and Lieutenant John C. Cantwell, USRM, had resulted in a comparatively fast and thorough investigation of a drainage system which in 1883 was unknown.

Neither service had any difficulty finding a precedent for operation in Alaska. Between 1880 and 1884, effective control of the territory was di-

---

1. Naval Records, NA, RG 45.
2. Healy, *Report of the Cruise of the Revenue Marine Steamer Corwin in the Arctic Ocean in the Year 1884* (Treasury Department, Washington, 1889), p. 5. Also published as *House Miscellaneous Document 602, 50th Congress: 1st session* (2583).

vided between them; the Navy ruled Southeastern—the Panhandle—
with a man-of-war at Sitka, and the Revenue Marine plied the westward
coast. Passage of Alaska's First Organic Act in 1884 did little to alter the
power structure, for the governor and a handful of civil officials were in
no position to police the vast territory. During the next decade the Navy
was still in and out of southeastern Alaska, independently and in cooperation with the Coast and Geodetic Survey, and in the West, the presence of
a Revenue cutter continued to be the only evidence of federal authority.
Though inland exploration was an unfamiliar activity to either service,
on the Kobuk the Navy was a trifle out of place geographically and his-
torically. Exploration that might lead to knowledge of the Arctic Alaskan
interior and thus facilitate rescue service was more in line with the mission
of the Revenue Marine.

From the beginning of United States' hegemony over Alaska, the Revenue Marine played a vital role. A Revenue cutter carried the first official
government scientific party to Alaska; direction of the expedition was
given to the Revenue officer in command. During the next year (1868),
the cutter *Wayanda* cruised the coast from Bering Sea to the southern tip
of Alaska with Thomas T. Minor aboard as surgeon. Minor had been instructed by the Smithsonian to collect natural history specimens and to examine into the territory's resources. Exploring parties were sent ashore
from the cutter to search for coal and other minerals, and one small boat
expedition went up the Kenai River a short distance. From the Alaska
Peninsula, Minor obtained specimens of petroleum. Both Minor and the
ship's captain were enthusiastic about the country and its resources.[3]

The main functions of the Revenue Marine, as an arm of the Treasury
Department, were collection of customs along the coast, regulation of
traffic in arms and liquor, and police duties connected with the management of fur seals on the Pribilof Islands; in 1889, by statute, it undertook
the surveillance of salmon fisheries.[4] Systematic work along the northern
littoral began in 1880 with assignment of the Revenue Cutter *Corwin*, a

3. Minor's testimony, March 26, 1880, in U.S. Senate Committee on Territories,
"Civil Government for Southeastern Alaska," *Senate Report 457*, pp. 31–34. SI, *Annual
Report, 1868*, pp. 24, 30, 57. J. W. White, "A Cruise in Alaska," *Senate Executive
Document 8, 40th Congress: 3d session* (1360), 3, 4, 7. B. L. Reed, "The Contribu-
tions of the Coast Guard to the Development of Alaska," *Proceedings of the U.S. Naval
Institute*, 55 (1929), 408.
4. D. H. Smith and F. W. Powell, *The Coast Guard*, Institute for Government Re-
search Service, Monograph No. 51 (Washington, 1929), pp. 10, 11.

wooden steamer rigged for sail, 145 feet long, with a draft of twelve feet.[5] The Secretary of the Treasury proudly boasted: "To thousands of half-civilized natives she represents the majesty and power of the nation, and dispenses such justice as humanity and the needs of the people call for." An annual appropriation of $25,000 kept the *Corwin* and her successor, the *Bear*, under way.[6] The cutters provided medical aid to the indigenes, carried and otherwise assisted scientist-explorers from all agencies, administered justice, and served as mail boats.[7] Ivan Petroff relied on the Revenue Marine to enumerate the northern Eskimos for the Tenth Census. Revenue steamers transported Sheldon Jackson, the government education agent, on his inspection tours of what probably was the largest school district in American history. And it was the *Bear* that carried the first reindeer from Siberia to Alaska as part of Jackson's plan to relieve destitute Eskimos.[8]

In 1881, E. W. Nelson and John Muir were aboard the *Corwin* on her cruise in the Bering Sea and the Arctic Ocean. Their efforts may be viewed as a logical extension of the work of Kennicott and Dall on floral and faunal relationships between Asia and America. Though Muir had small opportunity to explore inland geology, he returned from the voyage with an amazing geological hypothesis. He thought he had enough evidence to demonstrate (1) that the regions traversed were covered with a mantle of ice that moved south to discharge into the Pacific below the Aleutians; (2) that after the period of "universal glaciation" the coastal mountains of Bering Sea and the Arctic Ocean were freighted with distinct glaciers many of which had only recently disappeared; (3) that the main features of the region were due to glacial action; and (4) that the Bering Sea and nearby Arctic Ocean basins were "simply" those parts of the ice-sheet's bed which were deeply eroded and over which the ocean gradually extended as the ice retarded, "thus separating the continents of Asia and America, at the close of the Glacial period."[9] This astonishing thesis may

5. Reed, "Contributions of the Coast Guard," p. 408.

6. H. McCulloch, "Thanks of Congress to the Officers and Crew of the Steamer Corwin," *House Report 2507, 48th Congress: 2d session* (2328), 1, 2.

7. Reed, "Contributions of the Coast Guard," p. 408.

8. J. A. Lazell, *Alaskan Apostle* (New York, 1960), pp. 100, 101.

9. Muir, "On the Glaciation of the Arctic and Sub-Arctic Regions Visited by the United States Steamer Corwin in the Year 1881," in C. L. Hooper, *Report of the Cruise of the U.S. Revenue Steamer Corwin, in the Arctic Ocean, 1881* (Treasury Department, Washington, 1885), p. 147.

have been the most colossal bad guess that John Muir ever made. It challenged Dall's belief (later confirmed) that the Yukon regions of Alaska had escaped glaciation. If correct, Muir's thesis would affect certain large conclusions about plant and animal distribution that were in turn closely connected to problems of evolutionary biology. In response to an inquiry, Asa Gray wrote at once to Muir and volunteered to handle determination of the Arctic plant collection.[10] Among geologists, Muir's theory never enjoyed much vogue, but the presence of Nelson and Muir put the Revenue Marine squarely in the business of science. It was soon in the business of inland exploration also.[11]

The Treasury Department sent special agents and customs collectors to the Pribilofs, Kodiak, and the Panhandle. Some were competent, some incompetent; some were opinionated, some were not. Almost all at one time or another submitted reports on the country or parts of the country, or wrote books or articles on Alaska. "In all this activity there was of course much inferior work done by persons unqualified either by training or habits of accurate observation," wrote William Healey Dall in 1885. He continued: "Numerous petty agents of the Treasury have reported from time to time, in documents of fortunately limited circulation, some of which reveal to the student official Bunsbyism of the purest breed."[12] The reader has already met Henry Elliott, who challenged Dall's estimate of Alaska's value. He was preceded and succeeded on the Pribilofs by other Treasury agents, not all of whom agreed with him. Many did, though, and the fact leads to a conclusion that Pribilof agents who knew only the Seal Islands and the Aleutians were prone to belittle the hospitableness of Alaska. William Gouverneur Morris, Treasury agent assigned to southeastern Alaska, was as vocal an opponent of Elliott's views as Dall. Indeed, Morris was almost intemperate in his evaluation of the "marplot" Elliott, whom he accused of "gross and palpable ignorance" rather than "intentional design."[13] Morris' report on Alaskan resources was informative

10. W. F. Badè, *Life and Letters of John Muir,* 2, 191.
11. The Revenue Marine performed a number of spectacular rescue operations. One was a successful coastal trek from south of St. Michael to Point Barrow. This important event is an episode in the history of Arctic exploration and thus falls outside the purview of this study. See U.S. Revenue Cutter Service, *Cruise of the U.S. Revenue Cutter Bear and the Overland Expedition* (Treasury Department, Washington, 1899).
12. "Native Tribes of Alaska," AAAS, *Proceedings, 34* (1885), p. 367.
13. W. G. Morris, "Report upon the . . . Resources," *Senate Executive Document*

and vehemently favorable, but limited by an imprecise knowledge of the country north and west of the Panhandle. His career in Alaska reached a climax during the two-year interim between the Army evacuation in 1877 and the Navy's arrival in 1879. Without military supervision of any kind and without an organic act, Alaska was virtually untended except by Treasury Department collectors and an occasional visit by a small, lightly armed Revenue cutter.

It was an alarm in 1879 over the threat of an Indian uprising that brought a Naval man-of-war to Sitka, and the Navy lingered there. The commander of the first Naval vessel stationed permanently at Sitka, Captain L. A. Beardslee, policed the illegal manufacture of liquor, which had been at the root of the Indian disturbances, and tried (unsuccessfully) to organize a viable local self-government. He declined to make any specific recommendation on government for the country as a whole, but definitely favored some effective, simple form of civil rule. On most issues he sided with the anti–Alaska Commercial Company faction.[14] In the pages of *Forest and Stream*, for which he wrote under a pseudonym, Beardslee exchanged barbs with Elliott over Alaska's agricultural potential.[15]

Earlier, Beardslee while on duty elsewhere had made observations on the natural history and physical condition of ocean water for the Fish Commission. When he offered to continue the work in Alaska, the Smithsonian gladly accepted, and furnished him with instruments. He also collected and forwarded natural history materials to the Institution.[16] He and his successor conducted hydrographic surveys, the results of which were published by the Hydrographic Office and incorporated on USC&GS charts. Detailed meteorological records for Sitka were kept and published.[17]

Naval officers working in conjunction with the Coast and Geodetic Survey in southeastern Alaska also collected for the Smithsonian,[18] and

---

59, p. 121. For an exchange of insults between Elliott and Morris see *San Francisco Chronicle*, December 8, 1878, and January 18, 1879.

14. L. A. Beardslee, "Report Relative to Affairs in Alaska," *Senate Executive Document 71*, pp. 181–83.

15. April 22, 1880, and December 18, 1879.

16. SI, *Annual Report, 1879*, p. 45. Ibid., *1880*, p. 47.

17. Beardslee, "Report Relative to Affairs in Alaska," pp. 83–169.

18. For example, USNM, *Proceedings, 1881*, pp. 463–74.

made outstanding contributions to ethnology. During the seasons 1885–1887 Ensign Albert P. Niblack studied and collected among the Tlingits and Haidas; his results were published in the National Museum's report for 1887.[19] The monograph was partially illustrated by materials from the G. F. Emmons collection at the American Museum of Natural History in New York.[20] Emmons was also a Naval officer on duty in Alaska. About the same time, Franz Boas began work on the mythology and philology of the Northwest Coast Indians. Boas called the Emmons collection "one of the most complete, systematic, and consequently valuable, brought from the Northwest coast to the museums of our country."[21] The labors of the two young officers provided Boas with rich materials for his classic volume, *Primitive Art*.[22] Thanks to men like Niblack and Emmons, the Navy's record in science was laudatory—if limited geographically.

One example of Naval activity in Alaska beyond the geographic limits of the Panhandle began accidentally. Natives around St. Lawrence Bay, Siberia, had rendered aid to crew members of the Naval ship *Rodgers*, which had been sent in 1881 in search of the ill-fated *Jeannette*;[23] the *Jeannette* was crushed by Arctic ice while engaged on a north polar expedition that same year, and the *Rodgers* was destroyed by fire while in winter quarters. In appreciation of the natives' assistance, Congress appropriated money to buy gifts and entrusted their delivery to Naval Lieutenant George M. Stoney. In 1883, after distributing the tokens, Stoney found himself at Kotzebue Sound with time on his hands. With a boat and rations from Captain M. A. Healy's *Corwin*, and with a crew member from the cutter, the Lieutenant began a week-long examination of Hotham Inlet. From a native, Stoney learned of an interior river that led into an ocean filled with ice, and he surmised: "I think what he alluded to is either the Colvell [sic] or Mackenzie River." Reportedly, the head of

19. Niblack, "The Coast Indians of Southern Alaska and Northern British Columbia," USNM, *Report, 1887–88*, pp. 225–386.

20. H. F. Osborn, *The American Museum of Natural History* (2d ed. New York, 1911), p. 87.

21. Boas, "An Ethnological Collection from Alaska," *Science*, 11 (April 27, 1888), 199. See also Boas, "Gleanings from the Emmons Collection of Ethnological Specimens from Alaska," *Journal of American Folk-Lore*, 1 (1888), 215–19.

22. New York, 1955; originally published in 1927.

23. Stoney to W. E. Chandler, October 12, 1883, Naval Officer's Letters, NA, RG 45.

the northern river could be reached after a short portage from the source of another stream emptying into Hotham Inlet.[24] While exploring the Inlet, Stoney encountered the Kobuk delta, and traveled upriver some forty miles.

Stoney requested orders to explore the Kobuk further,[25] claiming the title "discoverer." As a matter of fact, the Kobuk was known to British officers who had been sent during the Russian period in search of Sir John Franklin, the great British explorer who disappeared in the Arctic in 1845. Furthermore, the Kobuk may have been navigated a short distance in 1874.[26] In any event, the river was effectively discovered in 1883, and it is unprofitable to argue whether the Navy or Revenue Marine deserves the credit. Stoney and Healy together were responsible for the Kobuk's identification; both reported the "discovery"; and both successfully promoted more detailed exploration of the stream.

While Stoney sought approval for a Naval expedition under his command, Healy prepared to have the river investigated—this time wholly under the auspices of the Revenue Marine. On July 8, 1884, John C. Cantwell was given command of a steam launch manned by a boat's crew, and accompanied by Assistant Engineer S. B. McLenegan, Quartermaster Horace Wilber, and Fireman J. Lewis. The duty was a lucky accident for Cantwell; he was placed in command when another officer, who was to have charge of the expedition, lacerated his hand before starting. The explorers were instructed to make as accurate a survey as time would allow, and to collect information on flora and fauna and resources of the countryside. Also, Cantwell was specifically ordered to investigate the supposed existence of jade in the region, based on reports of a mysterious "green mountain."[27] (The green mountain dominated a row of hills located not far from the north bank of the Kobuk, about halfway up the

24. Stoney to Chandler, October 15, 1883, in ibid. S. B. McLenegan, in Healy, *Cruise of the Corwin, 1884*, p. 105. Stoney, "Explorations in Alaska," *Proceedings of the U.S. Naval Institute*, 25 (October 1899), 533, 534, continued in ibid. (December 1899), 799 ff.; also published separately as *Naval Explorations in Alaska* (U.S. Naval Institute, Annapolis, 1900).

25. Stoney, "Explorations in Alaska," pp. 533, 535. Stoney to Chandler, October 15, 1885, NA, RG 45.

26. Stoney, "Explorations in Alaska," p. 534. Dall, "Exploration of the Kowak River," *Science*, 4 (December 19, 1884), 539.

27. Healy, *Cruise of the Corwin, 1884*, p. 10. Healy to Cantwell, July 8, 1884, in ibid., p. 49.

river. In 1884 both McLenegan and Stoney brought mineral specimens from the mountain and in 1886 Stoney confirmed the existence of jadeite, which was used by the Eskimos for various implements and is now a commercial source of Alaskan jade.)

Cantwell made remarkable time—nearly twenty-five miles a day against a strong current. Coal for the steam launch was mined along the way. On July 21, thirteen days after setting out, the explorers abandoned the steamer and continued upstream in skin boats. The natives were reluctant to accompany the party too far inland, because of superstition and a disinclination to interrupt their summer hunting and fishing. They were even more hesitant about directing the explorers to the jade mountain. At first, not even half pay in advance, plus a supply of ammunition, would satisfy them. They had seen Cantwell at work with the sextant and artificial horizon, and thinking he was a shaman they requested that, in addition to their pay, he guarantee a plentiful supply of game near their homes during the coming winter. Cantwell noted: "I had no alternative but to promise plenty of deer."[28]

By August 29, when the party was back aboard the *Corwin*, a rough survey of the Kobuk some 300 miles inland had been made, and Selawik Lake had been explored. Cantwell appended ethnological notes to his report, and McLenegan made observations on the natural history and ornithology of the region.[29] Cantwell apologized for not achieving the river's head, but he returned with an Indian report of short portages to the Koyukuk and to another river flowing into the northern sea. He, like Stoney, thought the latter stream might be the Colville. The importance of such communication routes for rescue purposes, Cantwell correctly observed, could not be overestimated.[30]

Given the time and instruments at their disposal, the Revenue Marine party prepared a creditable map and provided a body of approximate information on a hitherto unknown section of the continent. At Healy's suggestion, Cantwell explained in a letter to the Chief of the Service: "I was entirely ignorant of the obstacles which were to be surmounted and on this account made many mistakes which eventually compelled me to turn back without having attained the object for which I was sent." The

28. Cantwell, in ibid., p. 59; also pp. 55–59.
29. Ibid., pp. 60, 63, 67, 75–98, 109–25.
30. Cantwell to Healy, November 13, 1884, in ibid., p. 51.

letter continued: "I think it only an act of justice to myself to inform you of my earnest desire to be allowed to make one more attempt."[31]

On the downstream leg of Cantwell's journey, when he was investigating the jade mountain, George Stoney and a Naval party passed on the way up. Stoney had received authorization for a renewed attempt to explore the Kobuk; he was assigned the Naval schooner *Ounalaska* for the duty.[32] The schooner was slow to reach Hotham Inlet on Kotzebue Sound; the *Corwin* had already arrived. Stoney felt the Cantwell expedition would "only prompt us to make our work more thorough, if such was possible."[33] From July 20 to August 13, the Naval party traveled upriver in a steam cutter, and then transferred from the steamer to skin boats, as Cantwell had done. Neither expedition reached the headwaters, though Stoney got a few miles farther up than Cantwell.[34]

In 1885, Cantwell was back in the field. On his new expedition he was fortunate enough to be accompanied by Charles H. Townsend, from Spencer Baird's Fish Commission; Townsend's subsequent report on the ornithology, ichthyology, and entomology of the area, along with his general observations on natural history, helped to make the second Revenue Marine exploration a scientific success.[35]

31. Cantwell to E. W. Clark, October 29, 1884, NA, RG 26.

32. Log of the *Ounalaska*, 1884, in NA, RG 45. Miscellaneous field notebooks of the expedition are with records of the Hydrographic Office, NA, RG 37. Also, Stoney to Chandler, April 10, 1884, NA, RG 45.

33. Stoney to Chandler, May 26, 1884, NA, RG 45.

34. Stoney, "Explorations in Alaska," pp. 540–42.

35. Healy, "Report of the Cruise of the Revenue Marine Steamer Corwin in the Arctic Ocean in the Year 1885," *House Executive Document 153, 49th Congress: 1st session* (2400), p. 12; also published separately. The earliest systematic researches on the economic fishes of Alaska were undertaken by Tarleton H. Bean of the Fish Commission in 1880. Bean accompanied Captain C. P. Patterson and Dall on a Coast and Geodetic vessel from April to November. The ichthyologist reported seventy-five species of food fishes. Bean noted: "More than two-thirds of the whole number exist in great abundance where they occur." According to the Smithsonian report for 1881, fishes were "collected in Alaska and scientifically described long before any were made known from California." The work was in part a response to increased commercial interest in territorial fisheries. Exploitation of this marine resource before the Gold Rush led to further investigations, and to early federal conservation measures in Alaska. See the following works: R. Rathburn, *Summary of Fishery Investigations Conducted in the North Pacific Ocean and Bering Sea from July 1, 1888, to July 1, 1892, by the U.S. Fish Commission Steamer Albatross* (Washington, 1894), p. 127, extracted from the *Bulletin of the U.S. Fish Commission, 1892*, pp. 127–201. SI, *Annual Report, 1880,*

From experience of the previous year, the steam launch was improved. One day's journey above Stoney's highest point of 1884, Cantwell left the launch in charge of Townsend and continued upriver in a skin boat.[36] This time he attained the river's source, Walker Lake, or, to use the native name, "Big Fish Lake." According to legend, the lake contained fish of immense size and ferocity. In what must be one of the classic fish stories contained in a government document, Cantwell described how a native with the expedition plotted to capture one of the giants: "One of my party baited a hook, made of the antlers of a reindeer, with a goose, and attaching our towline he gravely threw it far out into the deep water, and making the shore end of this novel fishing-line fast to a stout tree he sat down and waited for some unwary fish to bite."[37] Cantwell did not report whether the fisherman succeeded in snaring his game.

The Revenue Marine Kobuk journey of 1885, though not without hardships, was made in relative comfort. The natives co-operated, the steamer performed well, and the explorers were well fed from their own provisions and from the comparative abundance of game of all varieties. The pioneer voyage on the Noatak River, which flows from the north into Hotham Inlet, was less of a pleasure excursion. S. B. McLenegan was chosen by Healy to head a reconnaissance of the Noatak to determine its size and general course. McLenegan won the duty, he explained later, because he was the youngest "and perhaps least missed."[38] With Seaman Nelson of the *Corwin* and no native guide, McLenegan set out in a three-hole kayak twenty-seven feet long. The seemingly endless, laborious, damp and cold tracking upstream eventually led into the bare, woodless plains of Arctic Alaska. McLenegan wrote: "The landscape was one of the bleakest imaginable; not a sign of life was anywhere visible, and the cold, piercing blasts which swept across the tundra caused us to realize

pp. 47, 25. Bean, "The Fishery Resources and Fishing Grounds of Alaska," *Senate Miscellaneous Document 124, 47th Congress: 1st session* (2000), 81. SI, *Annual Report, 1881*, p. 465. Bean, "Report on the Salmon and Salmon Rivers of Alaska," *House Miscellaneous Document 211, 51st Congress: 1st session* (2777), 5, 40. F. F. Barker and P. Charlton, "Compilation of the Acts of Congress and Treaties Relating to Alaska from March 30, 1867, to March 3, 1905," *Senate Miscellaneous Document 142, 59th Congress: 1st session* (4921), 30, 31, 50, 51.

36. Cantwell, in Healy, "Cruise of the Corwin, 1885," pp. 25, 31.

37. Ibid., p. 38.

38. McLenegan to Phillip S. Smith, May 1, 1911, Historical Documents, USGS Files.

keenly the solitude of our position and only increased our desire to see the end of the journey."[39]

After a month of such travel, the two men cached their boat and proceeded on foot for a dozen miles, until they were satisfied that the river at that point was only a creek or series of creeks. The return trip began August 3. Because of rapidly rising water, the men determined to make a canoe dash 125 miles to where they had stashed provisions. They made it, but had difficulty recognizing the spot because of the flooded river banks. The downward voyage was fast and exciting. "The wild rush of the river, mingled with the scream of the eagles and the madly dashing canoe, all contributed to the excitement of the moment."[40] McLenegan reported aboard the *Corwin* on August 27. Dall called the reconnaissance "extremely creditable."[41] By the end of the century, the sketch map made by McLenegan had not been superseded.[42]

On August 11, when Cantwell was on his way downstream, once again he met George Stoney on the way up—this time aboard the steam launch *Explorer*.[43] The unfortunate Naval officer had been upstreamed the second year in a row.

Stoney's final sojourn on the Kobuk was no mere reconnaissance. His party included three other officers, an assistant engineer, an assistant surgeon, and twelve men. Dall thought the expedition "dangerously large";[44] he must not have known Stoney's carefully laid plans. The expedition had provisions for twenty months, mainly leftover stores from another Arctic expedition. Two boats, one a small steam cutter and the other a specially designed sixty-foot flat-bottomed steamboat, were to provide transportation. The party was also equipped with a portable steam sawmill to be worked in connection with the boat boilers. Toward the end of August, the party began construction of a winter camp that Stoney named Fort Cosmos, after the exclusive scientific club of Washington, D.C. Cosmos was located well up the river to permit exploration in all directions— toward the Arctic, the Yukon, the Brooks Range, and back down the Ko-

39. McLenegan, in Healy, "Cruise of the Corwin, 1885," pp. 67, 59, 65.
40. Ibid., pp. 70–72.
41. "Geographical Notes," *Science*, 6 (October 30, 1885), p. 381.
42. A. H. Brooks, *Geography and Geology of Alaska*, p. 123.
43. Cantwell, in Healy, "Cruise of the Corwin, 1885," p. 46.
44. "Proposed Explorations in Alaska," *Science*, 5 (February 20, 1885), 154.

buk Valley. The sciences were divided among the officers and systematic investigations and surveys were projected.[45]

Once settled in at Fort Cosmos, Stoney organized a number of winter trips. Surgeon F. S. Nash was sent inland to collect ethnographic information. On December 26, Engineer A. V. Zane crossed over to the Koyukuk and descended it to the Yukon and St. Michael, returning in February of 1886. Stoney himself explored Selawik Lake and River, began observations for a base line to triangulate the Kobuk Valley, and examined the headwaters of the Noatak and the Alatna. He reached Chandler Lake and a tributary of the Colville, where he was told by natives about a route to Point Barrow.[46] By the end of the summer of 1886, Stoney had completed an instrumental survey of the Kobuk Valley, prospected the famous jade mountain, and sent a party to complete a survey of the Noatak.[47]

The most original exploration of the Stoney Expedition was undertaken in April by Ensign W. L. Howard. With two white men and two natives, Howard struck due north across the Noatak and portaged to a native village visited by Stoney earlier in the year. Howard then descended to the Colville and followed it a few miles before crossing to the Ikpikpuk, which took him to the Arctic Ocean near Point Barrow.[48]

As a result of work between 1884 and 1886 by Cantwell, McLenegan, and Stoney, the Kobuk region became to experts one of the best known slices of interior Alaska. Interservice rivalry had only resulted, as Stoney predicted, in a more complete examination of the area. The Naval operation of 1885–1886 may have been patterned in part after American experience during the First International Polar Year at Barrow. At any rate, Stoney's organization was a prototype for later Arctic and Antarctic explorations. The expedition was well equipped and provisioned, and under strict military discipline. Carefully scheduled explorations radiated from headquarters at Fort Cosmos. Stoney anticipated psychological problems of Arctic life and work and took novel means to alleviate them. For summer travel, he devised an ingenious hooded mask of wire gauze for protection against mosquitoes, the scourge of Alaskan explorers.

It was not until 1899 that the results of Stoney's expedition were pub-

45. Stoney, "Explorations in Alaska," pp. 549–52.

46. Ibid., pp. 561, 570.

47. Ibid., pp. 562, 563. Also, *Proceedings of the U.S. Naval Institute* (December 1899), p. 802.

48. Ibid., pp. 811–22.

lished, and even then the account was abbreviated and published privately; the full report with maps never did appear in print. Stoney hinted darkly about the "mysterious" disappearance of the papers.[49] Perhaps, as a recent student of Arctic exploration has suggested, service rivalry may be suspected.[50] Obviously the rivalry did exist; there is evidence that it may have been as much a personal matter between Healy and Stoney as it was a question of allegiance to either the Navy or the Revenue Marine.[51] Another possible explanation is related to the priority of Cantwell's report. The Navy Department may have been reluctant to risk criticism of what might be regarded on Capitol Hill as wasteful duplication of effort: the expeditions were competing on the Kobuk at the same time that the Allison Commission was investigating efficiency in the federal scientific establishment.

Stoney and the Navy were upstreamed by Cantwell and the Revenue Marine in 1884, in 1885, and in the publication of results. In 1897 Stoney again urged Naval interest in the interior of Alaska and asked for command of the expedition. In a memorandum to the Secretary of the Navy, Stoney outlined his fear of dramatic disorder among the gold seekers if the Navy did not build and operate a Yukon steamer and establish stations on the river manned by Marines. Stoney felt that Army experience in southeastern Alaska, and the Army's record in trying to relieve another Arctic expedition, indicated how much better qualified the Navy was for police duty in Alaska.[52] The idea received warm support from Theodore Roosevelt, then Acting Secretary of the Navy; the Revenue Marine, added Roosevelt, was unfitted for the duty, chiefly because it lacked military organization, military training, and military discipline.[53]

The government eventually authorized a federal steamer for the Yukon, and in 1899 the *Nunivak* was completed. She was a sternwheeler of 450 tons, 209 feet in length. Her seven officers, four petty officers, and crew of

49. Stoney, "Explorations in Alaska," p. 533.

50. J. E. Caswell, *Arctic Frontiers* (Norman, Okla., 1956), p. 200.

51. Healy to Secretary of the Treasury, telegrams, April 30, 1886 (two), NA, RG 26. Stoney to Chandler, October 12, 1883, NA, RG 45.

52. Stoney, "Memorandum for the Honorable Secretary of the Navy," in "Annual Report of Navy Department, 1897," *House Document 3, 55th Congress: 2d session* (3638), 272–74.

53. Roosevelt, "Memorandum on the Subject of a Naval Expedition to Preserve the Peace and Enforce the Law on the Yukon River," September 16, 1897, NA, RG 45.

thirty men were instructed to enforce customs and navigation law, aid destitute miners, assist in general law enforcement, chart the river, and collect specimens and data on the region's flora, fauna, traffic, and weather. Exploration of areas adjacent to winter quarters was ordered, to avoid idleness and for the sake of "health, harmony, and discipline." Ironically, the *Nunivak*, which introduced a period of relative luxury to Yukon exploration, was a Revenue Cutter commanded by John C. Cantwell.[54]

54. Cantwell, *Report of the Operation of the U.S. Revenue Steamer Nunivak on the Yukon River Station, Alaska, 1899–1901* (Treasury Department, Washington, 1902), pp. 9–12.

9. Diplomatic Exploration and Headlines: 1886–1896

SYSTEMATIC scientific investigation and exploration in Alaska by any federal agency or military service suffered during the decade from 1886 to 1896. In addition to bruises left by the searching inquiry of the Allison Commission into the whole governmental science establishment, politically the period was a crucial watershed in American history. The era was marked by the election of a Democratic president for the first time since before the Civil War, by the resumption of agrarian unrest that led to formation of the Populist Party, by currency manipulation, by a stiff McKinley tariff that to some indicated the true locus of power, by groping attempts to limit that power through monopoly regulation by the government, and finally by the Panic of 1893 and an aftermath of unemployment and economic distress.

The Republic struggled internally to find itself, after years of drift in almost every area except scientific, technological, and industrial growth. Preoccupied with domestic issues, the American people rarely looked outward toward their giant step-child in the north. Very soon national introspection would be thrust suddenly aside for a brief and uncharacteristic foray into overseas expansion. In the meantime, exploration in the Far Northwest derived its main support from the American press in search of hot copy and from the demands of a minor international dispute which, if not amicably settled, could become major.

The willingness of America to extend the remarkable work of Dall, Stoney, Allen, and the others was tested between 1886 and 1891. Allen and his colleagues actively promoted exploration of the territory, and Congress now and then deliberated on the wisdom of supporting the proposals.[1] By 1890 a plan was formulated and was officially recommended by the Secretary of War.[2] From a military post on the Yukon, expeditions

1. Allen to Dora Johnston, September 9, 1886, and Dolph to Allen, December 27, 1886, Allen Papers. J. H. Keatley, "The Gold Fields of Alaska," *Arena*, 1 (1890), 733.
2. I. C. Russell, "Mount St. Elias Expedition," *JAGS*, 22 (1890), 665.

manned from a staff of topographers, astronomers, and other scientific specialists were to be sent in all directions to survey and study the country.[3] P. H. Ray, who commanded the Army's Point Barrow station during the International Polar Year, recommended four posts. The idea of an Army garrison in the interior met with opposition, however; even Nelson Miles, then Adjutant General in Washington, testified against it. If a post were necessary at all, he thought it should be at Sitka.[4] A military affairs committee of the House of Representatives offered a substitute bill, eliminating the military post and proposing only that a well equipped party be dispatched to a central point on the Yukon and from there undertake systematic explorations. An estimated $100,000 was required to cover the cost of the expedition.[5]

The proposal was commented on widely in the domestic and foreign press. In the United States, the House committee found editorial opinion generally favorable. The New York *Tribune* felt that development of Alaska would lead to a revival of plans for a transcontinental railroad. The New York *Herald*, as might be expected, was flippant; it had sponsored Stanley's search for Livingstone in Africa. Said the Pittsburgh *Gazette:* "Its [Alaska's] careful, intelligent exploration is of far greater importance to us than that of Africa, in which so much interest is taken." The *Army and Navy Register* articulated the Army's claim to handle the job: "To the Army more than to any other single agent do we owe the transformation of the 'Great American Desert' into the 'Great Empire of the West,' and it is quite natural, therefore, that the Army should be looked to to explore the only part of our domain which remains unknown and unexplored."[6] The *Register* failed to mention that the report of one Army explorer, Stephen H. Long, had been largely responsible for the legend of a "Great American Desert" west of the ninety-fifth meridian.

Amid newspaper acclaim for the plan of 1890, the Sitka *Alaskan* viewed the Yukon-based exploration as a gift to the "ring" (that is, the

3. E. Diebitsch, "Explorations in Alaska," *Goldthwaite's Geographical Magazine,* 1 (1891), 203, 204.

4. U.S. Senate, Committee on Military Affairs, "Military Post in Alaska," *Senate Report 557, 51st Congress: 1st session* (2704), 1, 2.

5. U.S. House of Representatives, Committee on Military Affairs, "Military Post in the Interior of Alaska," *House Report 3166, 51st Congress: 1st session* (2816), 1, 2.

6. U.S. House of Representatives, Committee on Military Affairs, "Exploration and Survey of Alaska," *House Report 3760,* pp. 1–7.

A.C. Company). The *Alaskan* preferred to see the $100,000 spent nearer "our own homes . . . instead of being laid out in a portion of the Territory inhabited only by a sparse population of natives, and which is not at all likely to be settled up by white people for many years to come."[7]

More effective opposition came from the distrust of Army competence by civilian bureaus and rival service agencies, and from competition for funds by the National Geographic Society:[8] the Society was then also engaged in its investigation of Mt. St. Elias in co-operation with the Geological Survey. But failure of the plan for organized exploration should probably be traced to general rather than specific sources of opposition. The Congress, occupied with domestic concerns in a fundamentally conservative age, could not remain excited for long about a search into the unknown that promised to yield no immediate practical benefits. The enthusiasm of 1890 was transitory. It was due partly to the publicity attending private exploration financed and reported by the press, and partly to the coincidental rise of an international controversy over the Alaska-Canada boundary.

The boundary problem festered for a long time before Theodore Roosevelt dramatically forced the issue at the turn of the century. The first government reconnaissance of the interior by Charles Raymond in 1869 was motivated by the reluctance of the Hudson's Bay Company to admit it was trading in United States' territory. As long as the areas adjacent to the boundary were vacant or held no economic attraction for either country, the issue would lie dormant. Three years after Raymond's reconnaissance, President U. S. Grant, in his annual message, called attention to the potential threat to international amity: if precise determination of the boundary were deferred until nearby regions were populated, "some trivial contest of neighbors may again array the two governments in an antagonism." Grant recommended the appointment of a commission to work on the problem jointly with a British commission.[9] Grant's suggestion was apparently inspired by Canadian representatives working through the British minister in Washington.[10] An estimate made after Grant's

7. September 20, 1890.

8. E. Diebitsch, "Explorations in Alaska," p. 204.

9. Fourth Annual Message, December 2, 1872, in J. D. Richardson, compiler, *A Compilation of the Messages and Papers of the Presidents* (20 vols. New York, 1897–1922), 9, 4141.

10. J. B. Moore, "Alaska Boundary," *NAR, 169* (1899), 502.

recommendation put the cost of a complete boundary survey at $1,500,-
000, and the time required at nine years.[11] Congress failed to act—and
small wonder, in light of social values reflected in the allocation of resources. The estimated cost of the survey was more than one-half of all
the money appropriated to the State Department for international boundary surveys between 1798 and 1885.

Despite Congressional inaction, the problem did not disappear. In
1875 General O. O. Howard warned of probable complications, and
Schwatka's excursion of 1883 also raised the issue. Gold prospectors
panned along the Yukon in and out of Alaska. President Cleveland re-
vived Grant's suggestion. The discovery of mineral wealth, Cleveland advised, required a boundary survey to avoid jurisdictional disputes. He
recommended an appropriation of $100,000.[12] A diplomatic exchange
was initiated in 1885.[13]

In 1887–1888 William Dall met in informal conference with George
M. Dawson of the Canadian Geological Survey to discuss the matter. The
men differed on interpretation of applicable treaties insofar as they per-
tained to the southeastern boundary. Dawson felt any plan not allowing
Britain access to the sea would be unacceptable, while Dall thought that
such a cession was undesirable and not likely to be considered seriously in
the United States. The two scientists were in virtual agreement on the
methods to be used in the establishment of a line.[14] Dall, still a partisan
of civilian science, claimed that the whole line from Portland Inlet to
Chilkat could be run in two or three seasons by about four parties for
probably not more than $125,000 provided the methods employed by
the USGS, the USC&GS, or the Canadian Geological Survey were used,

11. T. F. Bayard to E. J. Phelps, November 20, 1885, in Bayard, "Frontier Line
between Alaska and British Columbia," *Senate Executive Document 143, 49th Congress: 1st session* (2340), 3. T. C. Mendenhall, "Boundary Line Between Alaska and
British Columbia," *House Executive Document 111, 52d Congress: 1st session*
(2954), 2.

12. First Annual Message, December 8, 1885, in Richardson, *Compilation*, 10, 4917,
4918, 4985.

13. Bayard to Phelps, November 20, 1885, and May 22, 1886, NA, RG 59. Bayard,
"Frontier Line," pp. 1–20.

14. Dawson to Sir Charles Tupper, February 11, 1888, and Dall to Bayard, February 13, 1888, in U.S. Department of State, "Report on the Boundary Line Between
Alaska and British Columbia," *Senate Executive Document 146, 50th Congress: 2d
session* (2613), pp. 7–12.

whereas by military methods and men the work would take twice as long and cost at least half a million dollars. "In regard to this matter of expense," he added, "I speak advisedly, having regard to estimates already furnished by military authorities."[15]

The frontier issue coincided with an Anglo-American dispute over fur seal hunting in Bering Sea. The seal question was at the time far more serious, and the two controversies combined could have disrupted British-American relations. Fortunately, in 1889, just before the Bering Sea issue reached a critical phase,[16] Congress finally responded to Cleveland's request for action[17] and passed an appropriation of $20,000 for the boundary survey.[18] Coast and Geodetic teams took to the field.

The Canadians were already there. The Canadian organization in charge of exploration in Yukon Territory bore in 1887 a ponderous name —the Geological and Natural History Survey of Canada—that openly recognized the utility of multipurpose scientific exploration. It attracted, as did allied agencies in the United States, young and talented scientists from every discipline. Yet Canada neglected the Far Northwest until well into the nineteenth century. It was the discoveries like those of Schwatka and Krause that moved George Dawson to urge an investigation of the region.[19] The immediate necessity for exploratory work, however, arose from the increasing number of miners in the district.

Dawson led the expedition of 1887. His general plan was threefold. He and J. McEvoy carried a survey line from the Cassiar district in northern British Columbia via the Dease, Upper Liard, and Frances rivers to the source of the Pelly, down the Pelly to the Lewes (Yukon), thence up the last river and across Chilkoot Pass. R. G. McConnell surveyed the Stikine and Lower Liard, wintered on the Mackenzie River, then descended it to

15. Dall to J. B. Moore, January 3, 1888, in ibid., pp. 3, 4.

16. C. S. Campbell, "The Anglo-American Crisis in the Bering Sea, 1890–1891," *Mississippi Valley Historical Review*, 48 (1961), 393–414. Campbell credits Henry Elliott with a pivotal role in the American acceptance of a temporary restriction of sealing. In 1891 opponents of restriction reiterated the charge that Elliott was motivated by financial ties to the Alaska Commercial Company, which had lost the seal lease in 1890.

17. Fourth Annual Message, December 3, 1888, in Richardson, *Compilation*, 11, 5366.

18. T. C. Mendenhall, "Boundary Line," p. 2.

19. Dawson, "Historical Note on Events in the Yukon District, Northwest Territories," *Rev of Historical Publications Relating to Canada*, 2 (1897), 182.

the delta and crossed over to the Porcupine, on which he traveled down to the Yukon. The third phase was in charge of William Ogilvie, who carried an instrumental traverse from Pyramid Island in Chilkat Inlet along the Yukon to the 141st meridian, where he established winter quarters and an observatory.[20]

The Canadian endeavor was the first systematic series of instrumental traverses to cover so wide an area in the northwest corner of the continent. The Canadians were also interested in economic geology and metereology. Dawson's report contained notes on vegetation, Indians, and zoology, as well as his specialty, geology. Ogilvie's work was made available to American geodesists; one C&GS party even occupied the Canadian's winter quarters and observatory on the Yukon.[21]

The two American parties were more elaborately equipped and staffed than their Canadian counterparts, but operations were, with one exception, limited to astronomical observations and to triangulation and topographical surveys immediately adjacent to the two camps, one on the Porcupine and one on the Yukon, where the rivers cross the 141st meridian. J. E. McGrath was in charge on the Yukon and J. H. Turner on the Porcupine.[22] Turner made the only foray of any distance away from camp. With one companion, he sledded from his base on the Porcupine straight north along the meridian to the Arctic Ocean. The journey was a rapid reconnaissance made with minimal supplies plus, Turner whimsically admitted, "a modicum of alcohol stowed away in the event of snake bite."[23] McGrath and Turner conducted the first geodetic surveys in Alaska's interior, and also kept valuable meteorological and magnetic records.[24]

20. Ibid., pp. 182, 183. Dawson, "Report of an Exploration in the Yukon District," p. 6B. McConnell, "Report of an Exploration in the Yukon and Mackenzie Basins, N.W.T.," *Annual Report of the Geological and Natural History Survey of Canada, 1888–89*, n.s. 3, 7D. Ogilvie, *Information Respecting the Yukon District from the Reports of Wm Ogilvie and from Other Sources* (Ottawa, 1897), pp. 10–13.

21. Ogilvie, *Early Days on the Yukon: The Story of Its Gold Fields* (London, 1913), pp. 60, 61.

22. T. C. Mendenhall, J. E. McGrath, and J. W. Turner, "Alaska Boundary Survey," *NGM*, 4 (February 8, 1893), 179, 180. A. B. Schanz, "The Alaska Boundary Survey," *Harper's Weekly*, 35 (September 12, 1891), 699, 700. A. H. Brooks, *Geography and Geology of Alaska*, p. 125.

23. Turner, in Mendenhall, McGrath, and Turner, "Alaska Boundary Survey," p. 197.

24. McGrath, Turner, and C. A. Schott, "Results of Magnetic Observations . . . ," USC&GS, *Annual Report, 1892*, Pt. 2, pp. 529, 533.

The few markers located on the Yukon by the USC&GS and by the Canadian survey did not of course solve the boundary controversy. The surveys on the 141st meridian were conducted independently, and the southeastern line had yet to be located. In 1892 the two governments signed a convention to delimit jointly the southeastern boundary.[25] Astronomical stations were established at the mouths of principal rivers flowing over the line, triangulation nets were run up the valleys, and topographical sketches were prepared.[26] The co-operative effort was so successful that Britishers and Americans urged another joint commission of experts to establish the location of the 141st meridian.[27]

The surveys were necessary to any clear settlement of the controversy, but the interpretation of treaties written before the surveys were undertaken kept the issue alive. T. C. Mendenhall, of the Coast and Geodetic Survey, observed grumpily in 1896 that boundary treaties were "usually framed by politicians rather than by geographers; the advice of the latter being often ignored."[28] Nevertheless, the scientists were as much in disagreement on the issue as the politicians. Dall and Dawson when consulted in 1888 took the position of their respective governments. George Davidson wrote a book on the subject; his conclusion was foursquare American.[29] The Canada-Alaska boundary controversy was a portent of twentieth-century developments, when science would become increasingly involved in political questions, and when scientist and politician would often fail or refuse to recognize the limit of the other's competency. That particular boundary question has yet to be negotiated.

A side benefit for science in 1889 came from the work of I. C. Russell, who accompanied the Coast and Geodetic teams to Alaska as "geological attaché." On an invitation extended to the USGS, and through the courtesy of the Alaska Commercial Company, Russell traveled free of charge to Fort Yukon, up the Porcupine and back, then from Fort Yukon upriver to Chilkoot Pass. It was Schwatka's route in reverse, parts of which had been

25. Barker and Charlton, "Compilation of the Acts of Congress and Treaties Relating to Alaska," pp. 40–43.

26. T. C. Mendenhall, "Alaska Boundary Line," *Atlantic*, 77 (1896), p. 524.

27. Lord Gough to Olney, August 20, 1895, *Foreign Relations* (1895), p. 723. Richard Olney to Sir Julian Paunceforte, March 11, 1896, ibid. (1896), pp. 291, 292. Cleveland's Third Annual Message, in Richardson, *Compilation*, 12, 6063, 6064.

28. "Alaska Boundary Line," p. 519.

29. *The Alaska Boundary* (San Francisco, 1903).

covered the previous year by Ogilvie, McConnell, and Dawson. Though only a summer reconnaissance on a well traveled path, the excursion permitted Russell to gather notes on the surface geology of the Yukon Valley. He questioned Muir's generalization that the entire Bering Sea region had been occupied by a vast continental glacier during the glacial epoch, and he confirmed Dall's conclusion that the central and northern parts of Alaska, like a large portion of the Northwest Territory as reported by Dawson and McConnell, had not been affected by glaciation in recent geological times. Mammoth remains in Alaska, Russell observed, were found in regions not glaciated during the Pleistocene; this corresponded to the situation in Siberia. N. S. Shaler and T. C. Chamberlain agreed that Russell's brief report had a "very important bearing on our general conceptions of the Pleistocene period."[30] The next year Russell continued his glaciological investigation south of the Alaska Range at Mt. St. Elias.

While Congress debated the wisdom of the Army's plan to explore the interior of Alaska, private enterprise stepped into the breach. Expeditions financed by *Leslie's Illustrated Newspaper,* in 1890 and 1891, were designed to capture the imagination and subscriptions of American periodical readers. Basic geographical research into the unknown opportunities of the country, announced as the reason for the exploration, was actually an incidental consideration: the editors wanted exciting copy. *Leslie's* hinted: "It is not unlikely that the result will be second only to that of Stanley's explorations in Africa."[31] Steps were taken to guarantee the hoped-for result: the executive officer and artist of the expedition was E. J. Glave, who had been with Stanley in Africa. E. H. Wells was chief of the operation and A. B. Schanz was "astronomer and historian." A photographer, a scout, and three "frontiersmen" made up the balance of the original party.

A further element of drama was introduced with the rumor that Heywood W. Seton-Karr's English expedition proposed to "race" the Leslie party to Chilkat and enter the St. Elias Mountains ahead of the American

30. Russell, "Notes on the Surface Geology of Alaska," *Bulletin of the Geological Society of America, I* (1890), 155, 103, 123, 137, 138. Russell, "Yukon River," *JAGS, 22* (1890), p. 140. Russell, "A Journey up the Yukon River," *JAGS, 27* (1895), 143.

31. *Leslie's,* April 5, 1890. The explorations were reported in over forty issues of the periodical during the years 1890 and 1891: E. H. Wells, E. J. Glave, and A. B. Schanz, "The Leslie Expedition to Alaska, 1890–1891," *Leslie's,* 70–73 (1890–1891).

group.[32] Seton-Karr arrived first, but he awaited the newspapermen in order to divide up the interior routes.[33] The Englishman turned back after penetrating the Alpine region a short distance by way of the Chilkat River.[34]

The Leslie expedition also entered via the Chilkat. Krause's Kusawa Lake in Canada was first explored. Here Glave and Jack Dalton, one of the "frontiersmen," left the party and crossed a divide to the upper Alsek River, a young, violent stream which they descended to the Pacific Ocean. Glave's narrative was the first to appear in print.[35] The narrative must have given heart to *Leslie's* editor, for the achievement was a daring, exciting exploration of a river until then entirely unknown. In the spring of 1891 Glave returned to the Alsek region and again with Dalton explored the area, this time using pack horses[36] and penetrating to Kluane Lake in the White River Basin. Glave, a restless individual, eventually lost his life in the Congo; his partner in the Far Northwest pioneered the famous Dalton Trail of Gold Rush days.

Meanwhile in 1890 Wells, Schanz, and the remainder of the Leslie party proceeded from Kusawa Lake to the Yukon and down it to Fortymile River, the scene of recent gold strikes. Wells turned off and Schanz continued downriver. From the old Russian post of St. Michael, in the company of one William Greenfield, Schanz traveled by canoe to a Russian mission on the Yukon and portaged to the Kuskokwim, which he descended to the coast; then by portages and coasting he arrived at Nushagak in October.

Wells and two white men began an ascent of the Fortymile that took them to the Tanana and across it to Tok River. Rude sketch maps were made en route.[37] Wells then traveled down the Tanana to the Yukon and St. Michael and followed Schanz' route to Nushagak, where the two men

32. Ibid., April 12 and May 17, 1890.

33. Sitka *Alaskan*, June 28, 1890.

34. Seton-Karr, "Explorations in Alaska and North-west British Columbia," RGS, *Proceedings*, n.s. *13* (1891), 65–86.

35. Wells, Glave, and Schanz, "The Leslie Expedition," *Leslie's*, September 6, 1890. Glave's report appeared in nine parts: November 15, 22, 29 and December 6, 13, 20, 27, 1890, and January 3 and 10, 1891.

36. Glave, "Pioneer Packhorses in Alaska," *Century*, *44* (September 1892), 671–82, and *64* (October 1892), 869–81.

37. Wells, "Up and Down the Yukon," in *Compilation of Narratives*, p. 513.

were reunited. In January of 1891 Wells crossed the Alaska Peninsula to Katmai and from there returned to the States.[38]

Schanz began a more important exploration on January 29, the day after Wells left Nushagak. With John W. Clark, a trader, and Innokente Shiskin, a young Russian, Schanz ascended the Nushagak and Mulchatna rivers and sledded to Lake Clark, which he named and placed definitely on the map, though its existence had long been known from Indian reports. Schanz returned to Bristol Bay and portaged across the Alaska Peninsula to Katmai in the first part of March 1891.[39]

The Leslie expedition stimulated interest in the Far Northwest and in Alaskan exploration. Over forty reports and articles on the expedition appeared in the sponsoring journal alone, and other newspaper explorations were projected. From the Leslie reports, one periodical noted with surprise that the opportunities for exploration in North America were as tempting as those in Africa.[40]

The actual geographic and scientific accomplishments of Wells, Glave, and Schanz were disproportionate to the publicity their exploits received. Original geographical investigations were limited to Glave's run down the Alsek of Canada, Wells' examination of a small area near the upper Tanana, and Schanz' investigation of the Lake Clark region. Although the over-all enterprise was aided by the New York Museum of Natural History and officials of the Coast and Geodetic Survey, few contributions were made either to science or to cartography. Nor was the undertaking as systematic as the final itinerary may suggest. Judging from the plans reported and the routes followed, numerous major decisions were made hastily in the field, decisions that resulted in less important work: early plans, for example, had called for a thorough exploration of the White River Basin and the St. Elias Mountains.[41] The Army exploratory plan of 1890 may have been abandoned because the Leslie party came first into the field, but the abandonment was a mistake.

38. Wells, Glave, and Schanz, "The Leslie Expedition," *Leslie's*, June 20, 1891. Wells' narrative appeared in nine parts: July 4, 11, 18, 25, August 1, 8, 29, September 5, 19, 1891.

39. Ibid., June 20, 1891. Schanz' narrative appears in *Leslie's*, September 26, October 3, 10, 17, 24, 31, November 7, 28, 1891. Also, A. B. Schanz, MS, Historical Documents, USGS Files.

40. Wells, Glave, and Schanz, "The Leslie Expedition," *Leslie's*, June 20, 1891.

41. Ibid., April 26 and August 16, 1890.

A second expedition financed by the private press, sponsored by a syndicate of some fifty newspapers, was organized in 1891 by Frederick Schwatka, the perennial publicist-explorer of Alaska.[42] The director of the Geological Survey was asked for a geologist, and the assignment was given to C. Willard Hayes, an assistant of I. C. Russell in the southern Appalachians. Hayes was a highly trained, acute observer.[43] The party entered Canada by the Taku River, crossed the divide to Teslin Lake, and, unfolding portable canoes, boated down the Teslin River to the Yukon and old Fort Selkirk. From Selkirk the men crossed to the White River, which they ascended to the headwaters in Skolai Pass, a short portage to the upper Chitina River. At Taral the expedition was joined by Allen's old Indian acquaintance, Nikolai, who traveled with the party down the Copper River to the coast. The trip was completed in one season.[44]

In terms of original discovery, natural obstacles, and contributions to science, this 1891 expedition was the most notable journey Frederick Schwatka made in Alaska, though it received less publicity than any other because Schwatka died before he could publish the results. To Hayes must go much of the credit for success: he definitely confirmed old reports of copper deposits en route;[45] his report included notes on topography, vegetation, geology, mineral resources, and volcanic and glacial phenomena; and his map, though based on a rapid foot traverse made under difficult conditions, was later found "remarkably complete and accurate."[46] Hayes' work is another example of a professional government scientist making a privately sponsored exploration more than just an adventure designed to titillate the reading public.

Toward the end of the period 1886–1896, the interest of the U.S. Geological Survey in Alaska quickened. In 1895 the Survey was ordered to report on the gold and coal resources of Alaska; $5,000 was appropriated for the study. G. F. Becker suggested that William H. Dall join him. The latter specialized in coal resources, the former in gold. The geologists spent a month in Southeastern working off the Naval steamer

42. Schwatka to the Secretary of the Navy, March 19, 1891, NA, RG 45.

43. *DAB*, 8, 444.

44. Hayes, "An Expedition through the Yukon District," *NGM*, 4 (May 15, 1892), 117–62.

45. A. H. Brooks, "The Copper Deposits of the White, Tanana, and Copper River Regions of Alaska," *Engineering and Mining Journal*, 74 (1902), 13.

46. Brooks, *Blazing Alaska's Trails*, p. 282.

Pinta, then hopped the mail boat to Kodiak, where they chartered a small tug for work around Kodiak, on the Alaska Peninsula, and among the Aleutian Islands. Investigations of mineral deposits were now and then interrupted for more exciting geological pursuits: Becker climbed the volcano St. Augustine in Cook Inlet, and a side trip was made to the new volcanic island of Bogoslof in Bering Sea.[47]

The following year another $5,000 appropriation financed a mineral survey of the Yukon gold regions by Josiah Edward Spurr, Harold B. Goodrich, and F. C. Schrader. They reached the diggings from Juneau, traveling across Chilkoot Pass and down the Yukon, and examined placers at Fortymile, Birch Creek, and other early workings.[48]

Dall and Becker in 1895 and Spurr and Goodrich in 1896 studied known mineral areas, some being actively mined and others where work had been discontinued, and investigated still others that had only been reported. Some general geology was done. The Director of the Geological Survey reported in 1896 that sufficient data were secured "to establish the presence of a gold belt 300 miles in length in Alaska." He incidentally recommended that the USGS Alaskan budget estimate of $2,500 for fiscal year 1897–1898 be increased to $25,000.[49] The superintendent's recommendation was made in the fall of 1896, when George Washington Carmack found gold in the Klondike, but before the significance of the strike was apparent in the States.

47. Becker, "Reconnaissance of the Gold Fields of Southern Alaska, with some Notes on General Geology," USGS, *Eighteenth Annual Report, 1896–97*, Pt. 3, pp. 1–86. Dall, "Geographical Notes on Alaska," *JAGS*, 28 (1896), 1–20. Dall, "Report on Coal and Lignite of Alaska," USGS, *Seventeenth Annual Report, 1895–96*, pp. 763–875.

48. Spurr and Goodrich, "Geology of the Yukon Gold District, Alaska," USGS, *Eighteenth Annual Report, 1896–97*, Pt. 3, pp. 87–392.

49. C. D. Wolcott to Secretary of the Interior, November 24, 1896, in U.S. Treasury Department, "Investigation of Coal and Gold Resources of Alaska," *House Document 171, 54th Congress: 2d session* (3524), 2.

10. Marking the Map's Void Spaces: The Gold Rush

Have you marked the map's void spaces, mingled
with the mongrel races . . .?

ROBERT SERVICE, "The Call of the Wild"

ROBERT SERVICE—now more often maligned than quoted by belletrists
—was more than a rough-and-ready rhymester of the Yukon Gold Rush.
He was the articulate spokesman of a real or imagined older, bolder frame
of mind that revolted against the mundane confines of a daily wage. The
revolt followed an extensive period of economic distress and political fer-
mentation that eventually boiled over into rude and heartless, though
brief, overseas expansionism. The Gold Rush was symptomatic of what
Richard Hofstadter calls a national "psychic crisis," the ultimate expression of which came in the "splendid little war" with Spain and the im-
perialism that followed. Expansionism in the late nineteenth century was
partly a revival of the moving force behind the Western Union Telegraph
Expedition and the purchase of Alaska itself. Now, after the doldrums,
Americans who could no longer obey the spirit of the injunction to "go
West, young man" could and did "go northwest." The going as well as
the gold was a vital element in the Klondike stampede: not the gold but
the getting there was a harvest in self-realization that an Emerson could
appreciate. Pierre Berton writes: "To thousands of others the Klondike
also became a sort of symbol. They strove to reach it as a matter of personal honor."[1]

The gold was found before Carmack's 1896 strike on the Klondike (a
stream which, incidentally, Schwatka had tried to rename). In 1895
Alaska itself produced over $800,000 from placers, mainly on the Yukon,
and $1,725,000 in lode gold.[2] Even in 1890 a knowledgeable writer in a

1. *The Klondike Fever* (New York, 1959), p. 432.
2. P. S. Smith, *Past Placer-gold Production from Alaska*, USGS Bulletin 857-B
(Washington, 1933), p. 96. Smith, *Past Lode-gold Production from Alaska*, USGS
Bulletin 917-C (Washington, 1941), p. 180.

national magazine could aver: "The truth is, that hundreds of thousands
of intelligent Americans are profoundly ignorant of the fact that some of
the largest and most profitable gold mining enterprises within the limits
of the United States are conducted in Alaska."[3] The author had in mind
particularly the Treadwell stamp mill at Juneau, which Becker found pro-
ducing half a million dollars in gold annually from low-grade ore aver-
aging only $2.50 to $3.00 a ton.[4]

By 1890 there were prospectors in the interior too. A southern pass
was probably crossed in 1875 or 1878 by a lone adventurer,[5] but the route
from southeastern Alaska was not effectively opened to prospectors until
1880. In that year the Navy's Beardslee negotiated with the Indians for
permission for nineteen miners to cross Chilkoot Pass over a trail controlled by the Chilkat-Chilkoot Tlingits, who jealously guarded the route
and their trade monopoly with the inland natives. The nineteen miners
were escorted into Chilkat country by a military detachment. The officer in
charge collected natural history specimens, and Marcus Baker of the Coast
and Geodetic Survey accompanied the party with a sextant, artificial horizon, and dip-circle.[6] The operation combined new and old elements of
westward expansion: the not uncommon North American obstacle of
hostile Indian middlemen, a military escort for independent civilian frontiersmen, an officer collecting specimens along the way, and a federal civilian scientist.

Prospectors also penetrated the Yukon Valley from the river's mouth.
One party led by Edward Schieffelin, the discoverer of Tombstone, Arizona, came north in 1882 with its own little steamer. J. A. Jacobsen, who
traveled upriver with the group, returned with ethnological treasures, but
the mining party failed to strike it rich. After one season Schieffelin sold

3. J. H. Keatley, "The Gold Fields of Alaska," p. 730.
4. G. F. Becker, "Distribution of Gold Deposits in Alaska," *JG*, 3 (1895), 960.
5. C. G. (George) Holt apparently crossed the pass to the Upper Yukon in that
year, or about then. The extent of Holt's wanderings in the Far Northwest is vague.
For a starter see M. P. Berry on Holt in *Weekly Astorian*, Oregon, October 16, 1875;
W. R. Quinan, "Discoverer of the Yukon Gold Fields," *Overland Monthly*, ser. 2, 30
(1897), 340–42; G. M. Dawson, "Report of an Exploration in the Yukon District,"
p. 179B; H. T. Allen, *Report of an Expedition*, p. 23; L. D. Kitchener, *Flag*, pp. 155,
156; and Brooks, *Blazing Alaska's Trails*, pp. 321, 322.
6. L. A. Beardslee, "Reports Relative to Affairs in Alaska," *Senate Executive Document* 71, pp. 59–65.

his boat and abandoned the country.[7] Others came after him. On the Alaskan Yukon, placers were found on Franklin Creek, followed by strikes in the Fortymile region, on Birch Creek, and near Rampart. By 1896 the river's mining population numbered about 1,000.[8] To service the new immigrants, seven steamers were operating on the river in 1896.[9] The Alaska Commercial Company's Yukon monopoly was challenged again, this time successfully, by the North American Transportation and Trading Company, organized in 1892 by John J. Healy and backed in part by the Cudahy family of Chicago.[10] Independent or "free" traders who had located on the river at an early date received supplies from the A.C. Company and in payment transferred gold dust and fur to the Company.[11] Among the free traders, L. N. McQuesten, Arthur Harper, and Al Mayo were particularly influential in the development of the Yukon Valley. All three came to the region from the east rather than by way of Chilkoot or the Yukon delta. Over the years they established trading posts, operated Schieffelin's steamer, and prospected the river and its tributaries, in and out of Canada. An A.C. Company man who knew the trio described them as "typically frontiersmen, absolutely honest, without a semblance of fear of anything, and to a great extent childlike in their implicit faith in human nature, looking on their fellow pioneers as being equally as honest as themselves."[12] McQuesten preferred trading, Mayo captained the group's small river boat, and Harper roamed and prospected. The latter, according to Alfred Hulse Brooks, was the first to appreciate fully the Yukon's mineral potential and the first to advertise the area through personal letters to the placer camps of British Columbia.[13]

Individual prospectors worked elsewhere in the territory. One was on the Kobuk with Cantwell and Stoney. Bremner, who had accompanied Allen, was murdered by Koyukuk natives in 1888. The Kuskokwim

7. Schieffelin, "Trip to Alaska," typescript MS, Bancroft Library.

8. Brooks, "History of Mining in Alaska," *Alaska-Yukon Magazine, 8* (1909), 150.

9. W. R. Siddall, "The Yukon Waterway in the Development of Interior Alaska," *PHR, 28* (1959), 366.

10. W. Ogilvie, *Early Days on the Yukon*, p. 68. Kitchener, *Flag*, pp. 92, 93.

11. Stewart Menzies, letter to C. L. Andrews, April 14, 1916, typescript MS, Andrews Collection, Sheldon Jackson Junior College, Sitka.

12. Stewart Menzies, quoted in C. L. Andrews, "Some Notes on the Yukon by Stewart Menzies," *PNQ, 32* (1941), 200.

13. *Blazing Alaska's Trails*, p. 317.

River was prospected as early as 1883, and parts of the Nushagak Basin in 1890. By 1892 mining districts had been organized on Cook Inlet, Kodiak, and the Alaska Peninsula, among other places.

The progress of geographical science was advanced but little in spite of all this activity.[14] The role of the Alaskan trader in exploration differs markedly from the previous American experience. Most of the early exploration in the first wave of westward expansion from the Atlantic seaboard was impelled by competition among colonial traders. The "discovery" of Cumberland Gap by Thomas Walker and the journey of Christopher Gist into the Ohio Valley were guided by Indian traders—either personally, or by previous instruction, or by recognition of trails and blazes.[15] Effective exploration of the Rockies was similarly the work of the colorful "Mountain Men," fur traders who explored every corner of the range and marked trails in the Far West. John C. Fremont, a government explorer, was guided by Kit Carson and Joseph Walker. By contrast, Alaskan traders conducted almost no original explorations. Though the Far Northwest found "men to match her mountains," there were no Mountain Men to guide the official explorers of the land. (A striking exception is Lukeen's service with the Telegraph Expedition during the Russian period.)

Although the prospectors traveled more widely than the traders, their contribution to geographical knowledge—as Brooks has indicated—also "is entirely disproportionate to the sacrifices of time and energy and often of human life which they have made."[16] Prospectors had two goals: to discover pay dirt and to pass safely through the country. "The information obtained by them is seldom exact, even when available," Brooks observed,

14. Stoney, "Explorations in Alaska," p. 824. Brooks, *Blazing Alaska's Trails*, p. 332. George Marks, "Trip Down the Yukon in 1883," typescript MS, from a conversation with C. L. Andrews, Andrews Collection. J. E. Spurr, "A Reconnaissance in Southwestern Alaska in 1898," USGS, *Twentieth Annual Report, 1898–99*, Pt. 7, p.96. L. E. Knapp, "Report, Oct. 1, 1892," in Governor of Alaska, *Reports*, 1, 43. The history of mining in Alaska-Yukon during the nineteenth century has captured the attention of numerous writers. Reliable accounts appear in the works of Brooks, of which the most readily available is *Blazing Alaska's Trails*, pp. 296–398. Pierre Berton's brilliantly written *Klondike Fever* is the best single account of the Gold Rush.

15. J. B. Brebner, *The Explorers of North America* (New York, 1955; originally published in 1933), pp. 219, 261.

16. "A Reconnaissance in the White and Tanana River Basins, Alaska, in 1898," p. 436.

"for their conception of where they have been is often as vague as their ideas as to where they are going."[17] The prospector took no notes (again according to Brooks), seldom even compass bearings.[18] In general, he carried no instruments and would not have known how to use them if he had; he was disinclined to carry them if furnished and probably would not have used them if instructed.[19] Consequently, the maps he might (if coaxed) draw from memory were often but slightly, if at all, more sophisticated than Indian sketches. Prospectors were occasionally reluctant to disseminate what little geographic knowledge they possessed if it meant competition for gold. Frequently, the prospector had no idea how to use a map, although this did not always prevent him from loud condemnation of existing charts.[20] In a word, if the prospector did make an original exploration, and if he could or would communicate his information, the results were of little practical use to geographers and of almost no use to science.

By further comparison with the Mountain Men and cis-Mississippi traders, the prospectors in the Far Northwest—especially prior to the Gold Rush—undertook hardly any original geographical journeys. There were of course exceptions, but few were notable; when they were, the matter of precision and availability of the information must be raised. Scarcely any records of original discovery by prospectors are available to the historian, and fewer still were available to the government explorer. Around 1889 Frank Densmore and about the same time Al King probably explored the Kuskokwim River, crossing to its headwaters from a southern tributary of the Tanana. Harper almost certainly examined the lower White and lower Tanana, and McQuesten a part of the Koyukuk.[21] These and other trips, scantily documented or unrecorded altogether, were no less difficult because they were not adequately reported. As Hayes wrote of a journey by Mark Russell, who had guided the Schwatka party

17. *Geography and Geology of Alaska*, p. 127. In this passage Brooks goes on to say that the prospector has "blazed the way" for the settler and explorer. The phrase must be rhetorical.

18. "Reconnaissance in the White and Tanana River Basins," p. 436.

19. C. W. Hayes, "An Expedition through the Yukon District," p. 119.

20. W. C. Mendenhall, "Reconnaissance from Resurrection Bay to the Tanana River, Alaska, in 1898," p. 288.

21. Brooks, "Geography of Alaska," *NGM*, *15* (1904), 215. Brooks, *Blazing Alaska's Trails*, p. 328. J. E. Spurr, "Journal, 1898," MS, USGS Files.

of 1891 along the Taku: "Less arduous or novel expeditions have brought fame to explorers better versed in the art of advertising than these unassuming miners."[22] (Hayes may have had Schwatka in mind.)

Beginning about 1896, it became commonplace for an explorer to learn he had been upstreamed by a prospector, especially in the Susitna-Chulitna basin. A mining party is said to have traveled up the Yentna, a tributary of the Susitna, in 1887, and in 1895 two prospectors apparently got as far as the Chulitna fork.[23] In 1896, W. A. Dickey led a small party up the Susitna to the forks. He probably went no more than fifty miles or so farther, but he reported information from prospectors who had traveled a distance up the Talkeetna (East Fork) and Chulitna (West Fork). As a Princeton graduate, Dickey was "better versed in the art of advertising" his exploits. Accounts of his journey appeared in the New York *Sun* and in the *National Geographic Magazine* for 1897.[24]

The trip is of additional interest because it was Dickey who named the continent's highest peak, which he estimated correctly to be over 20,000 feet. Though Dickey called attention to the mountain, he did not discover it. The Russians knew of its existence, and Cook Inlet Indians used the Russian name "Bulshaia"; interior natives called the peak "Denali," and prospectors called it "Densmore's Peak" and "Mt. Allen."[25] To this magnificent natural wonder, the monarch of North American mountains, Dickey gave the name "McKinley," after William McKinley, the Republican nominee for president; (the direct alternative, "Mt. Bryan," would hardly have been an improvement). After allowing his poetic imagination to soar in naming this crown of the Alaska Range, Dickey climbed Mt. Susitna near the river's delta and "confirmed" the "total absence" of the Alaska Range as marked on government charts.[26]

Generalization about the comparatively minor role played by prospectors as guides or sources of information for the official explorers of the ter-

22. "Expedition through the Yukon District," p. 119.

23. J. E. Spurr, "A Reconnaissance in Southwestern Alaska in 1898," USGS, *Twentieth Annual Report, 1898–99*, Pt. 7, p. 94.

24. "Discoveries in Alaska," New York *Sun*, January 24, 1897; and "The Sushitna River, Alaska," *NGM*, 8 (1897), 322–27.

25. Brooks, *Blazing Alaska's Trails*, p. 292. Brooks, "An Exploration to Mount McKinley, America's Highest Mountain," *JG*, 2 (1903), 443. C. L. Andrews, "Some Notes on the Yukon," p. 202. J. E. Spurr, "Reconnaissance in Southwestern Alaska," p. 48.

26. New York *Sun*, January 24, 1897.

ritory does not mean the Alaska-Yukon prospectors and traders played no role at all. Allen was better able to judge his chances for success after collecting information and intelligent geographical guesses from prospectors and traders, though he was not "guided" by the information. He was accompanied by Peder Johnson and Bremner, neither of whom had been above Taral. Allen became thoroughly convinced that prospectors were the most capable class of men available for wilderness duty.[27] During the Gold Rush, the prospector's contribution to exploration increased measurably. Army and Geological Survey explorers mined the miners for data about the country. Prospectors were hired to accompany various expeditions, and even when the gold-seeker had not actually traveled the route before, he often proved invaluable for his wilderness wisdom. H. H. Hicks, for example, did outstanding work for the E. F. Glenn expedition. Oscar Rohn, topographer on the Abercrombie expedition of 1899, could not induce members of the regular party to accompany him on one leg of his exploration and relied on the assistance of a young prospector.[28] And there are other examples.

The northern pioneer's record in science was not blank. One trader supplied the Canadian Geological Survey with mammoth remains used by George Dawson in his study of that extinct animal.[29] American traders manned meteorological instruments for the Signal Service. Mayo, Harper, and McQuesten gathered census information for Petroff.[30] E. W. Nelson received many upriver specimens and natural history data from Harper and McQuesten, including the sheep Nelson named after Dall. Harper took the opportunity his travels afforded to collect. Once, when he was away on a trapping expedition with Mayo, Indians broke into his quarters and uncovered some arsenic supplied by the Smithsonian for preservation purposes. Mistaking it for flour, the natives promptly cooked up a mess of flapjacks; the result was a collection of sick anthropological specimens.[31] The Gold Rush period saw an increase in the collection of scientific ma-

27. Allen, in *Compilation of Narratives*, p. 478.

28. Rohn, "A Reconnaissance of the Chitina River and the Skolai Mountains, Alaska," USGS, *Twenty-first Annual Report, 1899–1900*, Pt. 3, p. 399.

29. Dawson, "Notes on the Occurrence of Mammoth-remains in the Yukon District of Canada and Alaska," *Quarterly Journal of the Geological Society of London*, 50 (1894), 2.

30. Petroff, "Compendium of the Tenth Census—Alaska," page vi.

31. C. L. Andrews, "Some Notes on the Yukon," p. 198.

terials and information, some of it of special interest.[32] One wily prospector submitted to the Geological Survey a map drawn from compass bearings and the readings obtained from an odometric device attached to his
dog sled.[33]

By and large, the great gains to science and exploration came not from
amateurs but from professional scientists and explorers employed by the
federal government. That fact, however, in no way diminishes the courage
and daring of the prospectors and traders who ventured beyond the sea
coast or major rivers to face almost insurmountable natural barriers and
incredible hardships in the trailless interior.

The Rush focused world-wide attention on Alaska and lured many
nongold-seekers, political and civic figures, gentlemen scientists, and
sportsmen. The rushers themselves came from all parts of the United
States, Canada, and abroad. At the same time, government bureaus, some
new to Alaska, moved to fill the gaps in knowledge about the country and
to disseminate available data in their respective fields. The Bureau of
Navigation published a circular on navigational conditions on the Yukon
and Porcupine rivers.[34] The Labor Department issued bulletins on opportunities, prices, and problems of capital and labor in the gold fields.[35] And
at long last the Department of Agriculture promoted research by experts.

In light of the continual controversy over the territory's agricultural potential, it is a wonder that specialized investigations were not made earlier.
The first study devoted solely to the question was prepared by William
Dall in 1868 for the Commissioner of Agriculture. Dall's views were balanced and reasonable. He listed 118 species of useful indigenous Alaskan
plants, including grasses.[36] The Commissioner of the General Land Office,
using Dall's work, had high praise for Alaska's resources, but doubted
that its agricultural products would "soon attain such importance as to

32. For example, see M. L. Fernald, "Four Rare Plants from Alaska," *Ottawa
Naturalist, 13* (1899), 149.

33. F. J. Cuvier to J. E. Spurr, November 26, 1900, Historical Documents, USGS
Files.

34. Circular No. 24, Washington, 1898.

35. S. C. Dunham, *The Alaskan Gold Fields and the Opportunities They Offer for
Capital and Labor,* Department of Labor Bulletin No. 19 (Washington, November
1898); printed as *House Document 206, 55th Congress: 2d session,* Pt. 6, pp. 789–828.

36. Dall, "Report upon the Agricultural Resources of Alaska," in *Report of the
Commissioner of Agriculture, 1868* (Washington, 1869), pp. 187–89.

furnish any surplus." He estimated that sufficient arable land existed to provide farms for 150,000 families.[37] No further efforts by the Agricultural agency worth noting occurred until 1893. In that year, Frederick Funston—who had had some training in botany but was not a botanist—was commissioned to gather botanical specimens in the Yukon Valley. Entering the region over Chilkoot Pass, he wintered at Rampart House on the Porcupine River, and during that time he journeyed due north to the Arctic Ocean. For Funston, the Alaskan trip was mainly another opportunity for adventure in a long and adventurous career.[38]

The first serious attempt by the agency to evaluate the agricultural worth of the country came with the Gold Rush. For fiscal year 1898, $5,000 was appropriated for an investigation with special reference to the desirability of establishing experiment stations. Walter Evans, a botanist, and Benton Killin, a regent of Oregon Agricultural College, were appointed to visit the coast, and the peripatetic educator-missionary Sheldon Jackson was commissioned to examine the Yukon in connection with his annual inspection of reindeer stations and schools. Some collecting was done, and a few soil samples were sent back for analysis. From the report on their investigations came a recommendation that $15,000 be appropriated for further work and for the maintenance of experiment stations.[39]

The real pioneer of agricultural research in Alaska was C. C. Georgeson, a Dane, who did not conclude *a priori* that high latitudes automatically eliminated the possibility of soil cultivation. Georgeson was made special agent of the Agriculture Department with headquarters at Sitka. By 1900 he had surveyed plots for stations at Sitka, Kenai, Kodiak, Fort

37. J. S. Wilson, "Report of the Commissioner of the General Land Office, the United States Territories on the North Pacific," in "Report of the Secretary of the Interior," *House Executive Document 1, 41st Congress: 2d session*, Pt. 3 (1414), 202.

38. Funston, "Frederick Funston's Alaskan Trip," *Harper's Weekly*, 39 (May 25, 1895), 492. C. S. Gleed, "Romance and Reality in a Single Life—Gen. Frederick Funston," *Cosmopolitan*, 27 (July 1899), 322–24. Funston, "Along Alaska's Eastern Boundary," *Harper's Weekly*, 40 (February 1, 1896), 103. Funston later engineered the capture of Emilio Aguinaldo in the Philippines.

39. Evans, Killin, and Jackson, *A Report to Congress on Agriculture in Alaska*, Department of Agriculture, Office of Experiment Stations Bulletin No. 48 (Washington, 1898), pp. 1–3. Killin advised against establishment of stations; see p. 34. Also Evans, "Some of the Conditions and Possibilities of Agriculture in Alaska," *NGM*, 9 (April 1898), 178–80.

Yukon, and Rampart, and had discovered by experimentation that the Romanov variety of wheat could be grown with fair success.[40] But the myth of the icebox was not easily discredited, and Georgeson's early reports were a favorite object of jest.[41] Americans still thought in Jeffersonian terms: no land incapable of supporting a population of independent yeomen farmers could be fit for settlement or home rule. Georgeson's contribution was to diminish the old notion that all Alaska was an Arctic wasteland totally inhospitable to farmers.[42]

The Agricultural Department's Biological Survey took a special interest in Alaskan fauna. The Survey before 1896 had been chiefly concerned with the economic relations of birds to insects and plants. Beginning about 1896, biological explorations of North America became the bureau's main activity,[43] and in the summer of 1899 Wilfred Osgood and Louis Bishop carried the Biological Survey's investigation to the Yukon. The scientists concentrated on the Upper Yukon, an "absolutely virgin field." Nine new species and subspecies were described.[44] The next season Osgood studied the Cook Inlet district, where he identified twenty-four mammals and seventy-seven birds.[45]

The military agencies vied for police authority as well as for exploration duties. Stoney urged Naval supervision on the Yukon, with Marine garrisons and a river steamer. Though Cantwell's Revenue Service got

40. Georgeson, "Agricultural Experiments in Alaska" in "Yearbook of the U.S. Department of Agriculture, 1898," *House Executive Document 293, 55th Congress: 3d session* (3824), 523. Georgeson and Evans, *A Second Report to Congress on Agriculture in Alaska,* Department of Agriculture, Office of Experiment Stations Bulletin No. 62 (Washington, 1899), p. 2. Georgeson, *Fourth Report on the Agricultural Investigations in Alaska, 1900,* Department of Agriculture, Office of Experiment Stations Bulletin No. 94 (Washington, 1901), pp. 16, 17. Also, *Report on the Agricultural Investigations in Alaska in 1899,* Department of Agriculture, Office of Experiment Stations Bulletin No. 82 (Washington, 1900).

41. Brooks, "Value of Alaska," *Geographical Review, 15* (1925), 34.

42. Georgeson, "The Possibilities of Alaska," *NGM, 13* (March 1902), 81–85.

43. J. Cameron, *The Bureau of Biological Survey,* Institute for Government Research Service Monograph of U.S. Government No. 54 (Baltimore, 1929), pp. 22–32.

44. Osgood and Bishop, *Results of a Biological Reconnaissance of the Yukon River Region,* pp. 7, 8, 19.

45. Osgood, *Natural History of the Queen Charlotte Islands, British Columbia; Natural History of the Cook Inlet Region, Alaska,* Biological Survey of North American Fauna No. 21 (Washington, 1901), pp. 51–81.

the river boat, the Army was first to exert quasi-governmental functions on the river. Captain Patrick Henry Ray, who commanded the Point Barrow station during the International Polar Year, and who Dall had hoped would lead the expedition that was given to Allen,[46] was ordered to Alaska with Lieutenant W. P. Richardson in August of 1897—a move prompted by reports of disorder in the gold fields. The two officers were instructed to look into conditions and make appropriate recommendations; they were further charged to ascertain whether the winter food supply was sufficient to sustain the population.

In connection with the last duty, reports began to reach the States of impending starvation along the river. By December official opinion was aroused, and Congress appropriated $200,000 for relief, to be disbursed at the discretion of the Secretary of War. A unique plan conceived and directed by Sheldon Jackson was put into operation by the War Department. Jackson and an Army Officer proceeded to Scandinavia, where they purchased a herd of domestic reindeer, complete with sleds, harnesses, and Lap drivers. The strange cargo was brought to New York, shipped by rail to Seattle, and sent up to Alaska by boat. Meanwhile, before the animals got anywhere near the Yukon, the relief expedition was abandoned. New intelligence from the gold fields indicated that the earlier reports of impending famine had been exaggerated. Anyway, the Army had wearied of the whole reindeer experiment.[47] In retrospect, the scheme had elements of a gigantic, grotesque practical joke. Concern for the deer was one of Captain Ray's duties; there was talk of using the animals on the several exploring expeditions of 1898, and confusion about the reindeer's availability and utility delayed some of the explorations.

Ray recommended in 1897 the use of reindeer and soldiers to open a winter mail route from Cook Inlet via the Tanana to the Yukon. He planned to explore the country between the Gulf of Alaska and the Yukon that winter, if he were "able to obtain a sufficient number of dogs,"

46. Dall, "Proposed Explorations in Alaska," p. 154.
47. Ray, Richardson, et al., "Relief of the Destitute in Gold Fields," in *Compilation of Narratives*, pp. 497–501. This account is about the same as the official reports in Ray, Richardson, et al., "Relief of the People in the Yukon River Country," *House Executive Document 244, 55th Congress: 3d session* (3812). Both versions include Ray and Richardson, "Alaskan Gold Fields . . . ," *Senate Document 14, 55th Congress: 2d session* (3590).

but he never got around to it. Failing that, he hoped to make such exploration his "first work" should he remain in the territory;[48] he did remain, but made no exploration of the region. Ray was, however, instrumental in formulating the Army's justification for exploring the region between the Yukon and the Gulf in 1898, 1899, and 1900. Fearing commercial dependence on a British railroad to the Yukon Basin, Ray recommended that the government survey an "all-American route" north to the Tanana's mouth, from either Cook Inlet or Prince William Sound.[49] Congress decided to support the proposal. There was toward the end of the century a conspicuous political interest in Alaska, resulting in part perhaps from the wide origins of the stampeders.

Three Army expeditions were organized in 1898. The first was instructed to drive the reindeer north from southeastern Alaska, then to explore and mark trails from the Yukon to the Tanana. This phase of the operation was abandoned at the outbreak of war with Spain and the consequent demand for military personnel. A second expedition of some twenty men, commanded by William Ralph Abercrombie, was ordered to explore from Valdez to the Copper River and tributaries of the Tanana. The third expedition, slightly larger, under Captain Edwin Forbes Glenn was ordered first to Prince William Sound for the exploration of routes to the Copper and Susitna rivers, then to Cook Inlet. From the Inlet Glenn's party was to explore north from tidewater to one or more crossings of the Tanana.[50]

An anonymous commentator for the American Geographical Society saw in the explorations of 1898 evidence of the "stability of our Government" in the "calm indifference" with which plans were laid and executed in spite of demands of the Spanish war.[51] The war in fact had much to do with the outcome of the Army explorations that year, and their orderly execution. The expedition designed to explore south from the Yukon was abandoned. In southeastern Alaska, there was a train of pack animals in-

48. Ray to Adjutant General, September 15, 1897, in Ray and Richardson, "Relief," *Compilation of Narratives*, pp. 526, 527.

49. Ray to Adjutant General, October 7, 1897, in ibid., p. 534.

50. General Orders, March 16, 1898, in Glenn and Abercrombie, *Report of Explorations in the Territory of Alaska (Cooks Inlet, Sushitna, Copper, and Tanana Rivers) 1898*, pp. 5, 6. An abbreviated version of these reports is in *Compilation of Narratives*, pp. 561–709.

51. "Exploration of Central Alaska," *JAGS*, 30 (1898), 408.

tended for the transportation of relief stores, and when Glenn and Abercrombie learned that the reindeer allotted for their use were unfit, they requested the surplus pack mules; the officer in charge, however, had orders to ship the animals back to Seattle and would not release any of them.[52]

Abercrombie and Glenn proceeded to their posts at Valdez and Cook Inlet, where they dawdled in wait for pack animals. Abercrombie lost patience and returned to Seattle, where he requested permission to buy horses; in the meantime, pack mules had been sent north. "Explanation has been called for," his superior wrote of Abercrombie's action, "but it seems no justification is possible."[53] Abercrombie bought his pack horses and was ordered to return to Alaska immediately; his packtrain arrived on July 5. Since educated mules and horses were needed by the Army in Cuba, most of the horses were wild and needed breaking.[54]

Though a few parties were sent inland from Cook Inlet, Glenn also dallied. His men speculated on the possibility of his abandoning the work, something he threatened to do.[55] A geologist in the party asked of his journal: "Will Glenn come back or go on to Seattle?"[56] Men in both expeditions thought they had been forgotten by the powers to the south. Anxiety was heightened by the desire to participate in the fighting, such as it was. Glenn wrote: "That no authority was granted for returning to the United States to participate in the war with Spain, in which our regiments were engaged, augmented very much this universal feeling of despondency."[57]

William Abercrombie—who had vowed in 1884 never to return to Alaska—landed his oversized party at Valdez toward the end of April, and there he found seven feet of snow and hundreds of prospectors. The laborious task of unloading supplies, said Abercrombie, took up "one of the most trying nights that the expedition was to experience." Small parties were sent to scout the Valdez Glacier trail, then occupied by about 700 miners. One of the officers became snow blind and was led back to base

52. Glenn, in Glenn and Abercrombie, *Report of Explorations, 1898*, p. 12.

53. General Merriam to General Alger, June 3, 1898, AGO Files, NA, RG 94.

54. F. C. Schrader, "A Reconnaissance of a Part of Prince William Sound and the Copper River District, Alaska, in 1898," USGS, *Twentieth Annual Report, 1898–99*, Pt. 7, p. 354.

55. J. C. Castner, "Through Unknown Alaska," *Home Magazine*, 12 (1899), 520.

56. W. C. Mendenhall, "Journal, 1898," MS, USGS Files.

57. In Glenn and Abercrombie, *Report of Explorations, 1898*, p. 34.

camp. While Abercrombie had been in Seattle, topographical assistant Emil Mahlo and geologist F. C. Schrader had made topographic and geologic reconnaissances of some of the bays and islands of Prince William Sound. With Abercrombie's return, the expedition was split.

From Valdez, Schrader and Mahlo made a circuit comprising Klutina Lake and River and the Copper, Tasnuna, and Lowe Rivers. Coming down the Copper Valley on the west side, the Mahlo party fashioned a raft to cross the Tonsina River. When pushed out into the swift current, the craft was carried downstream. Two of the men, "apprehending danger," jumped for overhanging "sweepers." One made it; the other drowned. Others leaped from the runaway raft into the icy water and succeeded in reaching the banks. Schrader, Mahlo, two packers, and the cook remained aboard and eventually saved the cargo.[58]

Another party, a small one using pack horses, was led by Lieutenant P. G. Lowe, described by Abercrombie as "a man to be killed but not conquered." They traversed "in a bee line" the trail from Valdez to Mentasta Pass and the Tanana, following roughly Allen's old route. The trail through Mentasta Pass, Lowe remarked, was "well beaten" by prospectors. From the Tanana young Lowe continued in a northerly direction to the head of Sixtymile River, then over to Fortymile and down it to the Yukon. The trip was, he said, "a good-sized practice march, although by no means a picnic."[59]

Abercrombie got under way August 5 and reached Mentasta Pass by the same general route Lowe had followed. Abercrombie took a few bearings in the Pass, then returned south along Copper River. None of the separate journeys were "picnics." Abercrombie's account of one crossing of a glacial stream is illustrative.

> Prospectors and others who had attempted to cross the stream prior to my arrival had failed; but as I had already forded a number of very ugly-looking streams, and as it was absolutely necessary to cross this one if I went in via Lowe River, I disregarded all advice in the matter and rode my horse into the stream with a view of swimming it if it was too deep to ford, believing that if my horse could carry

58. Abercrombie, in ibid., pp. 299, 300. Schrader, "A Reconnaissance," pp. 350–54, 360, 361.
59. Lowe, in Glenn and Abercrombie, *Report of Explorations, 1898*, pp. 368, 382.

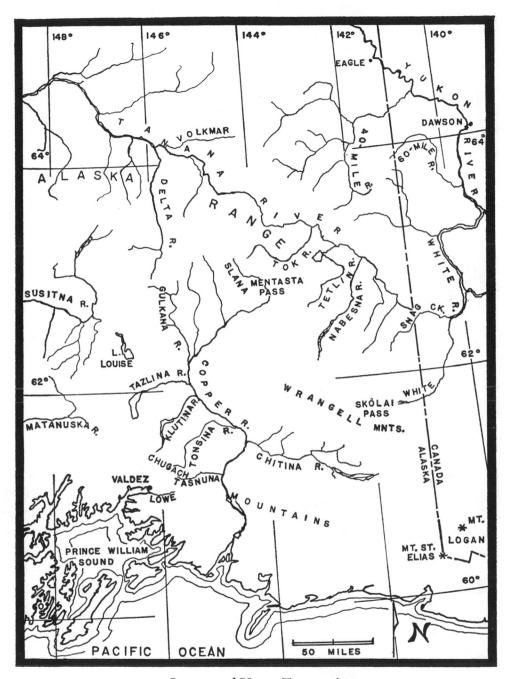

9. Copper and Upper Tanana rivers

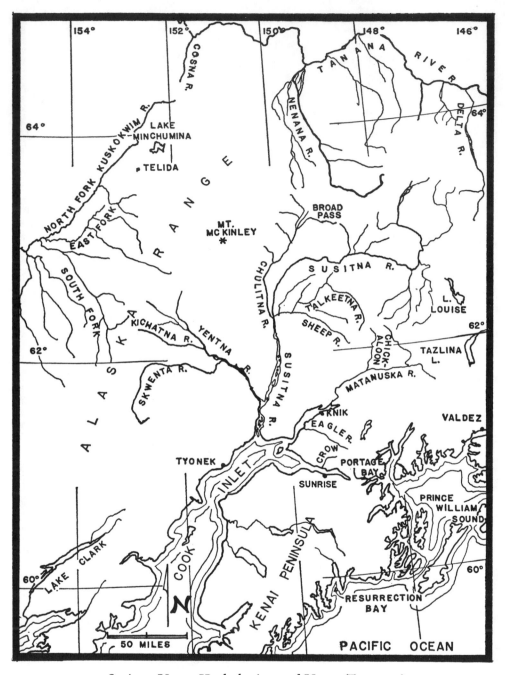

10. Susitna, Upper Kuskokwim, and Upper Tanana rivers

my weight (215 pounds), the pack animals, that I intended to load with but 150 pounds, could also cross. When in midstream I heard the bowlders being washed down the river bottom and knew that I was in serious trouble. I pushed on some 5 or 10 yards with the water up to my horse's shoulder, when the animal was struck by one of these bowlders, carried off his feet, and washed some 150 yards downstream, rolling over and over in the torrent, while I clung to his mane with my right hand, covering my head with the left. While struggling to gain a footing, the animal struck me on the left hand and head with one of his forefeet, mashing some of the bones of my left hand. At about the same time the horse lodged against a large rock with his feet uppermost, with my body pinned under him. I let go of the mane and grabbed the animal by the tail, when, minus my blankets and outfit, the horse scrambled up the bank and pulled me up with him. The water registered 35 degrees, so that when I reached the bank I was unable to stand.[60]

Leaving out the highly creditable work of Schrader and Mahlo inland and around Prince William Sound, the results of Abercrombie's Second Military Expedition of 1898 were not worth the hardships. Everywhere the soldier-explorers went they met prospectors or were preceded or accompanied by them. Abercrombie did get a good look at the country from the coast to the Tanana River. He recommended that the operation be continued in 1899. He believed a military trail could be built from Valdez to the Yukon for about $35,000; and a railroad, he reflected, was not only possible, but "a commercial proposition of great merit."[61]

Edwin Glenn's section proceeded first to Portage Bay (Whittier), where he found scores of miners encamped or en route over the short glacial portage to the Turnagain Arm of Cook Inlet. The stampeders at Valdez or inland, at Portage Bay, and at Cook Inlet knew the military expeditions carried some relief stores. Many believed, Glenn said, "that it was our duty to prevent them from committing improvident acts of all kinds . . . that we were to assume governmental powers of a most parental and charitable nature."[62]

After investigating the head of Portage Bay and the trail to Cook In-

60. Abercrombie, in ibid., p. 303.
61. Ibid., pp. 316, 349, 338.
62. Glenn, in ibid., p. 33.

let, Glenn's expedition re-embarked for the head of Cook Inlet and the Susitna River. A small party that included the geologist W. C. Mendenhall was landed in Resurrection Bay and ordered to explore overland to Turnagain Arm. Luther Kelly had in the meantime passed up Cabin Creek from Portage Bay to Glenn Lake, then gone over to Crow Creek and down it from the north to Turnagain Arm. Later, with Mendenhall, Kelly picked up his trail and continued toward the Knik Arm of Cook Inlet, which he reached by descending Eagle River Valley. From the mouth of the Susitna, Glenn dispatched Lieutenant H. G. Learnard upriver to the Talkeetna, where he tried but failed to connect with a party led by Sergeant Frederick Mathys up the Chickaloon River.

At the Talkeetna, Learnard detailed Sergeant William Yanert to explore northward. Yanert just missed discovering the Tanana route later used by the Alaska Railroad. He went from the Talkeetna up a northern tributary, then overland to the Susitna, which he crossed near Indian Creek, proceeding due north on the eastern flank of the Chulitna River and through Broad Pass as far as the Cantwell River. His route above the Talkeetna-Chulitna forks was roughly the same one followed earlier in the season by a USGS party, and in fact Yanert helped himself to some flour from the geologists' cache. Yanert's journey was lauded highly by Learnard, who recommended a promotion to Lieutenant.

The only section of the Glenn expedition to reach the Yukon was commanded by Lieutenant J. C. Castner. Castner was ordered to cut a trail from Knik up the Matanuska River. He continued beyond the river's headwaters, passed Lake Louise to the Delta River, then went down it to the Tanana. The main body of the Third Expedition under Glenn, accompanied by Mendenhall, overtook Castner on the Delta, and the two groups traveled together a few days until Glenn decided to return: it was late in the season, and moreover he hoped to save some of the livestock he had purchased without approval. Castner, with two men and two mules, was permitted to continue on.

Castner's journey nearly ended in tragedy. From the Tanana, he attempted to ascend the Volkmar River, became boxed in without adequate provisions to cross the mountains, and elected to retrace his steps to the Tanana, partly by raft. On September 10 the suffering men killed and began to eat their last mule.[63] With their clothing in shreds, their feet

63. Castner, "Through Unknown Alaska," pp. 521–23.

wrapped in strips of canvas, and shivering from exposure and hunger, they arrived at the Tanana, where they received succor from friendly Indians. Castner left a warm portrait of Tanana hospitality:

> In passing, it is but justice to say a word for these friends of mine, who found us all but dead in the wilderness, with the Alaskan winter closing in around us. Entire strangers and of another race, they received us as no friend of mine, white or colored, ever did before or since. They asked no questions and required no credentials. They were men. It was enough that their fellow-beings were starving. Unknown to them were the wrongs our race have done theirs for centuries. We were the first whites to visit their home. Their hospitality was the greatest I ever saw. . . . At each place we were royally entertained. From somewhere half a handful of rice would be brought out and cooked for us, giving each a mouthful. This had been kept stored up for months for some special occasion when someone was sick. It had been part of some stores they went 300 miles to get, in the dead of winter, and carried on their backs 300 miles in returning to their simple homes. Gladly they gave it all to us and asked nothing in return. Beaver tail is a delicacy with them, but they cooked all there was for us at each camp.[64]

Castner returned via the Yukon with a little topographic information and a negative report on the Volkmar route. Castner's journey, "which had cost so much suffering and privation," wrote Brooks, "yielded practically nothing of value."[65]

Glenn, like Abercrombie, thought he had the perfect route for a railroad. A portion of it had been cut and marked, and scraps of topographic information were brought back by Yanert, Mathys, and Learnard. An early mention of the agricultural value of the Matanuska Valley appeared in Glenn's report. Mendenhall reported coal in the same region.[66] The Matanuska-Delta trail was pioneered by the Glenn party, and the side trips of Kelly and Mendenhall, of Mathys, and of Yanert were useful—if minor—contributions to geographical knowledge. Mendenhall mapped the Resurrection Bay–Turnagain Arm trail and the Crow Creek–

64. Castner, in Glenn and Abercrombie, *Report of Explorations, 1898*, p. 259.
65. *Geography and Geology of Alaska*, p. 128.
66. Glenn, in Glenn and Abercrombie, *Report of Explorations, 1898*, pp. 116, 114.

Eagle River country. In addition to his geologic work, he also ran a route traverse up the Matanuska to the Tanana.

The geographic and scientific success of the expedition was due largely to Mendenhall. Glenn commended the geologist: "He was at all times enthusiastic in the performance of his work and most willing to render every assistance which by his technical education he was competent to give to the commands he accompanied." As for Mendenhall's topographic work, Glenn admitted: "This was no part of the duties he was expected to perform."[67]

Mendenhall and Schrader were civilian scientists on loan from the Geological Survey to the War Department. They were instructed "to ascertain the general distribution of rock masses, their relations, and . . . the character and origin of each formation; to observe and note all occurrences of valuable minerals." Observations were to be extended beyond physiographic and geologic features to the "fauna and flora, and to the determination of accessible routes for wagons and railroads."[68] The Geological Survey assumed that the Army would survey for a map. The USGS further recognized the necessity for tact and strict subordination to the Army's mission. The Director instructed both Schrader and Mendenhall to "undertake no surveys or other operations inconsistent with the purposes of the expedition, or likely to embarrass its commanding officer."[69] The two geologists kept the Survey's part of the bargain, though often surrounded by confusion and inefficiency. In general, Army results were disproportionate to the time, energy, suffering, size, and expense of the expeditions of 1898.

In 1899 the Army expeditions had no geologists attached, and an attempt to borrow topographic surveyors from the USGS was unsuccessful, though the Survey did recommend a topographer—Oscar Rohn.[70] Rohn's labor was the single most important exploratory effort of Abercrombie's Copper River Expedition of 1899. Abercrombie was ordered to open a military road from Valdez to Copper Center and Eagle City on the

67. Ibid., p. 123.
68. Mendenhall, "Reconnaissance from Resurrection Bay to the Tanana River," pp. 271, 272.
69. C. D. Walcott to Schrader, March 8, 1898, AGO Files, NA, RG 94.
70. C. D. Walcott to G. D. Meiklejohn, March 10, 1899, Secretary of War Files, NA, RG 107.

Yukon.[71] He hired surveyors and workmen on the spot. The project thus became a form of public relief work for unemployed and unsuccessful prospectors in the area:[72] it had been a hard winter in Valdez. The greeting Abercrombie received from his quartermaster was: "My God, Captain, it has been clear Hell!" The miners were crowded together in tiny, unsanitary cabins, and many were afflicted with scurvy. Abercrombie reported an Alaskan equivalent of the Abominable Snowman: "I noticed in talking to these people that over 70 per cent of them were more or less mentally deranged. My attention was first directed to this fact by their reference to a 'glacial demon.' "[73] Such could be the penalty of failure in the Gold Rush.

Rohn was charged to investigate the Chitina, and if possible cross to the headwaters of the Copper then descend it to Copper Center. His mapping and geologic work in the Wrangell Mountains and on tributaries of the Tanana added much valuable information concerning a physiographically complicated region. Abercrombie dispatched other, minor exploratory parties and surveyed parts of the wagon route. The final link, a pass through the coast mountains, had been discovered during the winter by prospectors.[74]

Abercrombie was explicitly ordered to open a military road from Valdez. Exploration was an incidental activity. In the prosecution of his central duty, Abercrombie did a good season's work. His mileage score was ninety-three miles opened for pack horses, thirty-five more in excavation, sixty-seven cleared and grubbed, and twelve additional miles cleared only. Twenty-six bridges with a total length of 856 feet were thrown over the area's turbulent rivers and creeks.[75]

Glenn's tour in 1899 was a continuation of his previous explorations rather than a road-building enterprise. Although he was instructed to mark the trail from Portage Bay to Knik Arm and to explore the west

71. Glenn and Abercrombie, *Report of Explorations, 1898*, p. 463.

72. Abercrombie, "Copper River Exploring Expedition" (1899), in *Compilation of Narratives*, p. 759; this is a shortened version of his official report of the same title printed as *Senate Document 306, 56th Congress: 1st session* (3874).

73. Ibid., p. 758.

74. Rohn, "A Reconnaissance of the Chitina River and the Skolai Mountains, Alaska," pp. 393–440.

75. Abercrombie, "Copper River Exploring Expedition" (1899), in *Compilation of Narratives*, p. 778.

side of Cook Inlet from open tidewater north to the head of navigation
on the Susitna for "the most practicable overland trail," Glenn's primary
duty was to find a direct route to the Tanana and from it to the military
posts on the Yukon.[76] To expedite the various sections of his command,
Glenn used a steamer on the Susitna and Yentna.[77] One party under
Lieutenant Joseph Herron was landed where the Kichatna flows into the
Yentna. A second party led by Private George Vanschoonoven and a third
comprised of Yanert and Mathys were landed on the Susitna River near
the forks. A fourth section, directed by the civilian topographer C. E. Griffith, proceeded from Knik to the Chickaloon. Griffith, according to his
own account, traveled up the Chickaloon (explored by Mathys in 1898)
and over to the Talkeetna (examined by Learnard the previous year).
From the Talkeetna's head he crossed to the Susitna and followed it to
Glenn's old trail of 1898. Griffith then investigated the Matanuska-Copper
regions, the Delta River, and finally passed north over well identified
trails. Of Griffith's detachment, Glenn wrote: "It was useless to explore
the valley of the Matanuska farther,"[78] and P. H. Ray, then in command
of Army operations on the Yukon, noted disconsolately: "It is a great
mistake to send such parties out under inexperienced civilians."[79] That
the subexpedition proved inconsequential was perhaps as much the fault
of Griffith's orders as of his leadership.

Sergeant William Yanert had originally been scheduled to head the
expedition that was assigned to Griffith.[80] Yanert's superior in 1898 had
recommended a commission for the resourceful sergeant; Alfred Brooks
later praised Yanert's ingenuity and skill;[81] and Glenn had rewarded
Yanert by leaving him in charge at Knik during the winter of 1898–1899.
When Glenn returned in the summer of 1899, Yanert declined to re-enlist
for Alaskan duty.[82] Apparently he feared the Chickaloon-Susitna itinerary

76. Glenn, in Glenn and Abercrombie, *Report of Explorations, 1898*, p. 464.
77. Glenn to Assistant Secretary of War, June 26, 1899, Secretary of War Files,
NA, RG 107.
78. Glenn, "Explorations in and about Cook Inlet" (1899), in *Compilation of
Narratives*, p. 718.
79. Ray's report, August 20, 1899, in U.S. War Dept., "Annual Reports," *House
Document 2, 56th Congress: 1st session* (3901), p. 119.
80. Glenn's report, in ibid., p. 80.
81. Brooks, *The Mount McKinley Region, Alaska*, USGS Professional Paper No.
70 (Washington, 1911), p. 29.
82. Glenn to Assistant Secretary of War, June 5, 1899, Secretary of War Files, NA,
RG 107.

might keep him in the Army longer than his enlistment would require. Instead, he and Mathys—the latter in charge—were given the task of finding a trail down the east bank of the Susitna to Cook Inlet. The two men, ignoring these orders without bothering to explain their actions, crossed from the head of the Talkeetna to the Chickaloon and descended it to the Matanuska. Their official published account consists of three short paragraphs from each man. Both say their orders called for a journey down the "west side of the foothills" to the Susitna station.[83] One is tempted to read between the lines and suspect that for some reason Yanert and Mathys deliberately sabotaged Glenn's plan for their party.

The work of traversing a route on the east bank of the Susitna was accomplished, but quite by accident. The Vanschoonoven party, reported Glenn, was "to have been personally conducted by me, but was of necessity turned over to another."[84] Glenn did not say why he relinquished the command. Vanschoonoven had distinguished himself the year before by making a forced march estimated at 140 miles, down the Matanuska, in a little over four days,[85] and Glenn called the achievement "one of the most severe tests that any of my party [in 1898] had been put to."[86] In 1899, however, Glenn was something less than satisfied with Vanschoonoven's performance. The Private, in the company of a "Doctor" George B. Thomas, went north up Indian Creek through Broad Pass, on the same general route Yanert and a USGS party had followed in 1898. To infer from the printed report just how far Vanschoonoven got in 1899 is difficult, but the chances are he turned back before descending the Nenana River valley. On the return trip, Vanschoonoven examined the region that had been assigned to Mathys.

Glenn claimed that the Vanschoonoven party, in failing to reach the Tanana, was intimidated by a swamp. "The sight of this unexplored swamp, like the cry of 'mouse' to the average female, caused an ignominious and inexplicable flight." Glenn vented his displeasure in his only printed report:

From a careful inquiry I am satisfied that this swamp could have

83. Yanert and Mathys, in Glenn, "Exploration in and about Cook Inlet" (1899), *Compilation of Narratives*, pp. 736, 737.

84. Glenn, ibid., p. 717.

85. Mendenhall, "Reconnaissance from Resurrection Bay to the Tanana River," pp. 288, 289.

86. Glenn, in Glenn and Abercrombie, *Report of Explorations, 1898*, p. 83.

been avoided by proper exploration of the high ground surrounding it, but even if this were not the case there is . . . no sort of doubt that the swamp could have been crossed by corduroying. This class of work was contemplated when the detachments were sent out. It was not considered necessary to specifically mention it, because the necessary tools for the work were sent along, and it was known that macadamized roads, paved streets, and railroad grades are not usually found in unexplored country.[87]

Three of Glenn's four expeditions thus failed to accomplish their goals. The fourth, under Joseph Herron, made an important contribution to geographical knowledge, but almost perished in the effort. With an assistant surgeon, two enlisted men, two packers, two native guides, and a pack train, Herron began an ascent of the Kichatna River on July 1. From the stream's head he crossed the Alaska Range through Simpson Pass and descended the Kuskokwim's South Fork. Here, his Indian guides deserted. Turning northeastward, he proceeded up the valley formed by the East and North Forks and soon became lost in the timbered lowlands. In September, the grass having withered, Herron abandoned his pack train. He decided to raft downstream in search of native assistance. The rafts were wrecked; rations were severely depleted by the accident and by foraging bears. The party nevertheless turned north again on foot, and was eventually overtaken by an Indian, who guided the wasted and weary explorers to Telida village. After a two-month layover, Herron, directed by Indians, continued north past Lake Minchumina and the upper Kuskokwim to the Cosna River, which he followed to the Tanana. He arrived at the Yukon on December 11.

Herron's journey was the first official exploration of the upper Kuskokwim. His report, he summarized correctly, represented "the earnest efforts of a small party in unknown regions against extraordinary obstacles, deserted by guides, caught by winter, deprived of transportation, and hampered by scarcity of food."[88] Of all the separate explorations by the Army in 1898 and 1899, Joseph Herron's was probably the most difficult and

87. Glenn, "Explorations in and about Cook Inlet (1899), in *Compilation of Narratives*, p. 717.

88. Herron, *Explorations in Alaska, 1899, for an All-American Overland Route from Cook Inlet, Pacific Ocean, to the Yukon* (War Department, Washington, 1901), p. 3; also published as *Senate Document 689, 60th Congress: 2d session* (5408).

the most original, if not the most profitable in detailed results or in terms of later development.

The Army was in 1898 and 1899 the wrong agency for the job of exploration. Military personnel seldom conducted any surveys, and rarely took any more observations than were necessary to get in or out of the country. The mapping was mainly done by either USGS geologists or civilian topographers. The Army parties were too large for primary exploration, and frequent back-tracking was necessary to carry up supplies. The longer expeditions were often actually a series of loops, stretching through the territory like a chain, rather than a solid line. There were too many delays in 1898 and not a few in 1899.

Part of the fault must rest with the two commanders; other difficulties were built into the Army system. There was a jurisdictional problem in Alaska. Ray on the Yukon made repeated recommendations about the work, strongly urging an end to seasonal expeditions and the substitution of a permanent station at Valdez, presumably under his command. After talking to the Griffith party, Ray was "fully satisfied" that the route from Cook Inlet was impracticable.[89] Interference from without was matched by friction within Glenn's organization. He had his troubles with Yanert and Mathys in 1899, and it must have pained the Captain in 1898 when Lieutenant Learnard compared the highly mobile and independent USGS parties with the Army's cumbersome and regulation-bound expedition.[90] There was even a jurisdictional squabble between Glenn and Abercrombie: the latter complained to the War Department about Griffith's "invasion of my territory."[91]

In 1900 an Army "Department of Alaska" was created. Thereafter Army activity was restricted principally to the construction and maintenance of military roads and telegraph lines.[92] Nearly half a million dollars was allotted for the telegraph.[93]

89. Ray, August 10 and 20, 1899, in U.S. War Department, "Annual Reports," *House Document 2, 56th Congress: 1st session*, pp. 117, 119.

90. Learnard, in Glenn and Abercrombie, *Report of Explorations, 1898*, p. 179.

91. Abercrombie to Assistant Secretary of War, August 26, 1899, Secretary of War Files, NA, RG 107.

92. Report of General G. M. Randall, in U.S. War Department, "Annual Reports," *House Document 2, 56th Congress: 2d session* (4072).

93. U.S. War Department, "Signal Service of the Army," *House Document 427, 56th Congress: 1st session* (3984), 3. U.S. War Department, "Telegraph and Cable Lines in Alaska," *House Document 365, 56th Congress: 2d session* (4163), 1, 2.

In 1898 and 1899 the Army amply demonstrated its inability to compete with the Geological Survey in scientific exploration and in the pursuit of original discovery. By the close of the century the major features of Alaska's portrait had been sketched, if not drawn in detail, and there were few problems of gross geography left unsolved; this success mainly resulted not from the work done by the Army, but from the labors of a small corps of USGS explorers.

11. Ascendancy of the Geological Survey

> Were the day clear I could see Mount McKinley from the window.
> As I picture in my mind its stupendous height, I compare it to our
> science. Many have assailed its flanks; some have proclaimed untruths
> about it; some have climbed by great effort well up the slopes; a very
> few, the best by natural selection, have reached the summit and there
> attained the broad vision denied those at lower altitudes. As for me,
> I am satisfied to have been able to traverse the great lowland to the
> base and to climb the foothills.
>
> ALFRED HULSE BROOKS[1]

IN 1878 John Wesley Powell submitted a statement to a special committee of the National Academy of Sciences. The committee, chaired by the great American theoretical geologist James Dwight Dana, was probing the organization of the western surveys. Powell spoke for a division of labor in the federal establishment along scientific lines, with geology in one department and mensuration in another. A successful survey organization should be further related, Powell thought, to the "industries of the people," to "utilitarian demands" analogous to the work of the Coast Survey and Naval Observatory. Ethnology was another important matter: the Indians were fast disappearing, and fundamental research into their customs was necessary to prevent a repetition of the "blunders we have made and the wrongs we have inflicted."[2] For other scientific pursuits, a problem approach was desirable. Powell felt that the primary function of a permanent geographical and geological survey should be the survey and classification of public lands. The Academy's report followed the main

1. Quoted in P. S. Smith, "Memorial of Alfred Hulse Brooks," *Bulletin of the Geological Society of America*, 37 (1926), 42, 43.

2. A. H. Dupree, *Science in the Federal Government*, pp. 205–09. Powell's view on the racial question had Alaskan equivalents in the quotation of Castner above, and in the comment of Fish Commission investigator Charles Townsend, who traveled with Cantwell on the Kobuk in 1885. Said Townsend: "In our management of these people . . . we have an opportunity to atone, in a measure, for a century of dishonorable treatment of the Indian." In Healy, *Cruise of the Corwin, 1885*, p. 88.

lines of Powell's argument. The term "geodetic" was added to the Coast Survey's title, and the separate civilian Geological Survey was established.

Powell's attitude toward science in government directly affected the course of Alaskan exploration after he became head of the USGS in 1881. The following year he explained why the Geological Survey had "thought best not to enter the field of Alaska until some . . . more urgent wants have been met." The "more urgent wants" were created by the growth of mining in the United States, an expansion of activity that required USGS attention but received limited fiscal support from Congress. The explanation came in answer to a Senate request for information on progress made by the Survey in the investigation of Alaska's mineral, agricultural, and economic resources; the Senate wanted to know whether a survey of the territory was not "within the class of work" belonging to the USGS. Powell admitted that his agency was organized for the specific purpose mentioned in the Senate resolution, but pointed out that a survey of Alaska could not be commenced for less than $25,000, an appropriation that must necessarily be continued for several years. The Congress was reluctant to finance the enterprise, and without Congressional support, Powell returned to the "more urgent wants."[3]

In 1886 Powell was quizzed again about Alaska, in connection with a bill to finance surveys for an intercontinental railroad to Bering Strait. Though he expressed no opinion on the wisdom of constructing such a railway, he did suggest that the terminus might best be located on Bristol Bay. He observed that a series of lines run by exploratory expeditions would cost more than an areal survey of the whole territory through which they ran. The USGS, he said, could possibly do an areal survey for no more than $2.50 per square mile.[4] Again Congress failed to support the project, and Powell's areal survey came to naught.

In retrospect, Powell's reactions in 1882 and 1886 failed to demonstrate the political skill that made him the number one scientific administrator in government. But if anyone could have pried funds loose from Capitol Hill in those years, Powell could have. He was perfectly willing to direct the exploration of Alaska, but only with additional appropriations and

3. Powell, "Letter of April 26, 1882," *Senate Executive Document 166, 47th Congress: 1st session* (1991), 1–3.

4. Powell, "Resources of Alaska," *Senate Miscellaneous Document 22, 49th Congress: 2d session* (2450), 1–10.

not at the expense of projects already under way in the States, where Powell was mainly concerned with "utilitarian demands" and research allied with the "industries of the people."

By 1892 Powell had made political enemies with his land classification and his irrigation survey, and one area of basic research that he had supported—paleontology—had come under heavy attack as the recipient of public funds. In the face of a business recession, tight money, Populist agitation for currency reform, and a change of presidential administrations, the ax fell. USGS, USC&GS, Naval Observatory, Smithsonian, and Bureau of Ethnology appropriations were slashed.[5] The wreckage of plans formulated in 1890 for systematic Army exploration of Alaska was an additional symptom of the diseases confronting federal science in the nation as a whole. Powell retired to the Bureau of Ethnology and C. D. Walcott became director of the USGS.

The Geological Survey had expressed a mild interest in Alaska before 1895. I. C. Russell made the Yukon circle route in 1889 as a guest of the USC&GS and the Alaska Commercial Company. The next two years he conducted geologic research at Mt. St. Elias in cooperation with the National Geographic Society. Dall, after 1884, was on the USGS payroll. Powell probably referred to Dall for specific advice on the prospect of Alaskan explorations. The USGS also published the results of Harry Fielding Reid's glaciological investigations. C. Willard Hayes of the Survey performed valuable work with the Schwatka expedition of 1891. But it was not until 1895 that the Geological Survey sent independent expeditions to Alaska.

The work of Becker and Dall in that year, and of Spurr, Goodrich, and Schrader in the next, was supported by two annual appropriations of $5,000 each. Though USGS activity had thus begun in a small way before the Gold Rush, the investigations of 1895 and 1896 nevertheless demonstrated the interest of Congress in Alaska's developing mineral industry. The primary emphasis on economic mineral deposits set the tone for all Survey operations in the Far Northwest during the century. The Geological Survey in Alaska was by law the scientific arm of the prospector and mining engineer. In the States, the USGS was authorized to make general "geologic surveys." For Alaska, appropriation bills specified "in-

5. Dupree, *Science in the Federal Government*, pp. 234, 235.

vestigation of the mineral resources."[6] In response, the USGS provided reports containing "useful information" in "untechnical language."[7] In some of them, the geologists even recommended the amount and type of provisions and the outfit with which the prospector should furnish himself.[8] The economic orientation was reflected in a letter from Hayes to the Director in 1903: "The success and value of the Alaskan survey are dependent, in a large measure, on the promptness with which it can meet popular demand for information in regard to any particular mining district."[9] The same year, a new branch of the agency was created and named the Division of Alaskan Mineral Resources.[10] The policy was consistent with Powell's philosophy of concentration on the "industries of the people."

The stress on mineral resources had little effect on the progress of USGS geographic exploration or general geologic investigation. Fundamental research in geology did not suffer, because individual investigators did general geological work anyway, and because it was difficult to separate applied from basic research, especially in an unexplored wilderness. In 1911, Alfred Brooks could assert from experience:

> As I see it, there lies no danger in the present trend toward applied geology, provided our applied geology rests on a broad basis of scientific research. If the spring of pure science is cut off, the stream of applied geology must soon run dry. There is no field of pure geology which will not yield results applicable to questions of material welfare. On the other hand, any given investigation in applied geology may lead to problems of paleontology, petrography, geophysics, or other branches of pure science.[11]

Insofar as exploration is concerned, the prospector's primary need in 1898 and 1899 was for maps and information to guide him through the coun-

6. Institute for Government Research, *The U.S. Geological Survey: Its History, Activities and Organization*, Service Monograph of the U.S. Government No. 1 (New York, 1918), p. 43.

7. C. D. Walcott, *Maps and Descriptions of Routes of Exploration in Alaska in 1898* (USGS, Washington, 1899), p. 12.

8. F. C. Schrader and A. H. Brooks, *Preliminary Report on the Cape Nome Gold Region, Alaska* (USGS, Washington, 1900), pp. 51–54.

9. June 20, 1903, Historical Documents, USGS Files.

10. Secretary of the Interior to Director of USGS, July 2, 1903, ibid.

11. Quoted in P. S. Smith, "Memorial of Alfred Hulse Brooks," p. 31.

try. The Survey expeditions therefore concentrated on the collection of general geographic and topographic data. In 1900 the agency suspended its exploratory activity temporarily to engage in area surveys of "regions having special economic promise" and to prepare maps from data collected during the first two seasons.[12]

The Geological Survey effort of 1898, exclusive of work done with the Army, was divided into four segments. E. C. Barnard traveled down the Yukon from its head to the boundary and, using the astronomic position and geodetic coordinates fixed by the C&GS, he extended triangulation into American mining regions of the Fortymile River basin. An area of over 2,000 square miles was topographically mapped at a scale of 1:250,-000 with a contour interval of 200 feet. In September Barnard proceeded downstream to St. Michael and returned to the States.[13] His comparatively detailed survey was a specific gesture of compliance with the Congressional injunction to undertake mineral investigations. Barnard was accompanied as far as old Fort Selkirk by a second USGS party under W. J. Peters, topographer, with Alfred Hulse Brooks, geologist, and four camp hands. For Brooks it was a long-hoped-for opportunity, and the beginning of his tenure as an Alaskan expert.

Brooks graduated from Harvard in 1894 with a Bachelor of Science degree. While at the University he was influenced by the geologist N. S. Shaler; he also met Spurr there. After graduation Brooks accepted employment with the USGS and worked under C. Willard Hayes in the southern Appalachians. Hayes inspired enthusiasm in the young geologist for the possibilities of Alaskan exploration. Brooks was in Paris studying at the Sorbonne when he received a telegram offering him the Alaskan job. He hurried back to begin a distinguished career in Alaskan geology and exploration, eventually becoming head of the Alaskan division. At one point in his career he refused a promotion to Chief Geologist of the Survey in order to remain in the Alaskan Branch.[14] One of his outstand-

12. Brooks, *The Mount McKinley Region, Alaska*, p. 11. Anon. [Brooks?] "Investigation of Mineral Resources of Alaska," *Engineering and Mining Journal*, 73 (1902), 585.

13. Barnard, "Report of the Fortymile Expedition," in C. D. Walcott, *Maps and Descriptions*, pp. 76–83.

14. P. S. Smith, "Memorial of Alfred Hulse Brooks," pp. 15–48. Mrs. A. H. Brooks, "Alfred Hulse Brooks," in *Blazing Alaska's Trails*, pages xix–xxi. *DAB*, 3, 72–74.

ing qualities, his biographer and colleague tells us, was intellectual honesty—

> honesty of purpose, honesty in the methods he practiced, and honesty
> in the support of the conclusions he reached. This quality is all the
> more remarkable because in exploratory work, whether that term
> applies to broad explorations in a new country or in a new realm of
> thought, there is neither time nor opportunity for the same minute
> scrutiny of details as there is in a restricted investigation in more
> thoroughly cultivated fields. In fact, the successful explorer must
> paint with broad strokes and bold outlines. Brooks did this, always
> leaving the picture clear and distinct, but at the same time, because
> he realized the necessary imperfection in his data, he pointed out
> those features that should be accepted only tentatively and that might
> require supplementary touching up or actual redrawing.[15]

Brooks, like William Dall, was interested in everything Alaskan: history, resources, political status, and all phases of scientific knowledge about the territory. In every field, he brought to his research and writing the same intellectual honesty evident in his geologic and geographic explorations. The years 1898 and 1899 were at once the youth and the maturity of both Brooks and the Geological Survey in Alaska.

The Peters-Brooks party began its survey at the confluence of the Yukon and White rivers. For six weeks the explorers laboriously dragged their canoes up the White, then up the Snag River and across the short portage to Mirror Creek near where the present Alaska Highway crosses the international boundary. Mirror Creek and the Tanana were then descended to the Yukon in a relatively fast, easy reconnaissance.[16]

A third Geological Survey party under George Eldridge and Robert Muldrow went up the Susitna, up the valley of Indian Creek, and through Broad Pass to the Nenana River, where it turned back for lack of provisions. The route ran parallel and to the east of Sergeant Yanert's exploration made during the same season.[17] Eldridge carried a rough survey

15. P. S. Smith, "Memorial of Alfred Hulse Brooks," p. 41.
16. Brooks, "A Reconnaissance in the White and Tanana River Basins, Alaska, in 1898," pp. 425–94. Brooks, *Geography and Geology of Alaska,* pp. 128, 129.
17. Eldridge, "A Reconnaissance in the Sushitna Basin and Adjacent Territory, Alaska, in 1898," USGS, *Twentieth Annual Report, 1898–99,* Pt. 7, pp. 1–29.

all the way. Muldrow's estimate of Mt. McKinley's height at 20,464 feet was, under the circumstances, amazingly accurate.[18]

Eldridge's instructions from the USGS reveal the quality of work the Survey expected from the expeditions of 1898. He was to determine general topographic features with a continuous stadia line over the whole route and by sketches of adjacent country made with a plane table. When practical, triangulation was to be substituted for the stadia line. Latitude stations were to be established at twenty-five-mile intervals. The instructions called for observation of magnetic declination, temperature, and climatic phenomena as well. Eldridge was to ascertain the distribution of rock masses, their relationships and characteristics, the occurrence of minerals, and the existence of good mountain passes. For a pioneer reconnaissance, it was an ambitious order.[19]

Another exploration—the longest (about 1,300 miles) made in 1898 by a Geological Survey party—was led by J. E. Spurr, geologist, and W. S. Post, topographer. The party included four "camp hands," a misleading label: one, F. C. Hinckley, had experience as a naturalist, and another, Oscar Rohn, who was to perform so well for Abercrombie the following year, had graduated from the University of Wisconsin and was qualified to act as an assistant geologist or assistant topographer if necessary. Spurr himself was possessed of a literary talent that was appreciated at USGS headquarters; he was asked to revise and even to rewrite the reports of a few of his more technically minded colleagues.[20] His own reports had the flavor of high adventure, and his popular narrative style was appropriate to the emphasis on practical matters in the Survey's northern operation. The report of the 1898 exploration contained notes on game and fish, native races, timber, zoology, and ornithology, in addition to the topographic, mineralogic, and geologic information.

Setting out in the summer of 1898, Spurr traced the Susitna to the Yentna and the Yentna to the Skwentna, then traversed a portage to the Styx River, an upper tributary of the Kuskokwim's south fork. The Kuskokwim was then followed to Bethel at the river's mouth, thence to where the Kanektok River empties into Kuskokwim Bay. The Kanektok was ascended and a portage was made to Togiak Lake and over the moun-

18. Muldrow, "Mount McKinley," *NGM*, *12* (August 1901), 312, 313.
19. Eldridge, "A Reconnaissance in the Sushitna Basin," p. 7.
20. A. C. Spencer to Brooks, October 15, 1902, Historical Documents, USGS Files.

tains to Nushagak. The party took the Naknek Lake portage to Katmai on the Alaska Peninsula. (Two original plans, one to cross from the Kuskokwim to the Yukon and another to return by way of Iliamna and Clark Lakes, were abandoned.) The party used light cedar Peterboro canoes, which nested for ease in transport. Each man was permitted forty pounds of personal baggage and monthly rations weighing eighty-six pounds, the latter including dried fruits, three-fourths of a pound of tea (the favorite wilderness beverage in Alaska since the Telegraph Expedition), beans, bacon, flour, and pemmican.[21]

On August 10, Spurr arrived at a Moravian mission on the Kuskokwim, and the party split. Three camp hands accompanied by Dr. J. H. Romig, a missionary doctor, went over to the Yukon and St. Michael, while the remainder of the group sailed down the Kuskokwim in a small sloop with another missionary.[22]

For a number of years, missionaries at various stations in Alaska had provided assistance and shelter to official explorers, prospectors, and casual travelers. The Presbyterian Sheldon Jackson deserves special credit for the whole missionary effort in the territory. With his encouragement in 1880 the country was divided among several Protestant organizations. The Presbyterians, except for a promise to establish a mission at Point Barrow, remained in Southeastern; the Episcopalians continued their work on the Yukon; the Baptists took an interest in the Kodiak and Cook Inlet regions, the Methodists in the Aleutians, the Congregationalists in Cape Prince of Wales, and the Moravians in the Kuskokwim and Nushagak valleys.[23]

Jackson, in his campaign for school facilities, appealed for help directly to the other denominations and to the public. His personal political influence was formidable. He had been introduced to Congressmen by Wendell Phillips, among others,[24] and President Benjamin Harrison, when he was a senator and chairman of the Committee on Territories, became a close friend of Jackson.[25] As Education Agent for Alaska, Jackson obtained both initial subsidies and maintenance funds from Congress for the various mission schools in the country. He also sponsored the importation

---

21. Spurr, "A Reconnaissance in Southwestern Alaska in 1898," USGS, *Twentieth Annual Report, 1898–99*, Pt. 7, pp. 43–45, 59–61.

22. Spurr, "Reconnaissance in Southwestern Alaska," p. 54.

23. J. A. Lazell, *Alaskan Apostle*, p. 65.

24. J. P. Nichols, *Alaska*, p. 73.

25. R. L. Stewart, *Sheldon Jackson* (New York, 1908), p. 339.

of domestic reindeer for the relief of natives.[26] Jackson's program to educate the natives met with considerable opposition. William Dall analyzed the situation: "Theoretically, every man is in favor of missionary work; but when, as in the present case, they take up available land for their schools, teach the Indian to work, and to build civilized houses, to ask a good price for his furs and fish, and on no account to sell his young daughters to white men, as was formerly the practice,—such innovations do not meet with universal favor."[27]

Sheldon Jackson has been called a pathfinder and a scientist but he was neither. It is true that on his tours of inspection he kept some meteorological and natural history notes; he journeyed on the Yukon River for the Agricultural Department in 1898; and his reindeer stations kept climatic records which were published in his reports on the animal.[28] But he did not "explore" any area, and his scientific contributions were insignificant and sometimes inaccurate. The importance of his reports lay in their social information, not in their inclusion of any exact data on natural history and ethnology.

The same general comment can be made of missionary attention to Alaskan science and exploration since Father Veniaminov's work during the Russian period. The missions were usually located near trading posts or on well established trade routes. Clerics seldom strayed from these highways, and if they did, the journeys were recorded inadequately or not at all. Not that American missionaries made no contribution. Jackson was instrumental in the Natural History Society at Sitka and was responsible for the founding there of an anthropological museum still in existence.[29] S. Hall Young was Muir's congenial traveling companion. Other missionaries aided in the census enumerations, and still others tended meteorological instruments.[30] Some natural history specimens were collected.[31]

26. Between 1891 and 1901, 1,280 animals were imported. The herd numbered half a million reindeer between 1930 and 1936. A. S. Leopold and F. F. Darling, *Wildlife in Alaska: An Ecological Reconnaissance* (New York, 1953), p. 69.

27. "Late News from Alaska," *Science*, 6 (July 31, 1885), 96.

28. A. H. Brooks, G. B. Richardson, A. J. Collier, and W. C. Mendenhall, *Reconnaissances in the Cape Nome and Norton Bay Regions, Alaska, in 1900* (USGS, Washington, 1900), p. 115; also published as *House Document 547, 56th Congress: 2d session* (4198).

29. Sitka *Alaskan*, October 29 and November 19, 1887.

30. A. B. Schwalbe, *Dayspring on the Kuskokwim*, p. 11.

31. For an example see W. J. Holland, "Alaska Insects," *Entomological News*, 2 (1900), 381–89, 416–23.

These contributions were peripheral and erratic, and in anthropology, where one would expect major accomplishment, the record is disappointing. A grammar and vocabulary of the Western Innuit dialect was compiled in 1889 and revised a few years later, based on notes furnished by John Kilbuck, who accompanied Spurr to the coast in 1898. A Jesuit, Francis Barnum, published a useful work on the same language in 1901.[32] Episcopalians on the Yukon were as active as any single denomination. Ketchum was accompanied by an English missionary on part of his Yukon reconnaissance in 1866. Even before that, in 1864, a British cleric reported to the Smithsonian on a journey in the Far Northwest.[33] During the American period, Episcopalian missionaries traveled the Yukon and portions of the Tanana, and one of them offered to collect for the Smithsonian.[34] John W. Chapman of the Anvik mission began soon after his arrival in 1887 to gather information and materials on the Athapaskans. He eventually collected for the American Museum of Natural History in New York, and he published Indian folk stories.[35]

Despite the seeming utility to missionaries of linguistic data and information on native customs, in general the contribution of American clerics to anthropology was not proportionate to their number and opportunity. The judgment is equally valid for missionary work in natural history and geography. A number of reasons can be advanced in explanation. First, missionaries were usually untrained in the sciences, and when missionary activity gained impetus in Alaska after 1880 the sciences had become increasingly specialized. Second, the churchmen were interested in education and conversion in a hard country, and these activities left them little extra time for attention to other issues. Third, in ethnology, Indian customs of interest to the anthropologist were often a source of revulsion to the Protestant missionaries. Such considerations put the missionary con-

32. Barnum, *Grammatical Fundamentals of the Innuit Language as Spoken by the Eskimo of the Western Coast of Alaska* (Boston, 1901), page xviii. Dall, "Review of *Alaskan Grammar and Vocabulary* by Agustus Schultze," *Nation*, 58 (June 21, 1894), 475.

33. W. W. Kirby, "A Journey to the Youcan, Russian America," SI, *Annual Report*, *1864*, pp. 416–20.

34. SI, *Annual Report, 1889*, p. 10.

35. H. F. Osborn, *American Museum of Natural History*, p. 93. Chapman, *Ten'a Texts and Tales from Anvik, Alaska*, Publication of the American Ethnological Society, 6 (Leyden, 1914), 14. Chapman, "Athapascan Traditions from the Lower Yukon," *Journal of American Folk-Lore*, 16 (1903), 180–85.

tribution to scientific exploration in roughly the same magnitude as the contribution of the prospector.[36] The Alaskan missionary's great achievement was in education. And his clean, warm mission station, combined with the aid and hospitality he extended to explorers like Spurr and Post, was a welcome respite from the hardship of wilderness travel.

Geological Survey work in 1898 was directed toward satisfying a public demand for maps of the main unexplored routes leading to or by mineral regions. The surveys were confined to the principal rivers and valleys. The summer work of 1899 supplemented this general plan.[37]

Peters and Brooks struck out in a northwesterly direction from the head of Lynn Canal and along the northern base of the St. Elias Mountains to the White River, on approximately the same route now followed by the Haines Road and Alaska Highway. Like Glave and Dalton, who explored part of the area in 1891, the geologists used pack horses, but only seven of the fifteen animals reached their final destination on the Yukon. Peters and Brooks ascended the White almost to its glacial source; then, continuing west along the foothills, the party crossed two divides to the Nabesna River, which they descended a few miles before cutting northwest to the Tanana. (Oscar Rohn, after crossing Skolai Pass the same season, came upon traces of the geological expedition.) From the Tanana River, the USGS explorers struck due north to the Fortymile and down it to Eagle on the Yukon, which they reached September 16, after covering 600 miles of rugged country in sixty-six days.[38]

A second USGS exploration of 1899, under Schrader and topographer T. G. Gerdine, first verified Raymond's astronomic position for Fort Yukon, then proceeded downstream a short distance to the Chandalar River, which they ascended 200 miles before passing to the headwaters of the Koyukuk River. Surveys were carried down the Koyukuk 700 miles

36. Not infrequently the information that churchmen published on Alaska was inaccurate. Dall cited one article by a missionary which asserted that Kodiak natives ate a dish composed of a mixture of bear's dung. Dall pointed out that the nearest thing to an oath in the native dialect was to tell an enemy to "eat dung." Dall thought the error arose from an Eskimo habit of making a type of salad from willowbuds found in the crop of the caribou where "they are as clean . . . as if in a basket": Dall, "Native Tribes of Alaska," AAAS, *Proceedings* (1885), p. 369.

37. Brooks, *Geography and Geology of Alaska*, p. 127.

38. Brooks, "A Reconnaissance from Pyramid Harbor to Eagle City, Alaska, Including a Description of the Copper Deposits of the Upper White and Tanana Rivers," USGS, *Twenty-first Annual Report, 1899–1900*, Pt. 2, pp. 331–91.

to Nulato, another known point. Stadia measurements were used in the lowlands and triangulation was used in rougher country. Every three or four days prominent triangulation stations were occupied in the hills, sometimes five or six miles from the river. The side journeys provided a limited opportunity for additional observations and for photography. The explorers found Yukon River travel uncomfortable, but not in the total lack of civilized facilities that Dall and Ketchum experienced. Said Schrader of the overcrowded river boats: "A short night's lodging in one's own blanket on the hurricane deck, on the floor of the cabin, or in the wood pile of the engine room was considered a luxury."[39]

While at St. Michael awaiting return transportation to the States, Schrader and Brooks decided to visit the recently discovered gold diggings at Nome. Some hasty topographic, geologic, and photographic work was done at the new placers. Information thus gathered enabled the USGS to issue maps and a report before the rush to Nome began the following spring.[40]

The demand for more detailed maps and geologic examination of important mining districts on Seward Peninsula and in the Copper River basin postponed further exploratory work in 1900. Schrader and A. C. Spencer mapped the Chitina copper district geologically.[41] Barnard was in charge of topography and Brooks of geology in the western part of Seward Peninsula, and Peters and Mendenhall in the east. Nearly 100 creeks in nine gold districts were included in the survey of mineral resources that embraced over 6,000 square miles. In their report, the geologists cast chapters on economic geology into "more popular form." "It is hoped that . . . [the] arrangement will make the results so far obtained of immediate and practical value to the average miner and prospector."[42] The concentration on practical economic matters was clearly in line with the Con-

39. Shrader, "Preliminary Report on a Reconnaissance Along the Chandalar and Koyukuk Rivers, Alaska, in 1899," USGS, *Twenty-first Annual Report, 1899–1900,* Part 2., pp. 448–49.

40. Schrader and Brooks, *Preliminary Report on the Cape Nome Region, Alaska.* Brooks, *Geography and Geology of Alaska,* p. 129.

41. Schrader and Spencer, *The Geology and Mineral Resources of a Portion of the Copper River District, Alaska* (USGS, Washington, 1901); also printed as *House Document 546, 56th Congress: 2d session* (4198).

42. Brooks, Richardson, Collier, and Mendenhall, *Reconnaissances in the Cape Nome and Norton Bay Regions, Alaska,* pp. 11–14. Brooks to C. D. Walcott, June 1, 1901, Historical Documents, USGS Files.

gressional authorization under which the Geological Survey labored in Alaska. Yet the work in 1900 by no means ignored "purely scientific ends," as Mendenhall phrased it.[43]

In 1901 areal mapping was continued on the Seward Peninsula, and Brooks investigated mineral districts in southeastern Alaska, but exploratory work was also resumed. Schrader and Peters traveled from the southern limit of Alaska to Point Barrow via the Koyukuk and Colville Rivers. Their party conducted the first instrumental survey from the Yukon to Alaska's northern coast and returned with the earliest reliable geologic information from the great Brooks Range. The same year, Mendenhall and D. L. Raeburn led an expedition up the Dall River and over to the upper reaches of the Kobuk, which they descended to its mouth.[44] Thus in 1901 a network of surveys connected the Yukon, Koyukuk, and Kobuk Rivers, the Arctic Ocean, and Kotzebue Sound. The next year's plan called for a traverse to the Yukon that would connect earlier surveys of the Susitna, Kuskokwim, and Tanana Rivers.[45] To accomplish that goal, Brooks directed a memorable expedition from Cook Inlet northwest across the Alaska Range, then northeast along the northern foothills of the range to the Nenana River, a tributary of the Tanana.[46]

Alaska was not thoroughly explored by 1903. Geologists would continue to study and map large wilderness areas well into the century. But by 1900 many gross geographical problems had been resolved, and the ascendency of the Geological Survey was firmly secured. Thereafter its pre-eminence in scientific exploration and mapping of the interior was not seriously challenged. The USGS appropriation went from $25,000 to $60,000 in 1900. The small, independent, mobile Geological Survey par-

43. Mendenhall to R. U. Goode, November 30, 1900, Historical Documents, USGS Files.

44. A. J. Collier, *A Reconnaissance of the Northwestern Portion of Seward Peninsula, Alaska,* USGS Professional Paper No. 2 (Washington, 1902). Brooks, *Preliminary Report on the Ketchikan Mining District, Alaska, with an Introductory Sketch of the Geology of Southeastern Alaska,* USGS Professional Paper No. 1 (Washington, 1902). Schrader, *A Reconnaissance in Northern Alaska Across the Rocky Mountains, along Koyukuk, John, Anaktuvuk, and Colville Rivers, and the Arctic Coast to Cape Lisburne in 1901,* USGS Professional Paper No. 20 (Washington, 1904). Mendenhall, *Reconnaissance from Fort Hamlin to Kotzebue Sound, Alaska, by Way of Dall, Kanuti, Allen, and Kowak Rivers,* USGS Professional Paper No. 10 (Washington, 1902).

45. Brooks, *Geography and Geology of Alaska,* pp. 129, 130.

46. Brooks, *Mount McKinley Region, Alaska.*

ties, staffed by highly trained civilian geologists and topographers, proved eminently suited to the job of primary exploration. Moreover, they were the logical units for mineral investigations. Though the crews were instructed to investigate territorial resources and flora and fauna in 1898 and 1899, the long distances covered and the absence of trained naturalists prevented anything but casual observations. No matter how informal, the observations were as useful as those of many previous explorers, and certainly more valuable than similar efforts by military personnel during the Gold Rush. The activity was stepped up by USGS investigators in 1900 and during the next few years, until technical specialization rendered "natural history" a historical term.

In the meantime, before the century ended, there came a spectacular achievement in Alaskan natural history that matched the quality of work done by the Geological Survey in interior exploration. The Harriman Alaska Expedition of 1899 is difficult to categorize. It was entirely financed by Edward H. Harriman, and therefore signalized the entrance of large-scale private philanthropy into Alaskan scientific research. Ostensibly, it was planned as a big game hunt and holiday outing for the Harriman family, and might be classed as a variety of tourism that produced incidental benefits to science. Yet the expedition was staffed by scientific personnel from the government and from the universities. Federal and university science therefore played a major role in the success that attended the cruise.

Furthermore, the true aim of the expedition may have been directly related to the earliest theme of American continental exploration in Alaska—the co-operation of science and business in the establishment of communication links between Europe and America via Alaska and Asia. Vilhjalmur Stefansson suggests that the excursion of 1899 might have been one phase of Harriman's grand design for a New York to Paris railway. The Stefansson hypothesis, though built on circumstantial evidence, is intriguing. Edward Harriman was perfectly capable of such imaginative planning.[47] Two years before the expedition, he arranged the merger of the Union Pacific Railroad with the Southern Pacific, and took on James J. Hill and J. P. Morgan in a struggle for control of the Northern Pacific. Harriman thought and acted on a grandiose scale. Whatever his real mo-

47. Stefansson, *Northwest to Fortune*, pp. 285–322.

tives for the Alaskan expedition, one thing is certain: it was the most luxurious reconnaissance in the history of nineteenth-century Alaskan scientific investigation.

In co-operation with the Smithsonian Institution and the Washington Academy of Sciences, Harriman gathered together more than a score of scientific specialists representing the universities, private institutions, and federal scientific bureaus. There were five botanists, a paleontologist, a mining engineer, a mineralogist, two geologists, three zoologists, including specialists in entomology and mammalogy, three ornithologists, a general biologist, an anatomist, a forester, and a geographer. The scientists came from Yale, Cornell, Amherst, Harvard, the University of Washington, and the University of California at Berkeley, and from the U.S. National Museum, the Geological Survey, the Department of Agriculture, and the Biological Survey. The Field Columbian Museum of Chicago, the Museum of the California Academy of Sciences, and the Missouri Botanical Gardens were represented. George Bird Grinnell, the editor of *Forest and Stream*, was along. To aid the scientific party there were two taxidermists, two photographers, and three artists, including Louis Agassiz Fuertes. The passenger list contained the names of many luminaries in nineteenth-century American natural history. The wise old Alaska hand, William Healey Dall, was in the party; so was John Muir. Henry Gannett, Chief Geographer of the USGS; C. Hart Merriam, Chief of the Biological Survey and then engaged in making mammalogy a respectable zoological specialty; John Burroughs, bird watcher and writer; Bernhard E. Fernow, formerly Chief of the Forest Service; D. G. Elliot, who had interested Harriman in the opportunity for hunting the Kodiak bear—all were aboard.[48]

Harriman brought his family—wife, two daughters, and two sons—and Mr. and Mrs. W. H. Averell, their daughter, and another young lady. Also included in the nonscientific segment of the expedition were the Harriman servants, two stenographers, a physician and his assistant, a nurse, a chaplain, eleven hunters, packers, and camp hands.

Scientists and members of the Harriman party were divided into committees. There were committees on the various natural history disciplines,

48. *Harriman Alaska Expedition* (12 vols. New York and Washington, 1902–1914), *1*, pages xxxiii–xxxv. H. Gannett, "The Harriman Alaska Expedition," *JAGS*, *21* (1899), 344, 345.

on routes and plans, on big game, on lectures, on literature and art, on music and entertainment. There was even a committee for the library of 500 volumes, provided by the Harrimans and supplemented by other members of the expedition. Hunting parties were expected to supply the expedition with venison and bear meat, Burroughs explained, "but to be on the safe side we . . . [took] aboard eleven fat steers, a flock of sheep, chickens, and turkeys, a milch cow, and a span of horses."[49]

The main body of the party left New York in a special train of palace cars. At Seattle the entire group boarded the recently overhauled and refurbished *George W. Elder*, an Alaskan cruise ship 250 feet in length with a 38.5-foot beam, registered at 1,709 tons.[50] The *Elder* carried a crew of sixty-five officers and men.

Except for a previously arranged stop at Kodiak to hunt bear, the precise itinerary was decided en route by the committees. The vessel stopped at Metlakatla, Wrangell, Juneau, Skagway, Sitka, Glacier Bay, Yakutat, and Prince William Sound. While in the Sound, the ship came upon the entrance to an uncharted fiord, which took Harriman's name.[51] At Kodiak, Harriman got his bear, a small female and her cub. (Naturally, Muir was distressed by the hunting.)[52] The expedition touched at the Shumagin and Aleutian Islands and the Pribilofs. According to Burroughs' account, the decision to visit Bering Strait was Mrs. Harriman's. Burroughs narrated: "We traveled two hours in Asia. I am tempted to write a book on the country, but forbear."[53] The *Elder* returned by approximately the same route though with fewer stops, and the journey ended July 30 in Seattle. In two months, the *Elder* had cruised some 9,000 miles and made about fifty stops for sightseeing or scientific investigation.[54]

The Harriman Alaska Expedition was not a voyage of geographical discovery; it was a scientific reconnaissance. Most of all it was a grand holiday excursion, and a floating university or scientific society. The evenings, when not taken up with dances and parties, were occupied with

49. *Harriman Alaska Expedition*, 1, pages xxix, xxxvi–xxxviii, 1.

50. G. H. Grosvenor, "The Harriman-Alaska Expedition in Co-operation with the Washington Academy of Science," *NGM*, 10 (June 1899), 225.

51. *Harriman Alaska Expedition*, 1, 71, 72. Also G. F. Kennan, *E. H. Harriman* (2 vols. Boston, 1922), 1, 201, 202.

52. *Harriman Alaska Expedition*, 1, 85. Muir, *John of the Mountains*, p. 416.

53. *Harriman Alaska Expedition*, 1, 98, 102.

54. H. Gannett, "Harriman Alaska Expedition," pp. 348, 349.

lectures. One night Dall might lecture on Alaska's history or geography, or someone else on sea life, or a geologist on volcanoes, or Muir on glaciers, or one of the ornithologists on bird life, or Grinnell on the Indians.[55] Somehow D. G. Elliot slipped in a lecture on Somaliland. According to Muir, the lecturer was cheered and greeted with shouts of " 'What's the matter with Elliot? He's all right! Who's all right?' etc." Muir reflected: "Interesting result of ice action." There was even a Harriman Alaska Expedition yell:

> Who are we? Who are we?
> We are, We are H.A.E.

On the way home, Muir reported: "We had a long talk on book-making, with much twaddle about a grand scientific monument of this trip, etc. . . . Much ado about little."[56] Actually, the "book-making" process elevated the expedition from a mere holiday coastal cruise to an important scientific event. Over fifty specialists were put to work on the specimens.[57] The collections were huge: for example, about 5,000 pinned insect specimens were brought back.[58] At an early stage of the study, thirteen genera and nearly 600 species "new to science" were described.[59] One investigator, while working over the shrimps, was obliged to review all the pertinent collections in the National Museum, including 50,000 specimens from Lower California to the Arctic.[60] From all this work came a dozen handsomely printed, bound, and illustrated volumes, published under the auspices of Harriman and the Smithsonian Institution. The first two volumes are devoted to the narrative, and to glaciers, the natives, history, geography, and resources. The third volume deals with glaciation, the fourth with geology and paleontology, and the fifth with cryptogamic botany. There are two volumes on insects, one on crustaceans, one on land and fresh-water mollusks and hydroids, one on shallow-water starfishes, and two on sea moss animals and sea and shore worms. "All in all," wrote Dall of the first two volumes, "it is a work of which America may

55. *Harriman Alaska Expedition*, 1, 63.
56. Muir, *John of the Mountains*, pp. 418, 420, 413.
57. C. A. Kofoid, "Our Land of the Midnight Sun," *Dial*, 31 (1901), 274.
58. Anon., "Discoveries in Our Arctic Regions," *World's Work*, 1 (1900), 152.
59. *Harriman Alaska Expedition*, 1, page xxvi.
60. Dall, "Review of the Harriman Alaska Expedition, Vol. 10," *Science*, 20 (October 7, 1904), 462, 463.

justly be proud."[61] Two other reviewers pointed out another value of the expedition, "as a sign post to our multi-millionaires."[62]

The story of science and exploration in the Far Northwest during the nineteenth century thus ended appropriately with the return of William Healey Dall to the field he knew so well and did so much to illuminate. There again was Muir, whose prose poems stimulated American interest in Alaska. One cannot help regretting that Henry Allen, Edward Nelson, C. Willard Hayes, Nelson Miles, John Cantwell and George Stoney, and I. C. Russell, to name a few others, were not free to make the trip. A complete list of deserving contributors to science and exploration, and to scientific exploration, would have contained too many names for the limited accommodations of the *Elder*, even excluding explorers then in the field. They were all brave men, men who exhibited a special type of courage in an unexplored wilderness. For all of Brooks' modesty, he and his fellow explorers of the Far Northwest in the nineteenth century climbed well up the slopes of distinguished achievement. A few reached the summit.

61. "The Harriman Expedition," *Nation*, 73 (October 17, 1901), 304.
62. Anon, "Discoveries in Our Arctic Regions," p. 156. G. W. L., "A Holiday Cruise to Alaska," *Nature* (London), 66 (1902), 176.

12. Conclusion

WITH THE BEGINNING of a new century, the last chapter in the history of North American geographical discovery came to a close. The last part of the continent to yield to man's curiosity was, logically, the corner lying farthest north and west from the spot first touched by Columbus. By 1900 the general facts of Alaska's relief and drainage were known, the major rivers had been traced, and the important mountains outlined. The pace of exploration, counting the years from 1865, was roughly equivalent to the speed of exploration in other continental areas, and progress of discovery was consistent with social attitudes in the United States during the nineteenth century, the remoteness of the territory, the economic interest expressed in the country, and the popular interest as evidenced by the population of the region. At the turn of the century, William Healey Dall could rightly aver: "It would require a row of stately volumes to contain an adequate account of the explorations and surveys made since the transfer [of Alaska]. . . . The amount done is marvelous, yet hardly known to the public. . . . A bibliography, far from complete, yet with fully 4,000 titles, does not cover the publications in book and serials upon the Territory and its adjacent regions."[1]

The American contribution began in 1865 with the Western Union Expedition, an abortive private attempt to link Europe with America by telegraph. The line was never built; but thanks to the plans of Robert Kennicott, the support of the Smithsonian Institution, and the field work of William Dall, the Telegraph Expedition was a bright start for American science and exploration in the Far Northwest. The next institution to take an active interest in exploration was the old Coast Survey, again represented by Dall. It was superseded by the Army: first, the Signal Service, with important work in scientific exploration, especially natural history and meteorology; and second, the Department of Columbia, which, under the direction of General Nelson Miles, sponsored a series of geographical

1. "The Discovery and Exploration of Alaska," in *Harriman Alaska Expedition*, 2, 204.

explorations that culminated in the remarkable journey of Henry Allen in 1885. In the meantime, the Navy and Revenue Marine had begun to compete in exploration above the Yukon. Both services had been and continued to be active on the coast, the Navy in Southeastern and the Revenue Marine along the western and northern littoral.

In 1889, the Coast Survey—newly named the Coast and Geodetic Survey—entered the interior to perform geodetic work connected with diplomatic concern over the international boundary. The period 1888–1891 also witnessed the vigorous exploration directed by George Dawson of the Canadian Geological Survey. United States activity during the same period was confined mainly to private or semiprivate expeditions sponsored by newspapers in search of exciting copy. Tourism had already brought incidental benefits to science and exploration. The Geological Survey, in the persons of I. C. Russell and C. Willard Hayes, contributed importantly to the significant private investigations. USGS interest quickened in 1895 and 1896 in response to increased mining activity. With the Gold Rush, popular and Congressional attention to Alaskan exploration multiplied as the population increased. The Army and Geological Survey competed for laurels in exploration. The Survey won. Distinguished work in natural history by the Harriman Alaska Expedition and in inland exploration by the Geological Survey was a fitting climax to nineteenth-century science and exploration in the Far Northwest.

The institutional pattern that emerged was in general similar to the pattern of American exploration south of the forty-ninth parallel. A private business enterprise first stimulated exploration, and was followed by the Coast Survey. The Army expeditions of 1883–1885 were the last breath of old-time military wilderness exploration of the American West. When the Army reappeared on the northern scene during the Gold Rush, its job was the more prosaic task of finding suitable interior routes for trails and roads. Even then, success of the exploratory phases of the Army's later work was due largely to civilian topographers and civilian scientists on loan from the Geological Survey. In 1898 and 1899 the USGS proved its superiority in interior exploration. The Smithsonian Institution was a constant factor in Alaskan exploration from the beginning. The Smithsonian recommended and instructed personnel; it helped to plan and to coordinate operations; and it received and studied materials collected by the various expeditions. The inland activities of the Navy and Revenue

Marine were institutional phenomena peculiar to the Alaskan experience. Perhaps their competition can be likened to the rivalry between the post-Civil War western surveys of Wheeler, Hayden, and Powell, which had prompted the National Academy's review of the federal scientific establishment. Thus the institutional sequence resembled the Stateside exploration phase of American westward expansion, but in Alaska the sequence occurred twenty to fifty years later.

In other ways, Alaskan exploration differed from the North American pattern. What Brebner called the "vain" incentive to exploration that came from missionary fervor before 1806 was not of major importance in Alaska.[2] Sheldon Jackson's efforts to provide schools helped satisfy the main social need of Alaska and so indirectly aided the cause of exploration,[3] but Jackson was no explorer and the Alaskan missionaries were not scientists. The traders and trappers, who had made significant contributions to exploration elsewhere on the continent before 1865, added only peripherally to geographical knowledge of Alaska during the American period. The prospectors' contributions were of approximately the same magnitude as the traders' and missionaries'. The existence of hostile Indian middlemen was a common obstacle to exploration of the continent and was present to a degree in Alaska, but was by no means as serious. The Navy negotiated peaceably the penetration of strategic passes in Southeastern. In the north, reported hostility of the Copper River Indians, the Tananas, and the Koyukons may have delayed examination of their territory, until Allen dispelled concern about all these tribes with his one journey.

The motives for Alaskan exploration are not easily isolated. The expectation of profit that was clearly present almost everywhere else on the continent, especially before the nineteenth century, was present in Alaska too between 1865 and 1900, but until 1895 it was frequently obfuscated. The profit motive was obvious in the Telegraph Expedition and in Raymond's reconnaissance, and it was the ostensible reason for Dall's Coast Survey expeditions, though science and the intellectual curiosity of William Healey Dall must also be taken into account. Dall's work along the

2. J. B. Brebner, *Explorers of North America*, p. 270.

3. When Dall was organizing his Coast Survey expeditions, the San Francisco *Alta California* commended the effort but regretted that "equally important" common schools were not promoted by the government: August 4, 1871.

Yukon after the Telegraph project was abandoned had purely scientific origins. Signal Service science in Alaska can be tied only tenuously to the economic motive; and the Army's geographic discoveries in the middle 1880s were chiefly the work of Nelson Miles and his aides, who desired only to learn about the country they were expected to defend. The Allen expedition was more the result of Henry Allen's desire to explore an unknown wilderness than it was the result of any single practical goal. In the Kobuk investigations by the Navy and Revenue Marine, two motives—aside from the competitive spirit—stand out: geographical needs of the Revenue Service's Arctic rescue function (indirectly a commercial consideration) and the personal drives of George Stoney, Michael Healy, and John Cantwell. The C&GS and Canadian Surveys of 1888–1890 were undertaken to settle an international problem that stemmed directly from an increase in mining along the border. Private explorations by the Leslie and Schwatka parties were designed to sell newspapers, a rather limited example of the economic motive. The glaciological investigations of Muir, Reid, and Russell had no incentive other than the desire to know the unknown and see the unseen. Research by the Fish Commission and the Department of Agriculture was plainly allied to the "industries of the people." With increased mineral exploitation, the Geological Survey began its independent work in the Far Northwest for commercial reasons. The Army's return was predicated on the assumption that military roads were a necessity. The Smithsonian Institution remained all the while a bulwark of basic research. Personal ambition and the pursuit of science and adventure appear in retrospect to be forces as potent as any in the motivational background of Alaskan exploration.

The direct injunction to satisfy practical and utilitarian demands under which the Geological Survey labored did not prevent its scientists from studying problems in general geology, any more than the hydrographic duties of Dall's Coast Survey expeditions prevented him from investigating natural history. Regardless of apparent motivation behind individual explorations in the Far Northwest, the less immediate needs of science were often met because of the interest and curiosity of the explorers. Their behavior was analogous to the behavior of personnel attached to the Army and civilian western United States surveys. Alaska served science in general as a field laboratory, a training ground for scientists, and a source of materials for study in the laboratories of the U.S.

Lord Rutherford liked to divide science into physics and stamp collecting. The sentiment expressed in that division gained currency in America during the twentieth century. Science in Alaska was closely connected to geographical matters, to the life sciences, to geology, to ethnology, and in a lesser degree to geophysics. In our modern era when physics, chemistry, and the mathematical sciences are the prestigious disciplines, the labor of the Alaskan investigator appears to be in the category of "stamp collecting." But in the nineteenth century a major impetus to scientific research was the theoretical progress in biology, geology, and ethnology, and those areas were central to American interest in geography. American science in the nineteenth century was no less "pure" than twentieth-century science by having followed a different pattern; its pattern was related to contemporary geographical interests and research opportunities.[4]

Exploration of the Far Northwest in the period 1865–1900 was an achievement of the federal government almost exclusively. Nearly every significant exploration was accomplished by a federal agency, and the government assisted others. The two large-scale private expeditions financed by Western Union and Harriman were both aided by the Smithsonian Institution, and the Harriman enterprise was staffed partly by government specialists. The success of the St. Elias investigations in 1890 and 1891 and of Schwatka's expedition in the latter year was due almost entirely to two government scientists. One extensive private endeavor, the Leslie Expedition, made few contributions to either geographic discovery or science. Furthermore, the part played by scientific societies and the universities was minor. The national government was indisputably the First Estate of science and exploration in Alaska during the last one-third of the nineteenth century. This fact has not hitherto been appreciated by general historians of Alaska, because it does not jibe with the emphasis on political history.

Modern political historians appear concerned about what might have been done for Alaska, rather than what was done or what could have been done in the context of the time. It should be remembered that in 1890 there were only 5,000 whites and Creoles in all Alaska, and about

4. Nathan Reingold, "American Indifference to Basic Research in the Nineteenth Century: A Reappraisal," paper read before the History of Science Society of Washington, D.C., February 19, 1962. The interpretation will be detailed in Dr. Reingold's forthcoming book.

three-fourths of them were in Southeastern and at Kodiak.[5] These two areas might have been provided with a more effective civil government, but it would probably not have induced much, if any, more settlement or development. Alaska's economic backwardness was related to its remote location and the diminished interest of Americans in frontier living. Even by 1895, in other parts of the territory the only Alaskans other than the indigenes were a handful of permanent traders and missionaries, semi-permanent prospectors, and the employees of a few small usually seasonal mining operations and several fishing concerns, all scattered along the main rivers or along the vast coast line. In sum, the sparse population rendered Alaska essentially apolitical during the century. Yet by 1895 the Coast Survey, the Army, the Census Office, the Navy, the Revenue Marine, and the USGS had all undertaken explorations; all were federal agencies.

In the second place, the social and economic atmosphere in the parent nation was not conducive to heavy federal expenditures in advance of population or economic needs—at any place, not just in Alaska. There were a number of special conditions that militated against large expenditures for earlier and faster systematic explorations. For example, the USGS appropriation of $5,000 for 1895 is interesting not because it was so small but because it came at all in the middle of a depression. Given the tiny population, the remoteness of Alaska, the limited economic inducement to development, and the national political, intellectual, and economic atmosphere, federal exploration of the Far Northwest was relatively fast, extensive, and progressive.

The progress of exploration is a logical and substantive theme for Alaskan history in the period 1865–1900. Commercial affairs—fur, fish, and mining—and missionary activity were limited geographically or chronologically, and the sparse civilized population precludes any emphasis on political evolution. The exploration embodied personal and national achievement of high order, and was a memorable chapter in the history of American science and geographical discovery.

5. U.S. Census Office, *Report on Population and Resources of Alaska at the Eleventh Census: 1890*, p. 3.

Index

Italicized page numbers indicate whole chapters.

Illustrations

1. Packtrain fording Lowe's River, about 1900

2. An Army expedition in high swamp grass

3. Yukon Valley at Eagle

4. Near the Ramparts, Yukon River, from Dall's narrative

5. Tanana Indian, by Whymper

6. Fort Yukon, by Whymper

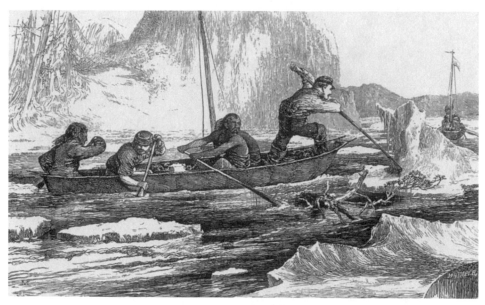

7. Western Union Telegraph Explorers on the Yukon, by Whymper

9. William Healey Dall at age 21

8. Robert Kennicott

10. F. E. Ketchum

11. Mike LeBarge

12. George Davidson

13. View of Sitka in the late 1860s

14. Fur Seals, 1872, by Henry Elliott

15. William Healey Dall in 1878

16. Henry Elliott, about 1865

17. Israel C. Russell

18. John Muir

19. Cadet Frederick Schwatka,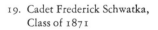
    Class of 1871

20. General Nelson Miles

21. E. W. Nelson

22. Schwatka's raft shooting the Miles Canyon rapids

23. Cadet Henry T. Allen,
Class of 1882

24. George M. Stoney

25. John C. Cantwell

26. The Cutter *Corwin*

27. C. Willard Hayes

28. John E. McGrath

29. Cadet Joseph Herron,
Class of 1895

30. Cadet Edwin F. Glenn,
Class of 1877

31. Frank C. Schrader

32. William R. Abercrombie

33. Landscape from the camp where Castner constructed a raft

34. Ladd's Station on Cook Inlet

35. Glenn's detachment at the point of separation from Castner

36. Learnard's detachment starting up the Susitna River

37. S. S. *Elder* near Wellesley Glacier

38. Walter C. Mendenhall

39. Alfred Hulse Brooks

40. John Wesley Powell

41. E. H. Harriman